Economic Analysis of
an Urban Housing Market

STUDIES IN URBAN ECONOMICS

Under the Editorship of

Edwin S. Mills
Princeton University

Norman J. Glickman. ECONOMETRIC ANALYSIS OF REGIONAL SYS-
TEMS: Explorations in Model Building and Policy Analysis

J. Vernon Henderson. ECONOMIC THEORY AND THE CITIES

Norman J. Glickman. THE GROWTH AND MANAGEMENT OF THE
JAPANESE URBAN SYSTEM

George S. Tolley, Philip E. Graves, and John L. Gardner, URBAN GROWTH
POLICY IN A MARKET ECONOMY

David Segal (Ed.). THE ECONOMICS OF NEIGHBORHOOD

R. D. Norton. CITY LIFE-CYCLES AND AMERICAN URBAN POLICY

John F. McDonald. ECONOMIC ANALYSIS OF AN URBAN
HOUSING MARKET

Economic Analysis of an Urban Housing Market

JOHN F. McDONALD

Department of Economics
University of Illinois at Chicago Circle
Chicago, Illinois

ACADEMIC PRESS

A Subsidiary of Harcourt Brace Jovanovich, Publishers

New York   London   Toronto   Sydney   San Francisco

ACADEMIC PRESS, INC.
111 Fifth Avenue, New York, New York 10003

United Kingdom Edition published by
ACADEMIC PRESS, INC. (LONDON) LTD.
24/28 Oval Road, London NW1 7DX

Library of Congress Cataloging in Publication Data

McDonald, John F   Date
    Economic analysis of an urban housing market.

    (Studies in urban economics)
    Bibliography: p.
    Includes index.
    1. Housing––Mathematical models. 2. Housing––
Illinois––Chicago––Mathematical models. I. Title.
II. Series.
HD7287.5.M23   301.5'4'0151   79–20969
ISBN 0–12–483360–8

PRINTED IN THE UNITED STATES OF AMERICA

79 80 81 82   9 8 7 6 5 4 3 2 1

TO THE MEMORY OF MY MOTHER

Contents

Preface   *xi*

Acknowledgments   *xiii*

Introduction   1

1   Models for the Demand for Urban Housing   7

1   The Demand for Housing and Residential Location: A Synthesis   7
2   The Demand for Housing and Residential Location:
      A Simplified Example   12
3   The Demand for Land: An Extension of Muth's Approach   14
4   A Survey of Studies of the Demand for Housing and
      Residential Location   14
5   Homeownership and the Demand for Housing   24
    Appendix: Access to Employment   29

2 The Value of Commuting Time 35

1 Introduction 35
2 Estimation of the Value of Reductions in Commuting Time 38
3 Driving Speed in Chicago 47

3 Race, Externalities, the Local Public Sector, and the Demand for Housing 51

1 Race and the Demand for Housing 52
2 Air Pollution, Neighborhood Income, and Other Externalities
  in the Chicago Housing Market 62
3 The Local Public Sector and the Demand for Housing 70
4 Conclusion 74

4 Models of the Supply of Urban Housing 75

1 Models of Long-Run Supply 76
2 Supply in the Market Period 88
3 Supply in the Short Run 92
4 Conclusions 98
  Appendix: Murray's Analysis of the Composite Good Housing 99

5 Analytical Models of the Urban Housing Market 101

1 Muth's Standard Model and Minor Extensions 101
2 Major Extensions of the Standard Model 106

6 Population Density in Chicago 117

1 Population Density in Chicago: The Historical Record 117
2 Population Density in Chicago: The Studies by Harrison and Kain,
  Muth, and Mills 123
3 Population Density in Chicago: 1970 128
  Appendix: Age Structure of the Housing Stock in Chicago
  Over Time 137

7 **Land Values in Chicago** 141

1 A History of Land Values in Chicago 142
2 Land Value Functions: A Reevaluation 146
3 Land Values and Zoning 159
4 Conclusions 166

8 **A Model of the Chicago Housing Market** 169

1 Population Density and Land Values in Chicago: A Summary 169
2 A Class of Vintage Housing Models 170
3 Conclusion 184

References 187

Index *197*

Preface

In the past 20 years urban economics has developed into an applied field within economics in which sophisticated theoretical models and empirical techniques are used. Such a comment applies particularly to the analysis of the urban housing and land markets. Today's urban housing economist must be familiar with Lancastrian models of demand, CES production functions, maximum likelihood estimation techniques, and a host of other topics. However, the rate of development of theoretical models has outstripped the progress in the empirical testing of these models. This is to be expected, of course. The primary task of this book is to provide some of the needed empirical testing of recent theoretical models of the urban housing and land markets. I attempt to determine how important are the various new theoretical models for explaining the basic patterns in the housing and land markets of one major metropolitan area.

The Chicago metropolitan area has been chosen as the laboratory for these tests because a great deal of empirical work has already been done on Chicago. These previous works provide a substantial body of information on the patterns of population density, land values, and housing prices. However, some of these works have not been related to modern theoretical models. Furthermore, some of these previous empirical studies have failed to uncover basic patterns in the housing and land markets in Chicago. This failure has left the empirical literature on Chicago in a rather confused state. I attempt to reduce the confusion.

This book is addressed to my fellow urban economists. Because I attempt to provide some perspective on recent research in the urban housing and land markets, the book should also be of interest to advanced students in urban economics (graduate students and, perhaps, advanced undergraduates). For the same reason, economists interested in applied microeconomics in general may find something of value here. Finally, those who are interested in the Chicago housing and land markets may wish to read the book because I have attempted to compile the significant empirical work on Chicago done by economists, and I have tried to tell a coherent story about the patterns in these markets over time. While the book is filled with the technical jargon of economics, the persistent reader will be able to discern my story.

The first five chapters of the book contain a survey of recent theoretical models of the urban housing and land markets and the empirical tests that have been conducted to attempt to verify these models. Chapters 1, 2, and 3 focus on models of the demand for housing, and Chapter 4 examines the supply models. Chapter 5 is a summary of recent extensions of the standard monocentric housing market model developed by Alonso (1964) and Muth (1969). In Chapters 1–4 I try to determine the level of complexity in urban housing models that receives the strongest empirical support. Wherever possible, empirical work pertaining to the metropolitan Chicago area is used. Chapters 6 and 7 contain the detailed empirical work that I and others have done on the patterns of population density and land values in Chicago. In Chapter 8, the final chapter, I have tried to develop a model for the Chicago housing and land markets that is consistent both with the conclusions reached in Chapters 1–4 and the empirical patterns observed in Chapters 6 and 7. While this effort is only partially successful, I think that a reasonably coherent story has been told and that some foci for future research have been provided.

Acknowledgments

This monograph is the result, in part, of work done in collaboration with H. Woods Bowman over a period of 4 years. His contributions are numerous, and he is the coauthor of a section of Chapter 7.

The data collection for the study was facilitated by a grant from the National Science Foundation (Grant GK 41663) to the College of Engineering at the University of Illinois at Chicago Circle for the study of the impact of high-rise buildings on the urban system. Harold Simon was the principal investigator, and his cooperation is deeply appreciated. The students who assisted in the project were Allen Adcock, Virginia Grey Aycock, and Sukdev Bains. Much of the empirical work would have been impossible without their attention to detail.

The data used to examine the value of commuting time in Chapter 2 were collected under the auspices of the Northwest Conference of Mayors, a group of mayors from towns in northwestern Cook County, Illinois. Pat Phillippi was the director of the survey, and I thank her for her efforts. The data on house values in Chicago used in Chapter 3 were provided by Lalitha Sanathanan and Robert Bednarz. Their assistance is appreciated. The manuscript was typed promptly by Alice Hatchett.

Finally, I wish to thank George Rosen, former head of the Economics Department, and Ralph Westfall, dean of the College of Business Administration, for providing me with sabbatical leave during the winter and spring of 1978. This time enabled me to produce this manuscript with reasonable promptness, something for which my wife Glena and I are grateful.

Economic Analysis of
an Urban Housing Market

Introduction

*Science never pursues the illusory aim of making its answers final,
or even probable. Its advance is, rather, towards an infinite yet attainable aim: that of ever discovering new, deeper, and more general
problems, and of subjecting our ever tentative answers to ever renewed
and ever more rigorous tests.*

—Karl Popper (1968, p. 281)

This study is an attempt to use the standard techniques of economic
analysis to understand some important empirical regularities in the housing
market of Chicago, Illinois. The study can be thought of as a study of the
Chicago housing market but, more importantly, it is an exercise in the use
of economic science. Consequently, this introduction is a brief discussion
of methodology in economics as it pertains to the study of urban housing.

At the conclusion of a recent paper that surveys recent developments
in the field of theoretical urban economics, Richard Muth (1977) has stated

> Surprisingly little attention has been paid to the empirical estimation and testing of models
> of urban spatial structure, relative to the amount of time we have spent on their theoretical
> development and elaboration. Yet it is principally through the former that shortcomings
> in such models are revealed and the way to their improvement is suggested [p. 396].

Similar sentiments have been expressed often by another eminent researcher
in the field, Harry Richardson, most recently in a book on the new theoretical
urban economics (1977a). Richardson (1977a) and Anas and Dendrinos

1

(1976) have surveyed the enormous literature in theoretical urban economics that has been produced recently. Indeed, there is a chance that, because of the faddishness that we researchers are subject to, the work of examining the empirical relevance of various theoretical models may not be done before researchers have moved on to another topic. The advancement of the science requires a closer cooperation between theorists and those who do empirical work. While it is counterproductive for theorists to be disinterested in empirical testing, it is equally problematical for empirical researchers to state beforehand that the real world of urban economics is too complex for reasonably simple and manageable models to capture most of the essential facts. This book is one attempt to respond to this problem as it pertains to the urban housing market.

At the outset I must acknowledge that the seminal book by Muth (1969), which has done so much to stimulate interest in analytical urban economics, is an unusually skillful blend of theory and empirical testing. However, much work has been done since Muth's book was completed. One of the few subsequent works that combines theory and empirical work is the distinguished book by Mills (1972a). The difference in the approaches taken by Muth and Mills is rather striking. Muth developed his theoretical analysis of the urban housing market in the first half of the book and presented his empirical findings in the second half of the book. Muth took care to relate many of his empirical tests to certain specific theoretical results. Mills, on the other hand, presented some broad empirical relationships in the first half of his book and then, in the second half of the book, developed a series of theoretical models that is consistent with these empirical findings. Among other things, Mills demonstrated that a number of models, with varying degrees of complexity and realism in the basic assumptions, are consistent with the broad trends in the distribution of population within metropolitan areas in the U.S. A third approach has been taken by housing researchers associated with the National Bureau of Economic Research. Kain and Quigley (1975) and Straszheim (1975), for example, have criticized strongly as seriously inaccurate the simplifying assumptions employed in work such as Muth (1969), and have attempted to demonstrate that the adoption of certain simplifying assumptions leads to empirically incorrect conclusions. Many of the issues raised by these fundamental disagreements are examined in the chapters to follow. However, it is clear that underlying the disagreements among housing researchers is, in part, a difference over methodology in economic science.

In a recent theoretical paper in which he relaxed an assumption made in his earlier work, Muth (1976) has stated

> One of the most frequently heard criticisms of economic models of urban residential land use is that they neglect the durability of residential real estate. Such a criticism is motivated

in part, perhaps, by a misguided desire for descriptive realism of assumptions rather than by limitations in the conformity of the implications of urban economic models to real world phenomena. By and large, current spatial models of urban residential land use which treat housing as nondurable agree rather well with patterns of urban population distribution in U.S. cities [p. 245].

Muth (1976, p. 245) went on to state that the spatial aspects of the durability of houses is a topic of interest in its own right and proceeded to develop a model for this purpose. The problem with the quoted statement is that other models that treat housing as durable may also agree rather well with the facts of population distribution. The empirical evidence used may fail to distinguish between alternative theories. It seems that Muth's statement places him in rough methodological agreement with Milton Friedman's essay on the methodology of positive economics (1953). Friedman's main point was that the adequacy of a theory must be judged by examining the conformance of the logical consequences of the theory with the phenomena it was designed to explain rather than by the realism of its assumptions.

There is an important way in which Friedman's argument is correct, and it is worthwhile, as a preliminary to the study of housing, to explore briefly the nature of theories.[1] In the philosophy of science it is common to distinguish between experimental laws, or empirical regularities, and theories. Theories by definition imply no overt empirical tests and, thus, cannot be put to a direct experimental test. The distinction between experimental laws and theories is a matter of degree, but is extremely useful. According to Nagel (1961), theories are best regarded as instruments for the conduct of inquiry, rather than as statements about which questions of truth or falsity can be usefully raised. Nagel (1961) further states that "the *raison d'etre* of the theory is to serve as a rule or guide for making logical transitions from one set of experimental data to another set [p. 129]." The theory is a statement form, not a statement nor a premise from which conclusions are obtained. Rather, according to Nagel (1961), ". . . evidence is sought for observational conclusions drawn from observational premises in accordance with the theory [p. 145]." However, an experimental law, or empirical regularity, that is explained by a given theory retains a meaning that can be stated independently of the theory and is based upon evidence that allows the law to survive the demise of the theory. The demise of the theory and its replacement by a new theory will involve a situation in which, according to Nagel (1961), "The new theory will presumably continue to explain all the experimental laws that the earlier theory could explain, in addition to explaining experimental laws for which the earlier theory could not account [p. 87]." On the other hand, a theory is capable of drawing con-

[1] This discussion is based upon Nagel (1961), who presents the instrumentalist view of theories.

nections between experimental laws about different subject matters and of suggesting more experimental laws. Nagel (1961, p. 90) suggests that a theory has three components: an abstract calculus or logical skeleton; a set of rules to assign empirical content to the logical skeleton; and an interpretation (or model) for the logical skeleton. These last two components are distinct; a theory may have an interpretation without a set of rules to assign empirical content.

Friedman's essay (1953) generated a great deal of debate and, while the last word on methodology in economics has not been spoken, Nagel's essay on Friedman (1963) seems to have settled matters fairly well.[2] Nagel pointed out that assumptions can be unrealistic in at least three senses:

1. A statement is not exhaustive, but mentions only some traits and ignores an endless number of other facts.
2. A statement is false or deemed to be highly improbable based on the available evidence.
3. A statement refers to a "pure" case or "idealized" conditions rather than phenomena that are actually encountered.

Nagel (1963) argued that Friedman did not distinguish among these types of unreality. Theory based upon the first type of unreality is highly useful, of course. Theory based upon the third type of unreality, the pure case, can be very useful so long as we recognize the incomplete nature of the conclusions derived therefrom. Theories based upon the second type of unreality are useless. Simon (1963) and Samuelson (1963) implored us to devote some energy to the testing of assumptions where possible so that improved theories can be constructed. A simple theory is not necessarily a good theory. On the other hand, we should wield Occam's razor to pare away needless complexity. It is my contention that in Muth's position there is the danger than bad theory will live on longer than it should, but that Kain and Quigley (1975) and Straszheim (1975) have probably introduced needless complexity into the analysis of urban housing for some purposes. It is my objective to steer a course between these two extremes and to develop a manageable model that is in better agreement with empirical evidence than the "standard" model of urban housing that is based on Muth's (1969) work. The theory in Muth (1969) will be used, however, because detailed examination of the available empirical evidence does not lead to its rejection in this application.

The standard microeconomic theory of the urban housing market includes these assumptions:

<hr>

[2] Rotwein (1959) also provided a penetrating analysis of Friedman's essay by contending that the testing of the realism of assumptions should be carried out where possible. A testable assumption loses its status as a theory and becomes an experimental law.

1. Consumers maximize utility
2. Producers maximize profit
3. The market is perfectly competitive
4. Housing is a single commodity that is produced by the services of capital and land

Only the fourth assumption has been extensively challenged as leading to incorrect conclusions. It seems to me that the other disagreements among housing researchers involve the specification of empirical laws. For example, there is disagreement over the functional form for production functions, demand functions, etc.[3] Furthermore, there is disagreement about whether it is more nearly correct to contend that the long-run implications of the theory should be used in preference to its short-run implications. Finally, there are extensive empirical investigations to determine whether a variety of environmental factors, broadly defined, influence the housing market.

The plan of the book is as follows. In the first three chapters I shall survey the available evidence to determine the assumptions upon which a theory of the demand for urban housing should be based. The first chapter is concerned with the issue of the degree of complexity needed in the specification of the commodity "housing." The second chapter examines the question of how many commodities in addition to housing should be included in the utility function of the urban household. New evidence on the utility of commuting time is presented. The third chapter continues this discussion by examining the evidence on the utility of environmental factors, public services, and racial factors in the context of housing analyses. The fourth chapter presents a detailed examination of the empirical evidence on the production function of housing services and other aspects of the theory of supply. Market period, short-run, and long-run competitive supply theories are considered. Chapter 5 contains a review of the existing analytical models of the urban housing market that derive from the Muth (1969) tradition. An exhaustive list of the assumptions employed by Muth (1969) is presented, and examples of models in which each of these assumptions is relaxed are given. Chapters 6 and 7 contain the basic empirical evidence upon which the choice of models is based. The evidence pertains only to the metropolitan Chicago area, so the objective of the study is to settle, at least temporarily, on a model for Chicago only. Chapter 6 presents time series and cross section data on the patterns of population density, and Chapter 7 contains both

---

[3] For example, Muth (1966) has based his conclusions about the implications of the theory discussed above upon a specific form of the production function for housing services. He assumes linear homogeneity for this function and is thus able to connect one type of empirical law with other empirical laws using the theory as a statement form. However, in this case, the empirical law concerning the functional form of the production function has not been tested directly.

types of data for land values. In Chapter 8 I present a model that attempts to be both consistent with the patterns of population density and land values and in agreement with available evidence concerning the underlying assumptions. In this way I hope that I have made contributions both to housing economics in particular and economic science in general.

1

Models of the Demand
for Urban Housing

In this chapter two critical issues in the formulation of a theory of housing demand are addressed. First, does the empirical evidence support the theory that housing is a single commodity produced by the services of capital and land? If this theory cannot be supported, how complex must the theory become to be consistent with the empirical evidence? Second, how important is the distinction between owning and renting the home? Can tenure choice be included in a reasonably simple theory of the demand for housing?

1 The Demand for Housing and Residential Location: A Synthesis

The purpose of this section is to provide a general analysis of the demand for urban housing and residential location. The model developed here is an attempt to include as special cases all of the hypotheses generated by other theorists. This analytical strategy allows us to isolate the particular assumptions that lead to each special case, thereby permitting a more rational choice from among the available models. The major recent empirical studies will then be compared using the general model.

The model begins with the specification of a utility function for the household. In this formulation we shall follow the new theory of demand

7

developed by Becker (1965), Lancaster (1966, 1971), and Muth (1966). In this theory the household purchases goods that are used, possibly in conjunction with the consumers' own time, to produce housing and residential location characteristics that enter the utility function. Rather than assume with Becker (1965) and Lancaster (1966, 1971) that the production of characteristics is done with fixed proportions of goods, we shall follow the more general model of Muth (1966) by assuming continuous possibilities for substitution of the input goods. As will be shown below, many housing studies have made use of the assumption of continuous substitutability. In addition, allowance is made for the fact that the household may contain more than one individual and one person who is employed. Recent work by Madden (1977) and White (1977a), for example, has examined the demand for residential location by households that include a second worker. Finally, to be general, we shall assume that the uses of time, other than home production, may enter the utility function. These uses of time include leisure, work, and commuting time.[1] Thus we express the utility function as

$$U = U(X, Y, N, C, H) \tag{1}$$

where X (a scalar) is units of a composite good, Y is a vector of n housing and locational characteristics, and N, C, and H are vectors of leisure, commuting, and work time, respectively. There is one element in each of these latter three vectors for each member of the household. The utility function is ordinal, continuous, real valued, and twice differentable.

Following Muth (1966), assume that the production function for each element in Y is homogeneous of degree one. The production function for Y_i, for example, is

$$Y_i = Y_i(Z, T^i), \tag{2}$$

where Z is the vector of m residential goods and locational attributes, and T^i is a vector of time inputs of the household. For generality, assume that all residential goods (floor space, bathrooms, etc.), all locational attributes (income level of neighborhood, air pollution, etc.), and time inputs of all household members contribute to the production of Y_i. Lancaster's model (1966, 1971) is based on the assumption that the consumers purchase each element in Z separately. However, Rosen (1974) has suggested that, in the case of housing, it is more reasonable to assume that the suppliers of housing sell packages of goods. To this package of goods the consumer may, of course,

---

[1] Several theoretical studies such as deDonnea (1972), Johnson (1966), Oort (1969), Owen (1969), and Yamada (1972) have suggested that utility may be a function of commuting time. Nonwork trips may be included in C, but such an assumption has not been included in any analyses of which I am aware.

choose to add his own time and/or other goods. Time and money spent shopping would be added, for example. In order to make this model empirically tractable, it will be necessary to make decisions concerning the number of elements in **Y**, the number of elements in **Z**, and the number of elements in **Z** (goods) that appear in the production function of each element in **Y**. Some of the complexities of these decisions are explored below.

The utility function is maximized subject to two types of constraints: money income and time.[2] The income constraint is

$$I = \sum w_j h_j + G = X + \sum^m q_k(u)Z_k + \sum t_j(u), \qquad (3)$$

where w_j is the net wage of the jth household member, h_j is hours of work of the jth household member, G is nonwage income,[3] $q_k(u)$ is the price for Z_k, which varies with residential location u, and t_j is the monetary commuting cost for the jth household member which also varies with residential location u. Residential location u is the distance from location to metropolitan center. The price of X, the composite commodity, is assumed to be 1.0. The time constraints are

$$T_j = \sum_{i=1}^{n} T_{ij} + H_j + N_j + C_j, \qquad (4)$$

where T_j is the total time available to the jth individual and T_{ij} is the time input by the jth individual to the ith characteristic.

The usual method of analysis is to maximize the utility function subject to the specified constraints. However, for purposes of this analysis we find it convenient to work with a minimization problem instead. The focus of the analysis is on the demand for the **Z** goods, the inputs into the production of housing and locational attributes. Furthermore, equilibrium will occur if the household can make no move that will increase its utility level. Using the terminology of Wheaton (1974), we can consider each location in the intraurban housing market as "open" in the sense that households can move costlessly to a location that will increase utility.[4] Given this

---

[2] See Henderson (1977, pp. 9–14) for a simpler version of this problem.

[3] Empirical studies of housing demand such as Muth (1960) and Reid (1962) emphasize that the appropriate measure of income is permanent income, or income considered over a span of more than one time period. This point represents a pitfall in attempting to conduct a study of housing demand based upon cross section data. Here we assume that the wage rates and nonwage income do not vary over the time period under consideration and that the time period is of sufficient length that past and future levels of wages and nonwage income do not influence current behavior.

[4] Below we consider the possibility that a household may not have perfect mobility to all locations in an urban area. This problem is called the supply restrictions hypothesis by Kain and Quigley (1972, 1975), McDonald (1974), and Straszheim (1975).

assumption, we can proceed to find the minimum cost of attaining the given level of utility U_0. As Nelson (1972) has shown, the solution to this minimization problem generates a bid-rent for each element in $\mathbf{Z}$. The theory of compensating rent differentials thus becomes the theory of the demand for housing and residential location. The supply of $\mathbf{Z}$ is considered in a later section.

The problem is to minimize the expenditures on goods other than housing and locational characteristics subject to the constraints that utility equals U_0 and that the amounts of housing, locational characteristics, and commuting times equal the amounts available at the location in question. We minimize

$$X + \sum_{j=1}^{r} t_j(u) + w_j(H_j + C_j), \tag{5}$$

subject to

$$U_0 = U(X, \mathbf{Y}, \mathbf{N}, \mathbf{C}, \mathbf{H}), \tag{6}$$

$$\mathbf{Z} = \mathbf{Z}^s, \tag{7}$$

and

$$\mathbf{C} = \mathbf{C}^s, \tag{8}$$

where $\mathbf{Z}^s$ is the vector of goods supplied at location s and $\mathbf{C}^s$ is the vector of commuting times at s. The Lagrangian expression is thus

$$L^* = X + \sum_{j=1}^{r} t_j(u) + w_j(H_j + C_j) + \lambda_0[U_0 - U(X, \mathbf{Y}, \mathbf{N}, \mathbf{C}, \mathbf{H})]$$

$$- \sum_{p=1}^{m} \lambda_p(Z_p^s - Z_p) + \sum_{j=1}^{r} \eta_j(C_j^s - C_j). \tag{9}$$

Minimization with respect to X, N_j, C_j^s, and Z_p^s produces the first-order conditions

$$\lambda_0 = \frac{1}{U_X}, \tag{10}$$

$$\lambda_0 = \frac{w_j}{U_{N_j}}, \tag{11}$$

$$\eta_j = \lambda_0 U_{C_j} - w_j \tag{12}$$

$$\lambda_p = \lambda_0\left(\sum_{i=1}^{n} U_{Y_i} \frac{\partial Y_i}{\partial Z_p}\right). \tag{13}$$

The Lagrange multipliers λ_0, λ_p, and η_j can be interpreted as the value of a marginal unit of utility, Z_p^s, and C_j^s, respectively. The third condition can be rewritten as

$$-\eta_j = \frac{-U_{C_j}}{U_X} + w_j, \tag{14}$$

which means that the value of a reduction in commuting time for the jth household member equals the wage minus the value of commuting time as a consumption good. As discussed by Nelson (1972), the fourth condition, written as

$$-\lambda_p = \left(\sum_{i=1}^{n} U_{Y_i} \frac{\partial Y_i}{\partial Z_p} \right) \bigg/ U_X, \tag{15}$$

is the change in rent the household is willing to pay for an additional unit of Z_p.

The expression for locational equilibrium in this model is complex, but is analogous to more familiar and simpler versions of the model. To derive the condition for locational equilibrium, consider the dual to the above problem. Here we maximize

$$U^* = U(X, Y, N, C, H) + \delta_0 \left[\sum_{j=1}^{r} w_j H_j + G - X - \sum_{k=1}^{m} q_k Z_k - \sum_{j=1}^{r} t_j(u) \right]$$

$$+ \sum_{j=1}^{r} \delta_j \left(T_j - \sum_{i=1}^{n} T_{ij} - H_j - N_j - C_j \right), \tag{16}$$

where δ_0 and δ_j are Lagrange multipliers. Maximization with respect to u yields

$$\sum_{j=1}^{r} \frac{\partial U}{\partial C_j} \frac{\partial C_j}{\partial u} - \delta_0 \left(\sum_{k=1}^{m} \frac{\partial q_k}{\partial u} Z_k + \sum_{j=1}^{r} \frac{\partial t_j}{\partial u} \right) - \sum_{j=1}^{r} \delta_j \frac{\partial C_j}{\partial u} = 0. \tag{17}$$

This equation can be rewritten as

$$\delta_0 \sum_{j=1}^{r} \frac{\partial t_j}{\partial u} + \sum_{j=1}^{r} \delta_j \frac{\partial C_j}{\partial u} = -\delta_0 \left[\sum_{k=1}^{m} \frac{\partial q_k}{\partial u} Z_k \right] + \sum_{j=1}^{r} \frac{\partial U}{\partial C_j} \frac{\partial C_j}{\partial u}, \tag{18}$$

which states that the marginal cost of moving a unit of distance equals the marginal benefit. As Yamada (1972) has pointed out, this condition for locational equilibrium may be satisfied at multiple locations. Indeed, the model presented by Mills (1972b, pp. 75–85) implies that a household is in locational equilibrium at *all* locations in the urban area.

2   The Demand for Housing and Residential Location: A Simplified Example

In order to fix ideas, let us examine the most commonly used model in the context of the synthesis provided above. This model was developed by Muth (1969). We assume that the household contains one individual who commutes to a job in the central business district (CBD). Utility is a function of the composite commodity X and housing services h, which are produced by the services of land L and capital K. Here housing is the only characteristic and land and capital are the goods purchased in the market. The individual's own time does not enter the production of h. Utility is not a function of commuting time. The composite commodity includes expenditures on leisure, wN.

The Lagrangian expression is

$$U^* = U(X, h) + \delta_0[Y - X - p(u)h - t(u)], \tag{19}$$

where Y is full income wT, $t(u)$ includes money and time cost of commuting, and δ_0 is the Lagrange multiplier. First-order conditions are

$$U_X - \delta_0 = 0, \tag{20}$$

$$U_h - \delta_0 p(u) = 0, \tag{21}$$

and

$$-\delta_0[p'(u)h + t'(u)] = 0. \tag{22}$$

Given that $\delta_0 \neq 0$, the condition for locational equilibrium becomes

$$t'(u) = -hp'(u), \tag{23}$$

which states that the marginal cost of moving a unit distance from the CBD equals the marginal benefit. The demand for housing can be written $h(u) = h(p(u), Y - t(u))$.

As Muth (1971a) has shown, this model can be used to derive the demand for urban residential land. The Nelson (1972) approach can be used to derive the marginal value of land. For the cost–minimization problem, the Lagrangian is

$$L^* = X + t(u) + \lambda_0[U_0 - U(X, h)] - \lambda_1(L^s - L), \tag{24}$$

where L^s is the amount of land supplied at location s. First-order conditions include

$$\lambda_0 = \frac{1}{U_X} \tag{25}$$

and

$$\lambda_1 = \lambda_0 U_h \frac{\partial h}{\partial L}, \qquad (26)$$

or

$$-\lambda_1 = \frac{U_h}{U_X} \frac{\partial h}{\partial L}. \qquad (27)$$

This final condition states that the marginal value of land equals the value of housing services on the margin times the marginal product of land.

Two essential features of this model should be emphasized. First, the goods that contribute to housing production, land, and capital, are distinguished by whether their price varies over space. The price of capital is assumed to be uniform over space. In a sense, capital can be thought of as a composite good that is elastically supplied everywhere. On the other hand, "land" may be a composite of those goods whose price varies over space. Thus, it is important to remember that in this simplified standard model we do not think of the housing market as being segmented because the price of one of the goods varies over space. Second, as pointed out by Muth (1966), the income elasticities of demand for land and capital must be equal because the production function is homogeneous of degree one. Own-price elasticities for land and capital may be different in Muth's model, of course. For example, assume that the production function has a constant elasticity of substitution σ. Then, as Allen (1967, p. 373) has shown, for a household

$$\frac{\partial L}{\partial R} \frac{R}{L} = -(S_K \sigma + S_L \eta) \qquad (28)$$

and

$$\frac{\partial K}{\partial r} \frac{r}{K} = -(S_L \sigma + S_K \eta), \qquad (29)$$

where R is the price of land, r is the price of capital, η is the household's price elasticity of demand for housing (defined as a positive number), and S_K and S_L are the shares of capital and land as percentages of the value of output ($S_K + S_L = 1$). Clearly, the two price elasticities are equal if and only if $S_K = S_L = .5$.

3   The Demand for Land: An Extension of Muth's Approach

For those researchers who are primarily interested in the demand for residential land, it is natural to specify that land itself is one of the housing characteristics in the utility function. In addition, the usual procedure is to assume that the housing characteristic land is produced only by the input good land and that the input good land does not enter into the production of any other characteristic. This approach has been used extensively by Alonso (1964), Harris *et al.* (1968) and Wheaton (1974, 1977a), for example. Altering the simple model presented above, a simple version of this approach can specify the utility function $U = U(X,h,L)$, where L is land and h, housing, is produced by various other input goods such as types of capital (square footage, hardwood floors, etc.) and variable inputs (fuel, maintenance, etc.). The budget constraint is now $Y = X - ph - R(u)L - t(u)$, where $R(u)$ is the rent on land. If δ_0 is the Lagrange multiplier, the first-order conditions include

$$U_X - \delta_0 = 0, \tag{30}$$

$$U_h - \delta_0 p(u) = 0, \tag{31}$$

$$U_L - \delta_0 R(u) = 0, \tag{32}$$

and

$$-\delta_0[p'(u)h + R'(u)L + t'(u)] = 0. \tag{33}$$

If we assume that all input goods for the production of housing are elastically supplied at all locations, then $p'(u) = 0$ and Eq. (33) implies that

$$t'(u) = -LR'(u). \tag{34}$$

The demand for land can be written $L(u) = L[R(u), Y - t(u)]$. Furthermore, if $p'(u) = 0$, housing can be included as part of the composite commodity if there is no interest in examining separately the demand for housing (as housing is defined here). This approach is certainly permissible (and even elegant) if the land market can be considered to be distinct from the housing market. However, this approach may not be as useful if the focus is on the short run, implying that we would assume that fixed housing capital and land are purchased together in a bundle. More discussion of this point is contained in Chapter 4.

4   A Survey of Studies of the Demand for Housing and Residential Location

This section is a summary of empirical studies of housing or land demand since the late 1960s that incorporate in the analysis the demand for residential location and/or neighborhood attributes (goods). Each study provides different answers to the questions listed above concerning the number of characteristics, the total number of goods, and the number of goods that contribute to the production of each characteristic. No empirical study has considered the possibility that time of the household members is an input into any characteristic, so no further consideration will be given to this issue.

The survey begins with a particularly interesting early study by Harris *et al.* (1968). In their formulation utility is a function of a composite good, lot size, leisure, and the amenities of the neighborhood measured in dollars per day. By specifying the utility function in this way, they assume implicitly that all features of housing, besides lot size and amenities, are part of the composite commodity whose price does not vary over space. The price of land per square foot is assumed to be the sum of two components; the value of travel savings and the value of amenities. The amenity value of a site is found by subtracting the value of travel savings (calculated by placing a standard value on commuting time) from the market price of the land. In their empirical results, the supply of amenity increases with the percentage of upper class residents and decreases with a location near nonresidential activity and percent occupants who are renters. The demand for amenity increases sharply with family income, and the demand for lot size increases with income but does not increase with family size. However, the equation for the demand for lot size includes a variable that measures the type of structure in which the household lives. This variable equals 1 if the structure is single detached, 2 if single attached, 3 if two to four apartments, etc. This equation is thus incorrectly specified because structure type should be considered endogenous. If structure type were omitted from the specification, it is likely that family size would be positively related to lot size because smaller families probably live in larger structures as defined above. In a way, then, this study raises the possibility that the taste for lot size varies with family size. In any case, the study by Harris *et al.* (1968) is highly innovative in its use of simplifying assumptions and deserves more attention than it has perhaps received.

Another study that is more clearly in the Muth (1969) tradition is the book by Evans (1973). In this formulation, household (individual) utility is a function of housing "space units," commuting time, work time, and a vector of other activities. Other activities are produced with fixed proportions of time and money expenditures. Housing space units are produced by the services of land and capital, as in Muth's model. Continuous substitution of land for capital is assumed. Evans (1973, pp. 88–97) devotes considerable attention to the possibility that utility is also a function of the density of development of an area (the number of dwellings per acre on a housing estate of several hundred houses or flats). Evans points out that, if the housing market is perfectly competitive, it will not be in the interest of an individual small supplier to take account of this external effect. Furthermore, it is reasonable to assume that no single consumer can influence the density of development. Thus, Evans concludes that market outcomes will not be influenced by the taste for the density of development. The situation is altered if a local monopolist controls the whole area in question. It would be in his interest to respond to a taste for low density. Evans believes that the instances of local monopolies are not frequent enough to have any significant impact. However, Evans (1973) neglects to examine the possibility that the taste for low density might be translated into a taste for the individual household's lot size. The existence of a preference for large lots per se would alter market outcomes from a situation in which households are indifferent to the alternative bundles of land and capital that produce the same number of housing space units. More discussion of this possibility is provided below.

Researchers who have been associated with the National Bureau of Economic Research have conducted studies that attempt to identify empirically the separate housing and residential location characteristics that should be included in the household's utility function. These studies have been conducted by Kain and Quigley (1970a,b, 1975), Straszheim (1975), and others. The NBER studies assert that housing should not be viewed as a single-valued commodity as Muth (1969) does, but that the demands for separate housing characteristics should be estimated. An early study by David (1962) estimated separate demands for housing quantity (measured as the number of rooms) and quality (measured by rent per room) and found that income and family size influenced the demand for these two characteristics differently. In particular, as family size increases the demand for quantity increases and the demand for quality decreases. The net result of an increase in family size is a decline in expenditures on housing. Kain and Quigley (1975) estimated separate demand functions for a large number of housing and locational goods that are assumed to contribute to three characteristics: dwelling unit quality and amenity, dwelling unit size, and neighborhood attributes. Furthermore, all of these demand functions were estimated separately by race (black and white). The goods that produce dwelling-unit quality and amenity are age of buildings, presence of hot water, presence of central heating, and interviewer ratings of interior and exterior quality. The production function for dwelling unit size includes the number of rooms, number of baths, first-floor area, and lot size. Neighborhood attributes are a function of interviewer ratings of the quality of adjacent units and the block face, median years of schooling in the census tract, percentage white in the census tract, miles from the CBD, school quality (achievement test scores), and crime (number of crimes per block). Kain and Quigley (1975) summarize their results by stating

Households with larger incomes and more education are seen to choose higher quality dwelling units, located further from the CBD. They also consume more of the attributes of neighborhood quality and prestige and units of slightly larger physical size. In contrast, at the same income, larger households consume substantially more of the attributes of physical size, particularly dwelling-unit size, and less of the attributes of dwelling-unit and residential quality [pp. 254–255].

In a further analysis, Kain and Quigley aggregate the various goods into measures of the three characteristics using the implicit prices of the goods found through the estimation of hedonic indices. Also, exterior space (parcel area) is examined as a separate characteristic. In this analysis, "Increases in income and education are associated with substantially greater consumption of exterior space and dwelling quality. Increases in family size are associated with greater consumption of interior space [Kain and Quigley, 1975, p. 282]." A serious shortcoming of the studies by Kain and Quigley is the failure to include the prices of the characteristics as explanatory variables. As will be discussed more extensively below, Kain and Quigley believe that there is variation over space of the prices of most, if not all, housing and residential location characteristics. Indeed, not even the price of exterior space (land value corrected for neighborhood quality) has been included in the analysis of the demand for exterior space. Nonetheless, Kain and Quigley seem to have identified some plausible patterns of demand for various housing characteristics.

The study by Straszheim (1975) followed the same general research strategy as Kain and Quigley in that separate demand functions were estimated for various attributes of houses: tenure type (own or rent), number of rooms, age of structure, and lot size. In addition, Straszheim allowed the demand for each attribute to be a function of household income, the own-price of the attribute, the price of a "standard" house, and (possibly) the prices of other housing attributes. The prices of housing attributes and the standard house are taken from the estimates of hedonic functions that allow the prices to vary over space. The derivation of these prices required a considerable amount of effort. Indeed, the more detail used in the derivation of these spatial price variations the better the results are likely to be. The model is, in Straszheim's judgment (1975, p. 95), a considerable simplification because of neighborhood effects and spatial discontinuities in housing prices, and Straszheim regards the estimates of the model as "largely a pedagogical exercise." Demand functions for each attribute were estimated separately for households in sixteen life cycle classes. Variations in income and price elasticities across life cycle classes were evident, although the statistical significance of these variations was not examined. Also, within life cycle classes, there appear to be variations in the income and own-price elasticities of demand for the various attributes. Again, the statistical significance of these variations is not calculated. As Straszheim points out in part, these results may be at variance with the assumptions made in Muth's model described above. Straszheim (1975, p. 20) argues that Muth's model implies homogeneity of tastes with respect to land–capital proportions. Furthermore, as mentioned above, Muth's model implies that the income elasticity of demand for land and capital are equal. Straszheim's evidence suggests that these elasticities may not be equal even after taste variations, as represented by life cycle grouping, are controlled.

For our purposes, one key question is whether there are substantial differences in the income and price elasticities of demand for the number of rooms (a proxy for amount of capital) and lot size. The income elasticities found by Straszheim (1975, pp. 174–182) for 16 life cycle groups of home-owners fall within the range of zero to $+.46$, with the income elasticity for lot size exceeding the income elasticity for number of rooms in 15 out of 16 cases. This average difference in income elasticities is .14 (.26 $-$ .12). This difference is not large. Furthermore, if a better measure of capital were used that included a measure of quality and a better measure of quantity, such as square footage, the income elasticity of the capital input would probably be higher than the average of .12 found by Straszheim. The own-price elasticities of demand for the number of rooms ranges from $-.09$ to $-.24$ over the 16 life cycle groups, while the range for lot size is (neglecting one positive and insignificant estimate) $-.40$ to -2.96. The difference in the average own-price elasticities is -1.0 ($-1.13 + .13$), a substantial magnitude. However, it is crucial to realize that Muth's model does *not* imply equality of own-price elasticities. Indeed, Muth's approach (1966) specifically allows for variations in own-price elasticities. Consequently, I conclude that, despite the monumental effort made, the evidence presented by Straszheim (1975) does not offer strong support for a more complex specification of housing characteristics and goods than that used by Muth and Evans.

Two other researchers, Davies (1974) and King (1976, 1977), have made careful studies that relate to the issue of the degree of complexity needed in the demand model. Both researchers explicitly specify a model of housing and residential location goods and characteristics of the Lancaster type. The study by Davies (1974) is interesting in that, given 19 measures of housing and residential location goods, factor analysis was used to determine the number of characteristics and the extent of the contribution of each of the 19 goods to each of the characteristics.[5] King (1977) has pointed out that "the mechanical technique might as readily combine as isolate specific characteristics [p. 1087]." However, because Davies (1974) assumed that

---

[5] Other studies that use factor analysis or principal components analysis for this purpose include Kain and Quigley (1970b), Little (1976), and Wilkinson (1973).

the prices of the goods do not vary with location, he did not estimate demand functions for the goods. Instead, he estimated an hedonic equation with the measures of the factors (characteristics) as independent variables. The significant variables in this hedonic equation ($t > 2.0$) are number of bedrooms, central heating dummy, plot size, and five factors shown in Table 1.1. The goods which contribute to these factors are also shown in Table 1.1. In general, there appears to be very little overlap in the sense that a good makes a significant contribution to more than one characteristic. In particular, the neighborhood amenities and the measures of the quality of the dwelling unit per se seem to contribute to separate characteristics.

The study by Kain and Quigley (1970b) followed a similar procedure and reached a somewhat different conclusion. The first factor identified was called basic residential quality and included variables that measure the quality of the exterior of the dwelling unit (structure and parcel), the quality of adjacent structures and parcels, and the quality of the block face. The second factor, dwelling unit quality, depends only upon the quality of the interior of the unit. Other factors supplement the explanatory power of the first factor to a small degree. These results suggest that the separation of exterior quality into a dwelling unit and parcel specific characteristic and a neighborhood amenity characteristic is difficult.

The studies by King (1976, 1977) are a notable contribution to this discussion because he found housing expenditure elasticities to be quite differ-

TABLE 1.1

Housing and Residential Location Characteristics and the Associated Goods as Identified by Davies

1. Open space (+)	a. Amount of open space within 1/8 and 1/4 mile radii
	b. Amount of residential land within 1/8 mile radius (negative sign)
2. Industrial land (−)	a. Amount of industrial land within 1/8 and 1/4 mile radii
3. General absence of industrial nuisance (+)	a. Amount of industrial land within 1/2 mile radius (negative sign)
4. Seclusion (+)	a. Distance to main road
	b. Distance to railway
5. Poor quality dwelling	a. Garage (negative sign)
	b. Age (negative sign)
	c. Central heating (negative sign)
	d. Plot size (negative sign)
	e. Density
	f. Terraced house type (negative sign)

Source: Davies (1974).

ent for four characteristics. In a procedure similar to that used by Straszheim (1975), King estimated an hedonic function that allowed the prices of the goods to vary over space. He then assumed that the goods could be aggregated into four characteristics as shown in Table 1.2. The results of the estimation of demand functions for the characteristics indicate that larger families purchase more interior space and less interior and exterior quality and site. These results agree with the results mentioned above obtained by David (1962). The housing outlay and own-price elasticities are also shown in Table 1.2. The outlay elasticities for structural features and interior and exterior quality are relatively high and relatively low for interior space and site. These results are of great interest if the purpose of the analysis is to predict the form in which additions to housing capital are made as income rises. However, the results, while suggestive, do not necessarily demonstrate that the income elasticity of demand for Muth's capital and land are different.

TABLE 1.2
Housing Characteristics and Their Goods as Defined by King

Characteristics	Outlay elasticity	Own-price elasticity	Goods
Structural features	2.04	−.15	Full insulation Number of garages Number of baths Basement laundry facilities
Interior and exterior quality	1.72	−.20	Hardwood flooring Number of fireplaces Modern electrical system Steam heat Rating of overall quality Type of exterior facing
Interior space	.64	−.14	Interior square feet Number of small special purpose rooms Basement characteristics One or two stories

Site	.54	−.82	Lot size
			Distance to CBD
			Perceived neighborhood
			  quality
			Provision of public garbage
			  collection and sewerage

Source: King (1977).

A recent study by Diamond (1978b) has focused specifically on the demand for various neighborhood amenities in the suburban areas of the Chicago metropolitan area between 1969 and 1971. Only new residences were included in the analysis so that Diamond could use the long-run implications of the theory he presents. Diamond extends the model of the demand for land discussed above to include neighborhood amenities. Suppose that some level of an amenity, designated $\bar{a}$, is exogenously supplied to consumers of land. The utility function for the household is now written $U(X, L, a)$ and the budget constraint can be written $Y = X - R(u, a)L - t(u)$. Maximization of utility subject to the budget constraint, where δ_0 is the Lagrange multiplier, produces the first-order conditions

$$U_X - \delta_0 = 0, \tag{35}$$

$$U_h - \delta_0 R(u, a) = 0, \tag{36}$$

$$U_a - \delta_0 \frac{\partial R}{\partial a} L = 0, \tag{37}$$

and

$$-\delta_0 \left[\frac{\partial R}{\partial u} L + t'(u) \right] = 0. \tag{38}$$

Here $\partial R/\partial a$ is the market equilibrium value at $\bar{a}$ of the marginal effect of the amenity on land rent. Manipulation of these conditions produces

$$V_a = \frac{U_a}{U_X} = \frac{\partial R}{\partial a} L, \tag{39}$$

the marginal value of the amenity. The key insight of this formulation is that the value of the amenity to the household is proportional to the quantity of land consumed. As King (1973) has explained,

> But consider the decision of a developer of vacant land. If his location enjoys a fine view, households will pay extra to live there. To maximize profits, the developer must select an optimal lot size; the smaller the lots, the more houses he will have available to sell at a premium. Consequently, a buyer wanting a double-sized lot must be prepared to pay the location premium for both small lots. Otherwise, the developer will prefer a sale to a second household. This suggests that payments for amenities will be proportional to lot size [p. 73].

This formulation assumes that lot sizes are continuously variable but, as King (1973, p. 73) has noted, this assumption may be inappropriate in the face of zoning restrictions and topographical irregularities.

For purposes of empirical estimation, Diamond (1978b, p. 12) writes

$$\int_{R^1}^{R^2} L(R, Y) \, dR = \sum_{i=1}^{n} \int_{a_i^1}^{a_i^2} V_{a_i}(a_i, Y) \, da_i, \tag{40}$$

where a_i is the level of amenity i and n is the number of amenities considered.[6] Assuming that the demand for land can be written $L = kY^bR^c$, the dependent variable in the analysis becomes $kY^b[(R^2)^{c+1} - (R^1)^{c+1}]/(c + 1)$. The right-hand side of Eq. (40) is a general functional form in which the independent variables are of the form $(a_i^2 - a_i^1)$. Interaction terms of the form $Y^p(a_i^2 - a_i^1)^q$ are also included, where p and q are exponents. After Eq. (40) is estimated, the income elasticity of the value of an amenity may be calculated as $(\partial V_{a_i}/\partial Y)(\overline{Y}/\overline{V}_{a_i})$.

In order to estimate Eq. (40), an estimate of the demand for land must first be found. Using the sample of 414 new homes (as of 1969–1971), Diamond (1978b) found that $L = e^{7.21}Y^{.64}R^{-.64}$. This demand function itself is of considerable interest in that both the income and price elasticities of demand for land in the Chicago suburbs are estimated to be .64. Using the estimated demand function for land, Diamond (1978b) paired the 414 observations on the basis of household income and calculated the differences in land rent per square foot and amenity levels for each pair. Using 207 observations, Eq. (40) was estimated and the income elasticities of the values of various amenities at the point of means were calculated, with the following results, where + indicates that the income elasticity is significantly different from zero at the 95% level.

Various amenities	Income elasticity
Access to CBD	2.11+
Access to commuter rail station	2.88
Within 5 miles of Lake Michigan	.72+
Lack of crime in municipality	2.36+
Air quality	.88
Topography (hilliness)	−.92

These results indicate that the income elasticities of the demand for access to the CBD and lack of crime are high relative to the income elasticity of demand for land, while the elasticities for proximity to Lake Michigan and air quality are relatively low. It would be of great interest to estimate such elasticities for other amenities such as goods produced by the local public sector. In any case, there appears to be a substantial variation in the income elasticities for various amenities in the Chicago suburbs. This result means that these amenities should be considered to be separate characteristics in the household's utility function.

A study by Wheaton (1977b) has been designed to estimate the variations in the price elasticities of demand for various housing characteristics while assuming that all the housing characteristics have equal income elasticities.

---

[6] The income term should be written $Y − t(u)$, where $t(u)$ is the amount paid for transportation at location u.

The model developed by Wheaton (1977b) posits a utility function $U = U(M,X)$, where X is a vector of housing attributes and M is the composite commodity. The utility function is assumed to be either a Cobb–Douglas or a CES function, implying that the income elasticities of all commodities are equal to 1.0. Wheaton's estimation of the parameters of the utility functions produces some interesting variations in the marginal value of housing attributes according to household income, age, and size. This approach to the study of the demand for housing attributes appears to be promising, although the necessity of making restrictive assumptions on the form of the utility function limits the scope of the conclusions.

Before concluding this review of empirical demand studies, it should be noted that a large number of hedonic studies have been completed that demonstrate the importance of various neighborhood amenities. In addition to the studies mentioned above, there are studies of racial price differentials, studies of the capitalization of the property tax and public services, predictive studies used for assessment purposes, and studies of air and noise pollution. These studies will be discussed in Chapter 3.

How complex must the demand model be to provide hypotheses concerning the operation of the urban land and housing markets that are reasonably accurate? This chapter has revealed that there are deep disagreements about the answer to this question. The extreme ends of a continuum of answers to the question are represented by Muth (1969) and Evans (1973) on the one hand and Straszheim (1975) and Kain and Quigley (1975) on the other. My preliminary conclusions include the proposition that neighborhood locational goods are important for the determination of the demand for locations. One should include such variables as the socioeconomic status of the neighborhood, crime levels in the area, the quality of the nearby housing stock, the presence of nearby industrial land use, open land, the property tax rate, the quality of public services provided, the amount of commercial traffic, the conditions of streets, alleys, and sidewalks, and the levels of air and noise pollution. No one has determined how to combine these "goods" into a smaller number of characteristics. The selection of which goods to include in a particular study must be based in part on the a priori judgment of the researcher based upon knowledge of the urban area in question and the purposes of the study. On the other hand, the demand for housing narrowly defined as the services supplied by the goods provided by the structure and lot (as opposed to the location) can probably be simplified to Muth's formulation. The studies surveyed do not provide clear evidence that the income elasticities of demand for housing capital and land are significantly different. There are great advantages in the parsimony achieved through the use of this assumption.

Another issue that should be addressed is the necessity to include in the utility function the amount of time spent working and commuting. Of particular importance to studies of locational choice is the proposition that utility depends upon the commuting time to and from work. The next chapter considers this question in detail.

5   Homeownership and the Demand for Housing

Another seemingly important feature of the housing market is that housing can either be owned or rented by the consumer. Is there evidence to suggest that including the distinction between owning and renting is important to the explanation of the basic patterns of population density and residential land values? Muth (1969, p. 19) believes that this distinction is unimportant except for the favorable federal income tax treatment accorded to homeowners and the existence of mortgage insurance and subsidy programs. On the other hand, Aaron (1970, p. 796) argues that owning and renting involve differences in responsibilities and risks, so that the consumer purchases packages of housing services that are different depending upon the decision to own or rent. MacRae and Struyk (1977) have worked out formally a theory of the demand for housing that incorporates the distinction between owning and renting. The purpose of this section is to present and extend this theory and to make a preliminary judgment as to its usefulness for the purposes at hand.

To keep the exposition simple, suppose that the utility function is the same as that used by Muth (1969), or $U(X,h)$, where X is the composite commodity (including leisure) and h is housing services. The budget constraint is $Y = X - p(u)h - t(u)$ as before. Now the simplest method for introducing the distinction between owning and renting is to assume that the price of a unit of housing services, $p(u)$, may vary according to the mode of tenure. The household selects its budget constraint by selecting the lower price of housing: either $p_o(u)$, the price of owner occupied housing, or $p_r(u)$, the rental price. The price of owner occupied housing is known to depend upon several factors: the interest rate on the mortgage (which depends upon the risk to the lender), the transaction cost of making the housing purchase, the expected length of occupancy, the expected change in the value of the house, the income tax treatment of the homeowner, and (perhaps) the quantity of housing purchased.[7] The risk to the lender depends upon a number of factors, including the income level and the variability

---

[7] Until recently, with the rapid increase in the number of condominium apartments, small quantities of housing services such as one-bedroom apartments were not generally available for purchase. One method for capturing this relationship is to assume that $p_o(u)$ depends upon h.

of income of the household. The demand functions for housing can thus be written as

$$h_o(u) = h_o(p_o(u), Y - t(u)) \quad \text{if} \quad p_o(u) < p_r(u), \qquad (41)$$
$$h_r(u) = h_r(p_r(u), Y - t(u)) \quad \text{if} \quad p_r(u) < p_o(u), \qquad (42)$$

and

$$h(u) = h(p(u), Y - t(u)) \quad \text{if} \quad p_o(u) = p_r(u), \qquad (43)$$

where $h_o(u)$ and $h_r(u)$ are the quantities demanded of owner occupied and rental housing, respectively.

It is useful to illustrate the quantitative importance of some of these factors that determine $p_o(u)/p_r(u)$. The illustration is an adaptation of the figures presented by Shelton (1968).[8] Assume that the renter and owner have equal income levels, so the fact that $p_o(u)$ may depend upon income initially is not being examined. Both households earn a $10,000 salary and both consider a "unit" of housing services to be a house valued at $20,000. These assumptions will be relaxed later. Further assumptions, using Shelton's data, are as follows.

1. Both houses have a $14,000 mortgage, or a down payment, or equity DP of $6000, which is 30% of house value HV.
2. The annual expenses for the housing services are

PT	Property tax	$300	1.5% of HV
I	Interest at 6%	840	
M	Maintenance for owner	200	1.0% of HV
D	Real depreciation	250	1.25% of HV
OC	Opportunity cost of down payment at 8%	480[9]	

Rental housing has additional expenses:

MN	Management	$100	.5% of HV
V	Vacancy allowance	60	.3% of HV
AM	Additional maintenance	120	.6% of HV

The renter is assumed to possess $6000, which earns 8% in the stock market.

Using the figures listed above, the annual real cost of providing the rental housing services is $2350 ($1590 + $280 + $480). The owner of the

---

[8] The prices in the example obviously reflect the state of the housing market in 1968 rather than current prices.

[9] The landlord is assumed to earn 8% on his portfolio. If the interest rate r charged on mortgages is the same as that which could be earned on investments, then the homeowner is indifferent to all debt–equity ratios for his house, assuming he values the return from his equity at its opportunity cost, the interest payments he would have to make if his equity were less. He saves $r(1 - t)$ by reducing his mortgage by $1, and earns the same amount by investing, where t is the marginal tax rate on income.

rental unit is allowed to take excess depreciation of about $150 (.75% of
HV), according to Shelton (1968). Thus the rent is $2200 per annum.[10]

Discovering the real cost of the services of owner occupied housing is
more difficult because some of the real cost does not involve a cash flow.
Real cost items which do produce a cash flow are the property tax ($300),
interest ($840), maintenance ($200), and real depreciation ($250). The
opportunity cost of the down payment ($480) should also be included, for a
total of $2070. The other three costs of rental housing (management costs
of $100, vacancy allowance of $60, and additional maintenance of $120) are
less for owner occupants. My conjectures for these costs are as follows.
Owner occupants cause less damage than renters, so I assume no additional
maintenance costs. The management of rental units consists of collecting
the rent and handling complaints. With an owner occupied unit the rent
transactions are not made, but the cost of handling complaints exists no
matter which type of tenure is used. For example, the repairmen must be
contacted if something breaks. Assume that the time spent making such
contacts is worth $25 per annum. The cost for vacancy arises from the turn-
over of tenants. Shelton (1968) demonstrates that owning is cheaper when
the length of tenure is $3\frac{1}{2}$ years or more because of the transaction cost of
the home purchase. Assume that the turnover of owners is much less than
for renters, so there is no vacancy allowance cost for owner occupied housing.
The resulting real annual cost of owner occupied housing is $2095.

Let us now find out how much the income tax laws reduce the private
cost of owner occupied housing below the social cost. The reduction in
private cost arises from the failure to tax the imputed income from the $6000
equity (net rent), allowing property taxes and interest costs to be deducted
from adjusted gross income (a deduction of $1140), and a failure to tax the
income from management services that the owner occupant performs for
himself, an amount of $25. Thus these real costs of $1645 appear to the
owner occupant as a cost of $1645(1 − t)$, where t is the marginal tax rate.
If t is .19, these deductions have reduced the private cost of housing by
$312.55 per annum, or 1.56% of house value. Compared to the renter, the
owner saves $417.55 per annum, or 19% of the annual rent of $2200.[11] Kain
and Quigley (1972) used Shelton's figures to arrive at a saving of 30% of
annual rent. Their estimate is higher because rent was underestimated at

---

[10] Shelton (1968) assumed the rent paid is $2000, based upon the usual rent-to-value rule
of 1 to 10. He did not notice the inconsistency in his data, but the one-to-ten rule is an approximation used instead of detailed calculations. Laidler (1969), for example, used 11% as the
gross rent-to-value ratio.

[11] It is assumed that both owner and renter itemize deductions. However, if the renter uses
the standard deduction and his real deductions are less than the amount of the standard deduction, then the advantage of homeownership is reduced.

$2000 and the down payment was assumed to be smaller. Aaron (1970, 1972) has made extensive calculations of this type. If the transaction cost of home purchase is $.07(HV)$, or $1400, as Shelton suggests, then it is cheaper to own if length of tenure exceeds 3.35 years.

A more general expression for the saving from homeownership can be derived by allowing income, house value, and down payment to vary. The cost of renting includes $PT + M + D + MN + V + AM$ minus excess depreciation, which equals $.044HV$. To this must be added interest and opportunity costs, or $.08(DP)(HV) + .06(HV)(1 - DP)$. The total cost of renting is thus $.044(HV) + .08(DP)(HV) + .06(HV)(1 - DP)$. The cost of owning includes the property tax of $.015(HV)(1 - t)$, the sum $M + D + MN = .0225(HV)$, and $.00125(HV)(1 - t)$, where this last term is the $25 of self-provided management services. The sum of interest and opportunity cost is is $.08(HV)(DP)(1 - t) + .06(HV)(1 - DP)(1 - t)$. Thus the total cost of owning is $.01625(HV)(1 - t) + .0225(HV) + .08(HV)(DP)(1 - t) + .06(HV)(1 - DP)(1 - t)$. Subtracting the cost of owning from the cost of renting yields

$$.00525(HV) + .01625t(HV) + .06t(HV)(1 - DP) + .08t(HV)(DP),$$

which can be written

$$.00525(HV) + .01625t(HV) + tr_b(HV) + t(r_1 - r_b)(HV)(DP),$$

where r_1 is the lending rate and r_b is the borrowing rate for the consumer. We may wish to write $r_b = r_b(Y)$ to indicate that, as MacRae and Struyk (1977) suggest, the mortgage interest rate depends upon the income level of the household. In this example we have considered the merits of owning or renting the same house, so we should add the increase in the value of the house in excess of the general increase in housing values over the year in question, written $\Delta(HV)/(HV) - \Delta P_H/P_H$, where the latter term is the general inflation in housing prices. Using $.07(HV)$ as the transaction cost of home purchase and N as the number of years of expected occupancy, the comparison of $p_o(\mathbf{u})$ with $p_r(\mathbf{u})$ can be made by comparing $.07(HV)/N$ with the saving derived from homeownership.

The effects of the favorable tax treatment of homeowners on the housing market can be examined. The analysis follows White and White (1977). To simplify the analysis, assume that units of housing services can be supplied to renters and owners at the same cost. Furthermore, assume that the supply of housing has a positive slope. In Figure 1.1 S is the supply of housing services, D_r is the renters' demand curve, D_o is the owners' demand curve, and D_t is the total demand for housing.[12] Initial equilibrium price and

[12] D_r and D_o are drawn assuming one price for housing, whether owned or rented.

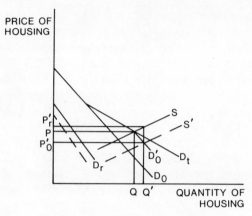

Figure 1.1.   Impact on housing market of a subsidy to homeowners.

quantity are P and Q, respectively. The tax subsidy to homeowners can be represented by a shift downward in the supply curve that owners face. This shift is shown by S'. It must be remembered that only homeowners can take advantage of the reduced cost of housing; the response is shown by demand curve D_o'. This response includes the shift of some renters to owner status, and D_r shifts slightly to the left as p_o/p_r declines. The end result is that the price of housing paid by owners falls from P to P_o', and the price paid by renters rises from P to P_r'. This increase in the price paid by renters is needed to generate the overall increase in housing supply brought forth in response to the subsidy to homeowners. In conclusion, because P_o'/P_r' is less than 1.0, we expect the consumption of housing to be greater for owners than renters at a given income level. As will be shown in Chapter 5, these results imply that population density will be lower for owners, ceteris paribus.

The subsidy to homeowners also influences the demand for amenities. If an amenity, designated a, is added to the utility function in the simple Muth (1969) model used in this section, it can easily be shown that

$$U_a/U_X = \frac{\partial p}{\partial a} h, \tag{44}$$

or the marginal value of the amenity is proportional to housing consumption. Now consider the effects of subsidizing ownership for one household. Lowering the price of housing for this household will increase h and leave $\partial p/\partial a$ unchanged, meaning that the marginal value of the amenity rises. Consideration of the impacts on the housing market of a subsidy to a substantial number of households is deferred to Chapter 5.

To summarize this chapter, we have concluded that we can reject the theory that housing is a single unobservable commodity if housing is meant to include neighborhood locational characteristics. However, it seems likely that we can assume that the goods housing capital, operating inputs, maintenance, and the residential lot produce a single characteristic, which I shall call *housing*. Other characteristics associated with the choice of residential location such as public services, air pollution, etc., cannot be conveniently aggregated. An examination of the impact of the subsidization of homeowners indicates that these subsidies influence the demand for housing (as defined here) and neighborhood locational characteristics. It remains to be seen how making the distinction between owners and renters will improve the explanatory power of a model of residential density and land values.

Appendix   Access to Employment

Access to employment is obviously a major factor determining the demand for housing at a particular location. Indeed, the standard monocentric model of the housing market (described in detail in Chapter 5) begins with the assumption that employment is concentrated at the center of the metropolitan area (CBD) and, thus, uses distance to the CBD as the measure of access to employment. For many purposes, the monocentric assumption is of sufficient accuracy. For example, Muth (1969, p. 215), in his study of the South Side of Chicago for 1950, calculated, for a sample of census tracts, the correlations between distance to the CBD and measures of access to employment. The correlations between distance to the CBD and access to manufacturing employment and access to retail employment were −.84 and −.98, respectively. However, it appears that the access to employment of residential sites has changed over time. This appendix provides a summary of the evidence to support this point.

Time series data on employment location are extremely difficult to acquire, so it is possible only to put together bits and pieces of the story. In 1960 the Census of Population began to collect data on place of work. Table 1.A1 contains for 1960 and 1970 the reported information on place of work for those people who lived in the Chicago SMSA. Assuming no one aged 14 and 15 was employed in 1960, we can conclude that employment reported as located in the city of Chicago declined by 235,695, or 14.9%, over the 10-year period. Employment reported to be located in the rest of the SMSA increased by 479,812, or 68.1%.

The Census of Manufacturers provides information on employment in the city of Chicago from 1899 to 1972. These data are shown in Table 1.A2. While the data for 1939 and before are not exactly comparable to the

TABLE 1.A1
Location of Employment (Residents of the SMSA)

	1960[a]	1970[b]
Total	2,481,094	2,790,485
City of Chicago	1,578,036	1,342,341
Rest of SMSA	704,751	1,184,563
Outside of SMSA	36,745	55,001
Not reported	161,562	208,558

[a]Employed persons aged 14 and over are included.
[b]Employed persons aged 16 and over are included.

TABLE1.A2
Manufacturing Employment in the Chicago SMSA[a]

	All employees			Production workers		
	Chicago	Cook County	SMSA	Chicago	Cook County	SMSA
1899	na	na	na	221,191	na	na
1900	297,624	326,111	351,993	262,621	269,748	292,202
1904	289,529	na	na	241,984	na	na
1909	356,954	na	na	293,977	na	na
1914	387,319	na	na	313,710	na	na
1919	502,100	na	na	403,942	442,193	481,161
1929	491,191	563,778	na	405,399	462,750	502,294
1939	402,840	na	na	343,903	389,261	422,705
1947	668,056	788,872	857,801	532,130	626,405	682,028
1954	614,847	765,678	889,784	469,010	581,674	644,101
1958	569,356	766,174	857,238	389,607	522,647	587,311
1963	508,797	747,990	860,637	350,368	513,485	593,600
1967	546,500	831,100	983,100	382,700	579,400	683,600
1972	430,100	738,700	909,300	293,100	492,000	605,000

[a]Proprietors and partners of unincorporated firms are excluded. Milk processors are included in 1954 and subsequent years, but excluded in previous years. In 1947 and subsequent years excluded were dried fruit packers, retailers that manufacture ice cream, retail bakeries, ready mix concrete makers, and machine shops that do only repair work. Employment figures for 1947 and before are averages for the year, and employment for 1954 and later years is as of the census week.

later figures (see the footnote to Table 1.A2), a reasonably clear pattern emerges. Employment growth is evident through the period to 1929. The figure for 1919 for all employees is slightly greater than the 1929 figure, but the effects of the World War I boom probably influenced the 1919 data. The next year reported was 1939, and the effects of the depression are still

TABLE 1.A3
Paid Employees in Retail Trade[a]

	Chicago	Cook County	SMSA
1929	204,828	na	na
1935	160,917	177,996	191,388
1939	184,449	207,802	226,135
1948	248,763	309,376	338,733
1954	223,545	273,490	306,803
1958	225,158	290,568	331,387
1963	210,064	299,064	352,622
1967	217,964	321,815	389,633
1972	193,096	332,725	429,845

[a]Employment for 1939 and before is the average for the year. Employment for subsequent years is as of the census week.

TABLE 1.A4
Paid Employees in Wholesale Trade[a]

	Chicago	Cook County	SMSA
1929	135,083	na	na
1935	83,349	na	na
1939	95,494	98,310	100,305
1948[b]	138,194[c]	139,162	142,658[c,d]
1954	131,194	142,979	148,306
1958	132,302	155,349	162,131
1963	121,407	158,532	170,973
1967	131,247	182,180	195,890
1972	101,175	169,102	194,193

[a]Employment for 1939 and before is the average for the year. Employment for subsequent years is as of the census week.
[b]Figures for 1939 and before not strictly comparable to figures for 1948 and later years.
[c]Figures for Chicago and SMSA for 1948 not strictly comparable to figures for 1954.
[d]McHenry County not reported. Employment figure was 289 for 1954.

evident. The peak of manufacturing employment in the city of Chicago in the table was in 1947, with a total of 668,000 for all employees. There has been steady decline from 1947 to the present, with the exception of the boom period of the late 1960s. The Census of Manufacturers recorded an increase in all employees of 37,700 from 1963 to 1967. Table 1.A2 also shows the available information for Cook County and the SMSA. Employment in manufacturing both in Cook County and the SMSA as a whole seems to follow national business conditions, although some shift from Cook County

TABLE 1.A5
Paid Employees in Selected Services[a]

	Chicago	Cook County	SMSA
1948	106,627	116,807	123,921
1954	111,847	126,048	135,088
1958	106,823	144,280	157,882
1963	123,742	149,655	168,382
1967	138,121	170,912	189,653
1972	157,315	208,513	245,152

[a]Selected services consist of hotels, motels, tourist courts and camps, miscellaneous business services, auto repair, auto services, and garages, miscellaneous repair services, motion picture firms, and amusement and recreation services except motion pictures. Employment is as of the census week.

to the rest of the SMSA is evident for the period 1947 to 1954. Both Cook County and SMSA employment peaks occurred in 1967, a boom year. It is revealing to note that, for all employees, the Chicago share of the SMSA was 77.9% in 1947 and 47.3% in 1972. It is likely that the absolute decline in manufacturing employment in the city of Chicago has reduced the accessibility to employment of many residential areas in the city.

Tables 1.A3, 1.A4, and 1.A5 provide the data from the Census of Business for paid employees in retail trade, wholesale trade, and selected services, respectively.[13] Employment in retail and wholesale trade in the city of Chicago declined slightly from 1948 to 1967, and then declined again from 1967 to 1972. Employment in both categories in the entire SMSA has steadily increased. Employment in selected services has increased in the city of Chicago over the 1948–1972 period. The pattern that emerges is that the decline in employment opportunities in the city of Chicago has occurred steadily since 1948 because of the decline in manufacturing employment. Employment in the suburbs has steadily increased. Other sectors in the city, such as selected services, have experienced increases, but these increases were not enough to offset the declines in manufacturing.

More specific information about the location of employment declines in the city of Chicago has been provided by Kain (1970) and B. Harrison (1974). Using data on employment covered by unemployment compensation, Kain (1970, pp. 27–29) has calculated the changes in employment by zip code areas for 1958–1963. Kain's figures indicate a decline of 1.5%, and that 70% of the decline in covered employment occurred in the area within approx-

---

[13] Inclusion of figures on proprietors does not change the nature of the results.

imately 4 miles of the CBD. The greatest decline occurred in the zone located approximately 2 to 4 miles from the CBD, a decline of 3.2%. Harrison (1974, p. 21) replicated Kain's study for 1963–1968 and found that covered employment increased by 1.3% in the city of Chicago during this boom period of the 1960s. However, during the period 1963–1968 employment in the zone approximately 2 to 4 miles from the CBD increased by only 0.1%. It is thus clear that the greatest declines in employment probably occurred in the zone 2 to 4 miles from the CBD. Consequently, the housing stock located nearby has probably experienced a decline in its access to employment since 1947.[14]

[14] See Kain (1968) for a study of the dispersion of manufacturing employment in Chicago relative to the center of the black housing ghetto. His data cover the period 1950 to 1960 and show that manufacturing employment was dispersing more rapidly than was the black population.

2

The Value of Commuting Time

1 Introduction

In the previous chapter the question is raised as to whether it is necessary to complicate the model of housing demand by adding commuting and work time to the household's utility function. The issue is not whether commuting and work time generate utility, but whether the fact that they do needs to be added to housing demand models to improve their empirical accuracy. In order to focus on these issues, it is useful to develop a simplified version of the demand model presented in the previous chapter. Assume that the household consists of only one individual and that Muth's model of the production of housing services provides sufficient detail. The utility function is now

$$U = U(X, h, N, C, H), \tag{1}$$

where h is housing services produced by the services of land and capital. The uses of time are leisure N, commuting C, and work H. Utility is maximized subject to the money and time constraints. The Lagrangian is written[1]

$$L^* = U(X, h, N, C, H) + \lambda[wH - X - p(u)h - t(u)] + \eta(T - N - C - H), \tag{2}$$

[1] Note the differences between this double-constraint formulation and the single-constraint model used by Muth (1969).

35

where w is the after tax wage, λ and η are Lagrange multipliers, and $t(u)$ is the money cost of commuting. The first-order conditions found by differentiating with respect to X, h, N, H, and u are

$$U_X - \lambda = 0, \tag{3}$$

$$U_h - \lambda p(u) = 0, \tag{4}$$

$$U_N - \eta = 0, \tag{5}$$

$$U_H + \lambda w - \eta = 0, \tag{6}$$

and

$$U_C \frac{\partial C}{\partial u} - \lambda[p'(u)h + t'(u)] - \eta \frac{\partial C}{\partial u} = 0, \tag{7}$$

respectively. Simple manipulations of these equations yields

$$w = \frac{U_N - U_H}{U_X} \tag{8}$$

and

$$-p'(u)h = t'(u) + \frac{\partial C}{\partial u}\left(w + \frac{U_H - U_C}{U_X}\right). \tag{9}$$

The first condition states that the wage is equal to the difference in the money values of leisure and work. The latter condition states that the marginal benefit of added commuting $-p'(u)h$ equals the marginal cost, which includes the money value of the net loss in utility that results from giving up leisure or work time. If we assume that commuting time and work time do not produce utility, then the marginal cost of commuting reduces to

$$t'(u) + \frac{\partial C}{\partial u} w,$$

or the value of a reduction in commuting *time* is simply equal to the after tax wage rate (holding money expenditures on commuting constant).

A large number of empirical studies of the value of reductions in intraurban commuting time contradict the conclusion that the wage rate is the correct value of time. Estimates provided by Beesley (1965), Claffey (1961), Dalvi and Lee (1969, 1971), Lave (1969), Lisco (1967), McDonald (1975), Quarmby (1967), Stopher (1969), and Thomas and Thompson (1970) tend to be less than 50% of the before tax wage rate, and some estimates are as low as 20% of the wage. In the context of the model under consideration here, this result has three possible explanations. Commuting may be a good and $U_C/U_X > 0$, there is a constraint imposed on hours worked for workers which makes $w > (U_N - U_H)/U_X$, or there is disutility in work meaning $U_H/U_X < 0$. Moses and Williamson (1963) have examined the second possibility extensively. However, the hypothetical constraint on hours worked implies that workers wish to work *more* than they do currently. It is not clear why workers should not be able to work more hours if they so wish. It is possible that there is disutility in work at the margin, but it should be realized that $U_H < 0$ means that the individual prefers to have his total time budget (his life span) reduced to working the marginal hour at no pay. Obviously the individual would rather have leisure than work, but it is doubtful that the individual would opt to have his life shortened.[2] Thus, if we assume that all uses of time contribute to utility in the relevant range, we are left with the notion that $U_C/U_X > 0$ is the best explanation for the observed empirical results. It thus seems reasonable to write the marginal cost of commuting as

$$t'(u) + \frac{\partial C}{\partial u}\left(w - \frac{U_C}{U_X}\right).$$

This formulation has important implications for the form of the marginal cost function. First, the marginal cost is obviously greater the greater is the wage. In addition, marginal cost is an *increasing* function of commuting time if U_C/U_X declines as C increases. However, it is likely that $\partial C/\partial u$ declines with distance to the CBD because travel speeds are greater on less heavily travelled routes. The remainder of this chapter is an empirical study devoted to the estimation of these hypothesized systematic variations in the value of reductions in intraurban commuting time.[3] A more precise marginal commuting cost function is needed for the further development of urban models.

---

[2] Using the same data as Thomas and Thompson (1970), a study by Guttman (1975) found a value of time in the same range (less than 50% of the wage) for trips to and from work taken at times off the peak traffic hours. His estimates for work trips on peak travel times are considerably greater (about 2.5 times larger) than for off-peak travel. According to Guttman (1975, p. 37), this difference in results can be explained by the disutility of driving during peak times. Given that Guttman's results are at odds with other studies of on-peak travel, this study will proceed on the conclusions enumerated above. It seems that theoretical issues that seek a resolution on empirical grounds are never completely settled. However, Guttman's results are also consistent with the hypothesis that the value of a reduction in commuting time increases with the total length of the trip measured in time units. This result is obtained below.

[3] This work is based on McDonald (1975).

2　Estimation of the Value of Reductions in Commuting Time

Several empirical studies have examined the variations in the value of intraurban travel time. (Beesley, 1965; Dalvi and Lee, 1969, 1971; Lave, 1969; Lisco, 1967; Quarmby, 1967; Stopher, 1969; Thomas and Thompson, 1970). However, none of these studies has first developed a formal model of consumer choice that yields qualitative hypotheses. The lack of a formal model may lead to omission of potentially important variables and thus may lead to biased estimates of the coefficients of included variables.

The model needed is a slightly altered version of the standard model of consumer choice in urban space. The standard model assumes a single central workplace and deduces a rent gradient. The data analyzed in this paper were collected at workplaces at various points in the suburban areas of the Chicago SMSA, and nearly all of the workers in the sample live in the suburbs. Because of the dispersed nature of the suburban workplaces and their distances from the Chicago CBD (20–30 miles), it is assumed that no rent gradient exists that is relevant to the model. The price of housing is not a function of commuting time. Therefore, housing is not made a separate good in the household utility function.

Since no rent gradient is assumed, another reason must be specified for the existence of commuting. First of all, zoning regulations do not allow industrial land use in the middle of residential areas, forcing a commute of distance greater than zero. Second, suburban communities offer different mixes of public services and property tax rate. The Tiebout (1956) hypothesis states that people "vote with their feet" to get the desired mix. Also, not all types of housing are available in all suburbs. Zoning regulations restrict the supply of certain types of housing, especially apartments and low-cost units. Thus some suburban residents choose a longer commute to obtain the desired public services or type of housing. The models developed here assume that residence location has been chosen partly for reasons other than workplace location and, thus, the commuter is constrained to commute a distance fixed by the residential location choice.

Now assume that time spent commuting C is an argument in the utility function. The commuter can spend more time commuting if he finds that the marginal utility of commuting exceeds the marginal utility of leisure. The problem is to maximize utility subject to three constraints; the income constraint, the total time constraint, and the commuting time constraint. The technique of nonlinear programming is employed. The formal statement of the problem is

$$\text{max} \qquad U(X, C, N)$$

$$\text{subject to} \qquad P_c + X - wH = 0, \tag{10}$$

$$T_0 - N - C - H = 0, \qquad (11)$$

$$C - C_0 \geq 0. \qquad (12)$$

The notation is

X = quantity of consumption goods,
C = commuting time,
N = leisure time,
w = wage rate,
H = work time,
P_C = money cost of commuting (total),
T_0 = total time,

and

C_0 = minimum commuting time.

The Lagrangian is

$$U = U(X, C, N) + \lambda(wH - X - P_C) + \eta(T_0 - N - C - H) + \phi(C - C_0). \quad (13)$$

The Lagrange multipliers represent

λ = marginal utility of money,
η = marginal utility of time (increase in T_0),

and

ϕ = marginal utility of a reduction in the commuting time constraint C_0.

The first-order conditions are

$$U_X - \lambda = 0, \qquad (14)$$
$$U_N - \eta = 0, \qquad (15)$$
$$U_C - \eta + \phi \leq 0, \qquad (16)$$
$$C(U_C - \eta - \phi) = 0, \qquad (17)$$
$$\lambda w - \eta = 0, \qquad (18)$$
$$C - C_0 \geq 0, \qquad (19)$$
$$\phi(C - C_0) = 0, \qquad (20)$$
$$wH - X - P_C = 0, \qquad (21)$$

and

$$T_0 - H - N - C = 0. \qquad (22)$$

Since C is always greater than zero (C_0 exceeds zero), the third and fourth conditions reduce to $U_C - \eta + \phi = 0$.

Case A: Commuters Not at the Boundary Solution

For commuters not at the boundary solution, C exceeds C_0. This means that ϕ equals zero, so the money value of a reduction in $C_0(\phi/\lambda)$ is zero. The relevant first order conditions are

$$U_X - \lambda = 0, \tag{23}$$
$$U_N - \eta = 0, \tag{24}$$
$$U_C - \eta = 0, \tag{25}$$
$$\lambda w - \eta = 0, \tag{26}$$
$$C - C_0 > 0, \tag{27}$$
$$\phi(C - C_0) = 0, \tag{28}$$
$$wH - X - P_C = 0, \tag{29}$$

and

$$T_0 - H - L - C = 0. \tag{30}$$

The comparative statics properties of the model are very simple. The value of reductions in required commuting time is zero and does not vary across individuals according to the wage rate and actual commuting time. Commuters who value a decline in C_0 at zero are excluded from the empirical work.

Case B: Commuters at the Boundary Solution

For commuters at the boundary solution, the first-order conditions are

$$U_X - \lambda = 0, \tag{31}$$
$$U_N - \eta = 0, \tag{32}$$
$$U_C - \eta + \phi = 0, \tag{33}$$
$$\lambda w - \eta = 0, \tag{34}$$
$$C - C_0 = 0, \tag{35}$$
$$\phi(C - C_0) = 0, \tag{36}$$
$$wH - X - P_C = 0, \tag{37}$$

and

$$T_0 - H - N - C_0 = 0. \tag{38}$$

Remember that the budget constraints imply $w\,dH + H\,dw = dY = dX$,[4] where $Y = $ income, and $dC_0 = -dN - dH$. The first-order conditions imply that the value of a reduction in commuting time ϕ/λ can be written as

$$\frac{\phi}{\lambda} = w - \frac{U_C}{U_X}. \tag{39}$$

[4] We assume that P_C is a constant because commuters in the sample studied were able to purchase a faster trip by taking a tollway, but not a shorter trip in terms of distance. Relaxation of this assumption implies that the value of a reduction in commuting time includes reductions in P_C.

Differentiation of this condition with respect to the wage rate w yields

$$\frac{\partial(\phi/\lambda)}{\partial w} = 1 - \left[\frac{\partial(U_C/U_X)}{\partial X}\right]\left(H + w\frac{\partial H}{\partial w}\right). \tag{40}$$

Let us assume that $\partial Y/\partial w = H + w(\partial H/\partial w) > 0$, or that earnings rise as the wage increases. If commuting is a normal good, $\partial(U_C/U_X)/\partial X$ exceeds zero, and if commuting is inferior, this term is less than zero. Thus the value of reductions in commuting time declines as income rises only if $\partial(U_C/U_X)/\partial X$ is greater than $1/(\partial Y/\partial w)$. For people who regard commuting as an inferior good, the value of reductions in commuting time definitely rises as income rises. Differentiation of ϕ/λ with respect to C yields the cost of increasing C,

$$\begin{aligned}
\frac{\partial(\phi/\lambda)}{\partial C} &= \frac{-\partial(U_C/U_X)}{\partial C} + \frac{\partial H}{\partial C}\left[\frac{\partial(\phi/\lambda)}{\partial H}\right] + \frac{\partial N}{\partial C}\left[\frac{\partial(\phi/\lambda)}{\partial N}\right] \\
&= \frac{-\partial(U_C/U_X)}{\partial C} + \frac{\partial H}{\partial C}\left[-w\frac{\partial(U_C/U_X)}{\partial X}\right] + \frac{\partial N}{\partial C}\left[\frac{-\partial(U_C/U_X)}{\partial N}\right]. \tag{41}
\end{aligned}$$

Let us suppose that $\partial H/\partial C$ and $\partial N/\partial C$ are both less than zero. We can further assume that $\partial(U_C/U_X)/\partial C$ is less than zero and that $\partial(U_C/U_X)/\partial X$ is greater than zero. If leisure and commuting are substitutes it may be that $\partial(U_C/U_X)/\partial N < 0$.[5] However, if N and C are complements, $\partial(\phi/\lambda)/\partial C > 0$. In summary, the value of a marginal reduction in commuting time may rise, fall, or remain unchanged as the wage or commuting time rises. Empirical tests are needed to establish these signs.

The data used to test the hypotheses of the model involve a choice situation for commuters who all use the private auto for the trip to work.[6] The commuters have the choice of taking a tollway (a faster trip) or using free streets and highways (a slower trip). Individuals who face this trade-off are not hard to find because, assuming people value their time, tollways should be less congested than freeways. Commuters filled out the questionnaire at their suburban places of work. If the commuter uses the tollway, he was asked to specify the toll paid and the amount of time saved. If the commuter uses a freeway, he was asked to specify the amount of toll he

---

[5] The Hicks definition of substitutes gives

$$\frac{\partial(U_C/U_X)}{\partial N}\bigg|_{u=u_0} = \frac{\partial(U_C/U_N)}{\partial N} - \frac{\partial(U_C/U_X)}{\partial X}\frac{U_N}{U_X} < 0.$$

Thus it is possible for C and N to be substitutes and to have $\partial(U_C/U_X)/\partial N$ exceed zero.

[6] The survey was conducted for the Northwest Suburban Conference of Mayors, a group of mayors from towns in the northwestern area of Cook County, Illinois. The questionnaire was prepared by the author.

avoids (if a tollway is relevant to him) and how much time is added to his trip to avoid the toll. Some 900 workers at 17 different firms filled out the questionnaire, and 115 persons indicated that they face the tollway–freeway trade-off situation (and responded to the other questions). The sample of 115 is used for the results reported here.

Using route choice data rather than modal choice data has become the standard technique for avoiding the problems arising from the taste for the comfort and convenience features of various modes. Route choice data give the closest approximation to the value of reductions in commuting time. The studies by Thomas and Thompson (1970) and Claffey (1961) used data of the type used here. The Beesley (1965) work used data that involved choice of alternative routes on public transit.

The model implies that the marginal value of reductions in commuting time may rise as income and commuting time rise and may fall as commuting time saved rises. These hypotheses stated in linear functional form are

$$\frac{-\partial X_2}{\partial X_1} = V' = v_0 + v_1 X_1 + v_2 X_3 + v_3 X_4, \tag{42}$$

where

V' = money value (cents) of a marginal reduction in commuting time,
X_1 = time saved if tollway is chosen (minutes),
X_2 = toll (cents),
X_3 = commuting time on freeway (minutes),
and
X_4 = income (units of $100)

(signs: v_1 less than zero, v_2 and v_3 greater than zero). From this function, the average value of X_1 (V/X_1) is written

$$\frac{V}{X_1} = v_0 + \frac{v_1}{2} X_1 + v_2 X_3 + v_3 X_4. \tag{43}$$

The commuter chooses the tollway if his real income will rise as a result. The change in real income is the value of the time saved minus the toll paid, written $\Delta Y = V - X_2$. Along an indifference curve, $\Delta Y = 0$. For purposes of empirical estimation, the theory can be stated as

$$Q = a_0 + a_2(\Delta Y) + u, \tag{44}$$

where

Q = number of trips taken by tollway (0 or 1),
ΔY = change in real income (cents),

and

$u = $ random error term.

Substituting for ΔY produces

$$Q = a_0 + a_1 v_0 X_1 + a_1 (v_1/2) X_1^2 + a_1 v_2 X_1 X_3 + a_1 v_3 X_1 X_4 - a_1 X_2 + u. \quad (45)$$

The estimate of this equation is shown below in Table 2.2. The marginal value of reductions in the commuting time function can be identified from this estimate. The estimate is a standard linear probability function, which can be interpreted as indicating the probability that a commuter with given values for the X's will choose the tollway.

The estimation of the equation may be difficult because of the likely collinearity among the independent variables. Variable X_1 appears four times in Eq. (45). Fortunately, other functional forms that reduce collinearity can be used to infer a value of reductions in commuting time functions. Note that the probability of choosing the tollway function implies that movement along an indifference curve is equivalent to holding constant the probability of choosing the tollway. In other words, given a change in the toll X_2, the change in the time saved X_1 that holds the change in real

TABLE 2.1
Alternative Functional Forms for the Probability of Choosing the Tollway Function

Function	Implied value of marginal reduction in commuting time $-(\partial X_2/\partial X_1)_{Q=\bar{Q}}$	Expected coefficient values
1. $Q = a_0 + a_1 v_0 X_1$ $+ a_1 (v_1/2) X_1^2$ $+ a_1 v_2 X_1 X_3$ $+ a_1 v_3 X_1 X_4$ $- a_1 X_2 + u$	$v_0 + v_1 X_1 +$ $v_2 X_3 + v_3 X_4$	$a_1 v_0 > 0, a_1 v_1/2 < 0$ $a_1 v_2 > 0, a_1 v_3 > 0$ $a_1 > 0$
2. $Q = b_0 + b_1 X_1 + b_2 X_1^2$ $+ b_3 X_2 + b_4 X_2 X_3$ $+ b_5 X_2 X_4 + u$	$\dfrac{b_1 + 2b_2 X_1}{-(b_3 + b_4 X_3 + b_5 X_4)}$	$b_1 > 0, b_4 > 0, b_5 > 0$ $b_2 < 0, b_3 < 0$ $b_3 + b_4 X_3 + b_5 X_4 < 0$
3. $Q = c_0 + c_1 X_1 + c_2 X_1^2$ $+ c_3 X_2 + c_4 X_1 X_3$ $+ c_5 X_2 X_4 + u$	$\dfrac{c_1 + 2c_2 X_1 + c_4 X_3}{-(c_3 + c_5 X_4)}$	$c_1 > 0, c_4 > 0, c_5 > 0$ $c_2 < 0, c_3 < 0$ $c_3 + c_5 X_4 < 0$
4. $Q = d_0 + d_1 X_1 + d_2 X_1^2$ $+ d_3 X_2 + d_4 X_1 X_4$ $+ d_5 X_2 X_3 + u$	$\dfrac{d_1 + 2d_2 X_1 + d_4 X_4}{-(d_3 + d_5 X_3)}$	$d_1 > 0, d_4 > 0, d_5 > 0$ $d_2 < 0, d_3 < 0$ $d_3 + d_5 X_1 < 0$

income constant is also the change in X_1 that holds the probability of choosing the tollway constant. This can be easily seen by solving for $-\partial X_2/\partial X_1$ holding Q and ΔY constant.

We shall assume that utility remains constant as X_1 and X_2 vary while keeping the probability of choosing the tollway constant. This assumption frees the functional form of the probability function. Table 2.1 displays the functional form derived above and shows three additional functional forms that imply that the value of a marginal reduction in commuting time is a function of income, commuting time on the freeway, and the reduction in commuting time. The form of the value of a marginal reduction in commuting time function and the expected coefficient signs are shown in each case.

The statistical technique used to estimate the probability functions is weighted least squares (Goldberger, 1964, pp. 248–251). The dependent variable is dichotomous; 1 if the commuter takes the tollway and 0 if the freeway is chosen. Then equations were estimated by ordinary least squares and then by weighted least squares to correct for heteroskedasticity. This linear probability model has a shortcoming because it is possible that predicted probabilities will not fall in the zero-to-one interval. However, the linear model is an appropriate technique in this case because interest

TABLE 2.2
Probability of Taking a Tollway (Weighted Least Squares)[a]

	1	2	3	4
X_1	.0184	.0369	.0203	.0359
	(1.99)	(4.24)	(2.24)	(3.42)
X_1^2	−.0019	−.0008	−.0018	−.0009
	(6.92)	(3.24)	(6.60)	(3.63)
X_2	−.0063	−.0167	−.0072	−.0150
	(4.55)	(6.53)	(4.38)	(6.83)
X_1X_3	.00081	——	.00081	——
	(9.33)		(9.44)	
X_1X_4	.000023	——	——	.000015
	(.94)			(.37)
X_2X_3	——	.00016	——	.00016
		(8.37)		(8.22)
X_2X_4	——	.000009	.000007	——
		(1.48)	(1.17)	
Constant	.2831	.4381	.2826	.4241
	(3.23)	(4.68)	(3.26)	(4.47)
R^2	.748	.664	.750	.632

[a] t statistics in parentheses: X_1, time saved on tollway (minutes); X_2, toll (cents); X_3, commuting time on the freeway (minutes); X_4, household income (units of $100).

TABLE 2.3
Correlation Matrix

	X_1	X_2	X_3	X_4	X_1X_3	X_1X_4	X_2X_3	X_2X_4
X_2	.43							
X_3	.61	.54						
X_4	.01	−.01	.09					
X_1X_3	.93	.56	.79	.01				
X_1X_4	.85	.36	.53	.44	.79			
X_2X_3	.55	.88	.81	.02	.75	.47		
X_2X_4	.34	.77	.46	.56	.44	.56	.69	
$(X_1)^2$	.93	.45	.58	.00	.87	.71	.56	.36

centers on the values of coefficients of independent variables and not on predictions made with the model. One statistical technique that has been widely used in similar situations and avoids the above problem is discriminant analysis (Warner, 1962; Quarmby, 1967; McGillivray, 1972). As is well known (Ladd, 1966) the coefficients produced by two-group discriminant analysis are proportional to the coefficients in linear regression analysis with a dichotomous dependent variable. Other statistical techniques that have been used in similar situations are probit analysis and logit analysis. Watson (1974) provided a review of these techniques. Domencich and McFadden (1975) have provided a formal model of choice with dichotomous (and polytomous) options. The functional form of the probability function is shown to depend upon the functional form of the error term, which Domencich and McFadden incorporated into the utility function. Choice among the alternatives for dichotomous choice problems is a matter of taste. If the Domencich–McFadden error term is uniformly distributed over the relevant range, the linear probability function is derived.

The results of the weighted regressions are in Table 2.2. All the coefficients in the regressions have the expected signs and only the coefficients of X_1X_4 and X_2X_4 are insignificant by conventional tests of significance. The other coefficients attain high levels of significance despite the collinearity problem that exists in the data[7] (see Table 2.3).

The results in Table 2.2 provide strong support for the hypothesis that the value of a marginal reduction in commuting time falls as the amount of time saved increases and rises with increases in the length of time spent commuting if the freeway is chosen. However, the value of time may not rise with income.[8] The t value for the terms that include income ranges

[7] Thomas and Thompson (1970), in a similar study, seem to have encountered a collinearity problem that was more harmful to the results than the problem encountered here.

[8] Other tests were run using a household per capita income variable rather than total household income, but the results did not change appreciably.

from $+.37$ to $+1.48$. Note that the t value of the income term in the estimate of column 1 in Table 2.2 is $+.94$, a figure that is exceeded by the t values for the income terms in two out of the three other functions.

In summary, the empirical evidence presented here provides reasonably strong support for the model, although the t value for the coefficient of the income variable is low in each case. The other empirical studies cited (Beesley, 1965; Dalvi and Lee, 1969, 1971; Lave, 1969; Lisco, 1967; Quarmby, 1967; Stopher, 1969; Thomas and Thompson, 1970) have all found that the value of reductions in commuting time rises as income rises. However, it should be noted that a test of statistical significance of the income variable is provided only by Dalvi and Lee (1969, 1971), Lisco (1967), and Thomas and Thompson (1970). In addition, only the studies by Dalvi and Lee include all of the variables suggested by the model. Dalvi and Lee found weak evidence that a longer commute means a higher value of reductions in commuting time. The other studies neglect this factor. For example, the Beesley (1965) study showed that a higher income group of public transit riders had a higher average value of time than did a lower income group of riders. The study did not control for the length of the commutation. Since all of the commuters in the sample work in Central London, it could be the case that the higher income group had a higher average commuting time than did the lower income group. Such a result would be consistent with the common observation that higher income people live farther from the CBD than lower income people.

TABLE 2.4
Variations in the Value of a Marginal Reduction in Commuting Time
(Computed from Table 2.2)[a]

		Function			
		1	2	3	4
$\dfrac{\partial V'}{\partial X_1}$	¢ per minute per minute	− .603	− .219	− .587	− .247
$\dfrac{\partial V'}{\partial X_3}$	¢ per minute	.129	.058	.132	.056
$\dfrac{\partial V'}{\partial X_4}$	¢ per minute per $100	.0037	.0332	.0031	.0021
V'	¢ per minute	3.81	2.70	3.38	2.59
	$ per hour	2.29	1.62	2.03	1.55
V/X	¢ per minute	6.73	3.88	6.53	3.90
	$ per hour	4.04	2.33	3.92	2.34

[a] X_1, X_3, X_4 are set at mean sample values.

The results in Table 2.2 can be used to compute point estimates of the value of the marginal and the average reduction in commuting time (see Table 2.4). At the point of means ($X_1 = 10.72$ minutes, $X_3 = 48.15$ minutes, and $X_4 = 153.3$), the estimate of the value of a marginal reduction in commuting time is computed to be 2.59¢ per minute to 3.81¢ per minute. The estimate of the average value at the point of means ranges from 3.88¢ per minute to 6.73¢ per minute. Table 2.4 displays the marginal changes in the value of a marginal reduction in commuting time at the point of means. Instability in these values exists, especially in the effect of a change in income on the value of a marginal reduction in commuting time.

In conclusion, the evidence presented in this chapter has shown that the commuter's willingness to pay for reductions in commuting time rises with the length of his trip and income. Also, the marginal value of reductions in commuting time falls as the amount of time *saved* increases. On the whole, the data show rather striking support for the model presented in this chapter.

3   Driving Speed in Chicago

In order to complete the analysis of the variations in the marginal cost of commuting distance, we need to examine the traffic volumes and average speeds at various distances from the CBD. In the expression for the marginal cost of distance from the CBD, written

$$t'(u) + \frac{\partial C}{\partial u}\left(w - \frac{U_C}{U_X}\right),$$

we shall investigate the term $\partial C / \partial u$, the marginal increase in commuting time as distance from the CBD increases. A detailed analysis of traffic volume and speed for the Eisenhower Expressway was conducted by Wilkie (1962). The Eisenhower expressway runs straight west from the Chicago CBD for a distance of 16 miles, with four lanes in both directions up to 7.5 miles from the CBD and three lanes thereafter. The field survey of traffic to the CBD during the period from 7 a.m. to 1 p.m. was conducted on March 16, 1961. The survey was conducted before a system of traffic lights to control entry to the expressway was installed. Table 2.5 shows the average speed on the expressway during the morning rush hour (7–8 a.m.) at various distances found by Wilkie (1962). From these figures for average speed we can compute the time cost per mile of added distance at each point along the expressway, and these marginal time cost figures are also shown in Table 2.5. These results show that marginal time cost does not decline monotonically with distance to the CBD. We see that traffic slows down appreciably as the distance to the CBD falls under 1.5 miles and that

TABLE 2.5
Marginal Time Cost of Distance on the Eisenhower Expressway

Location	Distance to CBD (miles)	Average speed (mph)	Time cost of added ½-mile distance (min)
Canal St.	.84	18	—
Morgan St.	1.46	19	1.58
Ashland Ave.	2.21	31	.97
Damen Ave.	2.71	34	.88
Oakley Blvd.	3.07	34	.88
Washtenaw Ave.	3.57	34	.88
Homan Ave.	4.45	44	.68
Independence Blvd.	4.95	34	.88
Kostner Ave.	5.70	34	.88
Cicero Ave.	6.25	29	1.03
Laramie Ave.	6.75	26	1.15
Central Ave.	7.25	26	1.15
Austin Blvd.	7.75	52	.58
Harlem Ave.	9.26	60	.50
Des Plaines Ave.	9.85	62	.48
1st Ave.	10.60	41	.73
9th Ave.	11.10	40	.75
17th Ave.	11.60	33	.91
25th Ave.	12.10	36	.83
Mannheim Rd.	13.10	26	1.15
Harrison St.	14.60	25	1.20

Source: Wilkie (1962).

traffic speeds up over the interval 9.85 to 7.75 miles to the CBD. Otherwise, the marginal time cost curve appears to be flat, with some variations. It is likely that marginal time cost falls as distance to the CBD increases beyond 16 miles (past the intersection with the circumferential Tri-State Tollway). Unfortunately, speeds on the other expressways in Chicago have not been studied in the detail represented by the work of Wilkie (1962). The marginal time cost of driving on side streets may vary greatly, of course. It is reasonable to assume that these costs are less in suburban areas than in the central city. For example, Lisco (1967, p. 53) assumed that driving time is 30 seconds per block in the Loop after 8:15 a.m. and 20 seconds per block in a suburb (Skokie). However, except for people who live on the southwest side, most drivers make relatively short trips on side streets if the CBD is the destination.

Since the focus of the entire study is on the housing market and not on transportation costs, further efforts to refine the analysis of the marginal cost of distance to the CBD seem unwarranted. I shall simply assume that marginal money costs $t'(u)$ are constant for auto drivers.[9] If the marginal time cost of distance $\partial C/\partial u$ is fairly constant over a wide range, then the marginal cost of distance rises with distance because of the rising money value of a reduction in commuting time. This form of the commuting cost function will be employed in the model developed in Chapter 8.

[9] Marginal money costs are zero for those residents of the central city who ride public transit (or 10¢ for a transfer).

3

Race, Externalities, the Local Public Sector, and the Demand for Housing

In this chapter consideration is given to additional goods that might be included in the utility function of the urban household for purposes of housing demand analysis. The general category of goods considered in Chapter 2 is the allocation of time associated with the choice of residential location. We now turn attention to the goods the supplies of which are exogenous to the individual household or housing supplier: neighborhood amenities and local public services. The purpose of this investigation is to determine which of these goods have been established as being of empirical relevance in the analysis of the housing market. Where possible, studies of the metropolitan Chicago area will be used for this purpose. For each good considered, we also wish to discover whether it is possible to represent its supply in a manner that is analytically tractable. For example, it will be convenient if the supply of a neighborhood amenity is a function of distance to the CBD. The three neighborhood amenities that have received the most attention in the empirical literature are racial segregation, crime, and air pollution; these will be examined in the first two sections of this chapter. The activities of the local public sector are examined in the final section. Both local public services and the property tax are considered.

1   Race and the Demand for Housing

There is a large and growing body of evidence to support the notion that the demand for housing expressed by white households is influenced by the racial composition of the area in which a house is located. In particular, the importance of the black residential population on white demand is reasonably clear. It appears that white demand is reduced both by the percentage black population in the area immediately surrounding a housing site and by the distance from the closest predominantly black neighborhood. Both of these effects arise from racial prejudice, an aversion to an individual member of a racial group regardless of the attributes of that individual. Furthermore, there is evidence of discriminatory behavior against blacks that takes the form of exclusion and price discrimination on the part of housing suppliers. The purpose of this section is to review briefly some recent econometric studies of these phenomena, and to examine in detail the recent studies of race and housing prices in Chicago. As King and Mieszkowski (1973) pointed out, it is important to separate the effects of demand and supply factors on racial price differences. If prejudice on the part of white households is the only racial factor operating, the aversion of whites for blacks will lead to supply adjustment, which brings about lower housing prices for blacks than for whites who avoid blacks, ceteris paribus. Such a result would make the task of this section relatively easy. However, if housing suppliers discriminate against blacks by limiting access as black demand grows, for example, then we may find that blacks pay more than whites for equivalent housing while, at the same time, white demand for housing in some areas is reduced by racial prejudice. In order to overcome this problem, King and Mieszkowski (1973), in their study of rents in New Haven during 1968–1969, examined the rents paid by white and black households in two types of areas, the black interior and the racial boundary, compared to the rents paid by whites in the white interior. In the hedonic regression results, white rents in the boundary areas were found to be 7% lower than white interior rents, a statistically significant result. Black rents in the boundary areas were equal to white interior rents, indicating a 7% price discrimination. Both white and black rents in the black interior were about 9% higher than white interior rents, suggesting limitations on the expansion of the black residential areas during a period of demand growth.

One of the main objectives of the study by Kain and Quigley (1975) was to establish the existence of a racial price difference in St. Louis during 1967 caused by restrictions on the supply of housing of various types available to blacks. Both rental and owner occupied housing in black areas were found to be more expensive than in white areas, and the size of the difference was found to increase with the quality of the housing bundle. Kain and

Quigley (1975) did not test for the effect of white prejudice on demand. This task was undertaken by Yinger (1978) for the St. Louis data on homeowners. Yinger's results showed clearly that, while blacks pay 15% more than whites in any neighborhood and the prices were higher in the black interior and boundary areas, the prices were *negatively* related to the percentage black population in a given area type (black interior, boundary, white interior). These results suggest prejudice against blacks on the part of whites and, perhaps, blacks as well.

A study by Schafer (1976), using data on Boston previously examined by Schnare (1976), also showed that whites pay less for a house, ceteris paribus, in the black ghetto and areas of racial transition than elsewhere. Also blacks were found to pay more than whites for equivalent housing in all types of areas. Only the three studies cited (King and Mieszkowski, 1973; Yinger, 1978; Schafer, 1976) have demonstrated the depressing effect of black neighbors on white housing demand. Numerous other studies have demonstrated that the price of housing is greater in a black neighborhood than in a white neighborhood, but failed to separate the effects of supply restrictions on blacks from the effects of prejudice. The studies by Little (1976) and Schnare (1976) are recent examples.

Now let us turn to the studies that have used data from Chicago. The first study to be published was the study of the Hyde Park and Kenwood areas for 1948–1951 and 1954–1956 by Bailey (1966). In that study Bailey found that the price was unrelated to the racial composition of its own block, and negatively related to the percentage black in the surrounding blocks. This latter result suggested that prices may have been lower in black areas, but no firm conclusions can be reached because the race of the purchaser was not known and because the racial composition of the block in which the house was located was not a significant factor. Indeed, if the sample consisted of white purchasers, the importance of the racial composition of the surrounding blocks suggested that prejudice on the part of whites lowered their demand. In short, the study by Bailey (1966) cannot be used as a basis for the assumptions in a model with racial factors included.

Muth (1969, pp. 284–303) has examined the change in median rent and house value from 1950 to 1960 for a sample of census tracts on the south side. The distinction was made between tracts that were over 80% black at both times, tracts that changed from over 80% white to over 80% black, and tracts that were over 80% white at both times. The change in rent was unrelated to these racial variables, but the price of houses increased more in changed areas than in white tracts.[1] This result is consistent with the

---

[1] Curiously, Muth (1969, p. 204) did not report the results of a regression for house value that included dummy variables for both changed and black tracts.

notion of restrictions on the supply of houses available for purchase by blacks during the period from 1950 to 1960.

According to Berry (1976), this situation changed completely during the decade of the 1960s. As Berry (1976, p. 417) stated, 482,000 new housing units were built in the Chicago SMSA during the 1960s, but the number of households increased only 285,000. As a result, 128,000 units were transferred from white to black occupancy and 63,000 units were demolished. The number of black households in the city of Chicago increased by 80,000, while the number of white households in the city declined by 119,000. The Latino population increased by 35,000 households. Berry (1976) claimed that these massive changes in the racial geography of the city, as the whites relinquished neighborhood after neighborhood to blacks, has resulted in substantially *lower* prices for blacks and Latinos than whites in their traditional neighborhoods. Berry (1976) also found that prices were lower in white areas near black and Latino areas than in the white interior areas. This combination of results suggested to Berry that, in effect, the model of white prejudice was operating and that there were no barriers to a rapid increase in the aggregate supply of housing available to blacks. A detailed examination of Berry's study follows.

The primary data source used by Berry (1976) are the title transfer records for the 30,000 single-family houses sold in the city of Chicago during 1968–1972. For each house the sale price, property tax assessment, and location were known. The race of the buyer was unknown. The houses were grouped into 231 census tract or tract group observations, and the analysis used the mean price of the houses sold in each of the 231 areas. Each of the 231 areas falls into one of the following racial categories:

1. Black residential area in 1968
2. Zone of black expansion during 1968–1972
3. Latino residential area in 1968
4. Zone of Latino expansion during 1968–1972
5. Contiguous white residential areas in 1972
6. Removed white residential areas in 1972

These categories were established by visual monitoring of key neighborhoods during the period of the study. The 1970 Census also provided data on median family income, percentage of population that lived elsewhere in 1965, and percentage of multifamily dwelling units for each of the 231 tracts or tract groups. The analysis also included a measure of particulate air pollution in 1969 and distance to the CBD. The assessed value of the house was used as a proxy for the quality and size of the housing unit and lot. A representa-

TABLE 3.1
Analysis of Market Prices of Single-Family Houses: 1968–1972[a]

Constant	28,908.00
Total assessed value	2.43
	(11.57)
Median family income	.06
	(2.00)
Percentage living	−73.0
elsewhere in 1965	(3.32)
Percentage units	132.0
multifamily	(3.07)
Contiguous white area	−1244.0
	(2.01)
Zone of black expansion	−1102.0
	(3.72)
Black area in 1968	−4305.0
	(6.76)
Zone of Latino expansion	−1826.0
	(2.52)
Latino area in 1968	−2985.0
	(2.74)
Distance to CBD	81.0
	(.79)
Particulate pollution	−149.0
	(7.84)
R^2	.72

Source: Berry (1976, pp. 408–409).
[a] t values are in parentheses. Dependent variable is mean selling price.

tive regression result is shown in Table 3.1. The results may be summarized as follows:

1. Prices were highest in removed white areas.
2. Prices were about the same in the contiguous white areas and the zones of black and Latino expansion.
3. Prices were considerably lower in the black and Latino areas of 1968.

Indeed, the difference between the prices in the white interior and the black interior was $4305, or 19% of the mean selling price of the 30,000 houses.

One potential problem with Berry's procedure is the use of the property tax assessment as a proxy for all of the physical features of the house and the lot. Berry (1976, pp. 402–406) first presented a test of the assumption that the assessed value of improvements is a good proxy for the housing characteristics. To conduct this test, he obtained from the Society of Real Estate Appraisers a sample of 275 single-family houses sold in Chicago during 1970–1972 for which both housing characteristics and assessed values are available.[2] These data contain information on many attributes of the house such as age, floor area, number of baths, lot area, and presence of air conditioning, improved attic, improved basement, and garage. The data on the houses were merged with 1970 Census data, which provide median family income in the census tract, percentage of homes in the census tract that are multifamily, percentage of tract population that lived elsewhere in 1965, and percentage of black, Latino, and Irish in the tract. Distance to the central business district in kilometers was measured, and a measure of air pollution (particulate concentration) was added. The selling price of the property was considered to be a function of these variables, and the regression equation was calculated (Berry, 1976, p. 405). Berry noted that the selling price of the property depends significantly upon the attributes of the house and upon several characteristics of the neighborhood. Next, he examined the assessment on improvements as a function of the same set of housing and neighborhood variables (Berry, 1976, p. 405). Berry (1976) concluded that

> It was confirmed that tax assessments on improvements did in fact reflect structure characteristics and not characteristics of location or environment, as they should if the latter are capitalized into the value of land. This finding permitted assessments to be substituted for the mass of Society of Real Estate Appraisers' data in the study of the full data set [pp. 404–406].

An examination of the regression results upon which this statement is based (Berry, 1976, p. 405) leads one perhaps to question the conclusion since median family income, distance from the CBD, and particulate pollution are significant determinants of the assessment on improvements. However, Berry's procedure raises a more fundamental issue.

The objective of the Berry study is to obtain unbiased estimates of the racial price differences in Chicago during the period 1968–1972, holding housing quality constant. Thus, the question is one of bias in the estimated coefficients of certain included variables (percentage black or Latino, in particular). The test conducted by Berry does not examine the biases in these coefficients introduced by substituting a proxy variable (assessment on improvements) for several housing characteristics. However, the data used by Berry for his test contain the variables necessary to conduct the appropriate test. Before this test is conducted, the econometric theory of proxy variables must be examined to cover the issue raised by Berry.

---

[2] These data are described in detail and extensively analyzed by Bednarz (1975) and Berry and Bednarz (forthcoming).

The fundamental hypothesis in the procedure used by Berry (1976) is that the omitted variables bias can be reduced by the use of a proxy variable that is (assumed to be) a linear combination of those omitted variables. This section provides a brief discussion of the problems in using a proxy variable. The discussion summarizes the presentation in Maddala (1977, pp. 158–161). To simplify, suppose that the true model is the two-regressor case

$$y = \beta x + \gamma z + u, \qquad (1)$$

where x is observed and z is unobserved, and u is the normal error term. Suppose we have the proxy variable $p = \alpha x + z + e$, where we allow correlation between p and u by allowing correlation between e and u. Correlation between p and x is also allowed. McCallum (1971) and Wickens (1971) proved that the bias in the estimate of β is less if the proxy is used in the ordinary-least-squares (OLS) estimation of the equation above, assuming $\alpha = 0$ and the correlation between e and u is zero. However, both of these assumptions may be violated in the case of Berry's data. As noted above, the assessed value of improvements is significantly influenced by three neighborhood variables (median family income, distance from the CBD, and particulate pollution). Thus it seems that α is not equal to zero. Also, the results presented by Berry and Bednarz (1975) indicate that the ratio of assessment to selling price is correlated with percentage black population. This may also be interpreted to mean that p is correlated with x. Furthermore, it would not be prudent to rule out a correlation between e and u. Maddala (1977, p. 161) presents the expression for the bias in the estimation of β given this two-regressor model; the bias can be larger or smaller depending upon the magnitude of α and the correlations of p with x and e with u. The interested reader should consult Maddala (1977). The point is that the issue is strictly an empirical question, to which we now turn.

The data used by Berry (1976) have been obtained for the purpose of comparing the biases present when a proxy variable for housing characteristics (assessed value of housing improvements) is included or excluded. In addition, a proxy variable for neighborhood characteristics (assessed value of land) is tested. The data consist of 275 observations of single-family homes sold in Chicago during the period 1970–1972. This section presents a direct examination of the extent to which inclusion of the proxy variables mentioned above "corrects" for omitted variables bias.

The full regression results are presented in Table 3.2. The dependent variable, selling price, is in natural log form. In column 1 of Table 3.2 the independent variables included are the same as those used by Berry (1976, p. 405), but the functional form of most of these variables has been changed to facilitate interpretation of the results. A few independent variables are in natural log form as in Berry (1976, p. 405), but the dummy variables and

TABLE 3.2
Regression Analysis of Selling Price[a]

Independent variable	1	2	3	4	5
Constant	1.098	−1.260	.160	6.767	7.120
	(1.21)	(1.09)	(.17)	(15.56)	(17.70)
Age (years)	−.007			−.011	−.011
	(7.60)			(10.67)	(11.85)
Square feet (natural log)	.296			.484	.228
	(5.57)			(7.28)	(3.22)
Number of baths	.095			.084	.111
	(2.97)			(1.84)	(2.62)
Improved attic (dummy)	.110			.158	.146
	(3.08)			(3.05)	(3.08)
Improved basement (dummy)	.078			.080	.084
	(3.04)			(2.16)	(2.45)
Air conditioned (dummy)	.047			.124	.109
	(1.36)			(2.53)	(2.42)
Garage (dummy)	.056			.100	.104
	(2.04)			(2.69)	(3.04)
Area of lot (natural log)	.155	.216	.210		
	(4.13)	(4.99)	(5.83)		
Particulate pollution	.001	.003	−.002		
	(.25)	(1.15)	(.68)		
Median income (natural log)	.555	.924	.654		
	(5.64)	(7.59)	(6.26)		
Multifamily units (%)	.154	.027	.211		
	(1.81)	(.26)	(2.41)		
Migrants (%)	.071	.331	.148		
	(.47)	(1.68)	(.90)		
Black (%)	−.276	−.225	−.292		
	(5.16)	(3.23)	(5.02)		
Latino (%)	−.749	−.857	−1.061		
	(2.24)	(1.96)	(2.91)		
Irish (%)	−1.726	−1.412	−2.015		
	(3.44)	(2.16)	(3.69)		
Distance to CBD	.025	.036	.018		
	(3.87)	(4.29)	(2.51)		
Assessment on improvements (natural log)			.249		
			(10.85)		
Assessment on land (natural log)					.208
					(7.13)
R^2	.802	.644	.754	.561	.631

[a] t values are in parentheses. Dependent variable is in natural log form. Sample size = 275.

the variables bounded by 0 and 1 have not been converted to natural logs. The results in column 1 are comparable to Berry's results and are satisfactory from the point of view of normality of the residuals. Using a chi-square test, the probability of rejecting the normality assumption is .83. It is further assumed that the specification in column 1 of Table 3.2 is correct in that no variables have been omitted that cause omitted variables bias in the results. The only coefficients that require some explanation are the very large and negative coefficients of percentage Irish (-1.726) and percentage Latino ($-.749$). These coefficients are also negative in Berry's study. However, the variables in Berry's study are in natural log form so that the magnitudes of the estimated coefficients do not appear to be large. The results in column 1 of Table 3.2 indicate that if percentage Irish rises from 0 to 100, the price of the house falls by 173%. However, the actual range of the variable percentage Irish is 0 to .14. The actual range for percentage Latino is 0 to .33.

The basic procedure to test for omitted variables bias and the correction for this bias is (a) run the regression omitting selected variables; and (b) run another regression including the proxy for these omitted variables. Columns 2 and 3 of Table 3.2 present the relevant test for the omission of housing characteristics: the age of the house, square feet of floor space, number of baths, improved attic (dummy variable), improved basement (dummy variable), air conditioned (dummy variable), and garage (dummy variable). The area of the lot is not omitted because it is not a characteristic of the house. As shown in column 1 Table 3.3, there are substantial biases introduced into some coefficients, especially median income, percentage multifamily units, and percentage migrants. The coefficient of percentage black, a major focus of the Berry (1976) study, changes by $+.05$, or 5%, for a change

TABLE 3.3
Analysis of Omitted Variables Bias

	Bias introduced by omitting housing improvements	Bias after including assessment on improvements
Area of lot	.061	.055
Particulate pollution	.002	−.003
Median income	.369	.099
Multifamily units	−.127	.057
Migrants	.260	.077
Black	.051	−.016
Latino	−.108	−.312
Irish	.289	−.289
Distance to CBD	.011	−.007

in percentage black from 0 to 100. The positive direction of this particular omitted variables bias is perhaps unexpected, indicating that blacks in the sample occupy houses of higher "quality" than other ethnic groups.

In column 3 of Table 3.2 the natural log of the assessment on improvements is added to the variables used in column 2 of Table 3.2. The assessment variable is highly statistically significant ($t = 10.85$), and the coefficient is .25. The biases still present (comparing columns 1 and 3 of Table 3.2) are shown in column 2 of Table 3.3. Comparing columns 1 and 2 of Table 3.3, the absolute value of the bias is reduced for six out of nine coefficients. Note that the sign of the bias changes in five out of nine cases. The biases in the coefficients of median income, percentage multifamily units, and percentage migrants are reduced substantially. Also, the bias of the coefficient of percentage black is reduced to only −.016. However, the bias in the coefficient of percentage Latino increases substantially from −.108 to −.312.

Column 4 of Table 3.2 contains the results of omitting lot area and the neighborhood characteristics: the measure of particulate pollution, median income, percentage multifamily units, percentage migrants, percentage black, percentage Latino, percentage Irish, and distance to the CBD. The omitted variables biases appear in the coefficients of square feet and air conditioned. Berry (1976, p. 406) contends that the assessed value of land is possibly a good proxy for neighborhood characteristics (and land area, of course), so this variable is added in column 5 of Table 3.2. The natural log of assessment on land is highly significant ($t = 7.13$) and has a coefficient of .208. However, as indicated in columns 1 and 2 of Table 3.4, the omitted variables bias is reduced in only three out of seven cases. The bias in the coefficient of square feet is substantially reduced (from .188 to −.068), but the large bias in the coefficient of air conditioned remains.

TABLE 3.4
Analysis of Omitted Variables Bias

	Bias introduced by omitting neighborhood characteristics and lot area	Bias after including assessment on land
Age (years)	−.004	−.004
Square feet (natural log)	.188	−.068
Number of baths	−.011	.016
Improved attic	.048	.036
Improved basement	.002	.006
Air conditioned	.077	.062
Garage	.044	.048

This investigation has demonstrated the potential hazards in using a proxy variable to replace several independent variables. The author strongly suggests that tests of the kind reported here be used on a smaller sample before a larger sample is analyzed using a proxy variable. It is possible that the omitted variables bias can be made *worse* when the proxy is included compared to results obtained when the proxy is excluded. Such a perverse result seems to occur in the Chicago data for the coefficient of percentage Latino population. The omission of the variables that measure the attributes of the house causes a negative bias in this coefficient, but the inclusion of the proxy (assessment on improvements) makes the bias more negative. On the other hand, the tests lend further support to Berry's conclusion that prices in all-black neighborhoods were significantly below the prices in peripheral white neighborhoods. However, this conclusion rests upon the assumption that there are no relevant variables omitted from the set used in column 1 of Table 3.2. Many would be unwilling to make this assumption. In particular, the expectations that home buyers have for the future quality of neighborhoods probably play an important role in the determination of housing prices.[3] No variables have been included to capture these effects. In any event, the methodological points stand.

Despite the technical problems with the study by Berry (1976), it is reasonable to conclude that white aversion to living near blacks was a powerful force operating in the Chicago housing market. A more tentative conclusion reached by Berry is that the degree to which black access to housing in border white areas is restricted depends upon the phase of the residential construction cycle. During a period of high levels of new construction in the suburbs such as 1968–1972, we would expect the racial borders to shift rapidly as whites act upon their basic aversion to blacks. Berry has thus suggested that the racial price differences with blacks paying more than whites found by studies such as King and Mieszkowski (1973), Kain and Quigley (1975), Schafer (1976), and many others are transitory.

The remaining issue is to determine whether there are factors that determine the direction in which the black–white border moved. A study by Steinnes (1977) has examined this question for the near northwest side of the city of Chicago during the period from 1960 to 1970. Using a sample of 62 census tracts, Steinnes (1977) estimated the probability that a tract "tipped" from white to black occupancy. A tract has tipped if the tract went from zero, or virtually zero, blacks in 1960 to 10% or more black in 1970. In a multivariate probit analysis, the probability of tipping was strongly negatively related to the distance from the closest black area in 1960, percentage of population foreign born in 1960, and percentage of

---

[3] I am indebted to Professor Marcus Alexis for this point.

housing units owner occupied in 1960. The probability of tipping was increased by increase in the median income in the tract and the percentage of houses in sound condition. These results indicate that, at a given distance from the black residential areas, the tract that was most likely to tip contained native-born, higher income whites in sound rental housing. This means that the expansion of the black housing areas is not necessarily into housing of poor quality. However, that expansion did tend to be into rental housing. This is probably the expected result because higher income white renters are probably very mobile and lower income whites of foreign birth who own their homes are relatively immobile. Furthermore, the blacks who were the first to move into the white areas were likely to be relatively mobile and high-income persons. For the present purposes, however, the most important finding is that except for percentage foreign born, distance from the black areas is the most important variable.[4] The expansion of the black housing areas is largely confined to contiguous areas, as Berry's study (1976) showed indirectly. This pattern necessarily places constraints upon the quality of the housing stock available to blacks. This interpretation will be incorporated into the final model developed in Chapter 8.

2 Air Pollution, Neighborhood Income, and Other Externalities in the Chicago Housing Market

In this section we review briefly the literature on the impact of air pollution, neighborhood income, and other externalities on the demand for housing, and examine in more detail some empirical results for Chicago.

There is a growing body of literature in which the negative effect of air pollution on the demand for housing is demonstrated empirically. The usual procedure is to perform a cross section analysis of a sample of census tracts or individual houses drawn from one metropolitan area. An hedonic equation is estimated and measures of air pollution are then added to the specification.[5] Early studies that showed that at least one measure of air pollution was a significant determinant of property values include Ridker and Henning (1967), Zerbe (1969), and Anderson and Crocker (1971). Empirical researchers in this field have faced some difficult problems. Adequate control variables must be included in the hedonic equation so that the relatively

---

[4] The variable percentage foreign born reflects the existence of some white ethnic communities that are unique to the area studied.

[5] An exception to this procedure is the work by Wieand (1973), who used the value of housing per unit of land as the dependent variable. The expected result, that pollution lowers land use intensity so defined, did not appear, This failure may stem from the lack of an explicit vintage model of housing supply. See Chapters 4 and 6 for further discussion of this issue.

minor effect of pollution on property values can be detected, and high correlation between the measures of various pollutants makes the isolation of the impact of one pollutant difficult. However, since the objective of this study is to develop an empirically verified approach to the study of the housing market, the fact that the demand for the reduction of one air pollutant is empirically uncertain is not a serious limitation. All we need to know for now is that air pollution in general effects housing demand and that the variations in pollution have a particular spatial configuration in the Chicago area.

There has been a debate over the proper interpretation of the regression coefficients for pollution variables obtained in the hedonic technique. Straszheim (1974), as we might expect from the discussions in Chapter 1, has stated that unbiased estimates of the coefficients of pollution variables are not possible unless one first takes account of the compartmentalization of the housing market. As was concluded in Chapter 1, this interpretation will be discounted for the purposes of this study. The debate has also centered on the question of how unbiased regression coefficients can be used to calculate the benefits of a reduction in air pollution throughout a metropolitan area. This issue was raised by Freeman (1971), who pointed out that a general equilibrium model of the city would be needed to simulate the total effects of the reduction in pollution. Contributors to the debate include Anderson and Crocker (1972), Small (1975), and Polinsky and Shavell (1975, 1976). This theoretical debate has established that

1. The cross-section regression results *can* be used to estimate the marginal rate of substitution between pollution reduction and other goods for an individual household.
2. Explicit general equilibrium models of the housing and land markets are needed to generate correct measures of the total willingness to pay (market demand) for a general reduction in pollution.

As Polinsky and Shavell (1976) have pointed out, if the general equilibrium model assumed is one with an "open" city (instantaneous migration of population in response to changes in utility in the city), then the cross-section regression results can be used directly to calculate the change in the aggregate land value. The change in aggregate land value equals the demand for cleaner air in this case. The calculations are more complex if a "closed" city (constant population) is assumed. The purpose of this section is to discuss the empirical results for Chicago concerning the individual's willingness to pay for cleaner air. The purpose of the entire study is to develop an improved general equilibrium model of the housing and land markets.

Studies by Anderson and Crocker (1970), Bednarz (1975), Diamond (1978a,b), and Smith (1978) have used data on individual houses in Chicago to estimate hedonic equations that include measures of air pollution. The

TABLE 3.5
Regression Analysis of House Values: 1967[a]

Constant	4.1532
Particulate pollution	−.3998*
(annual mean, 1966, by volume)	
Sulfur dioxide	.0601
(ppm by volume per 72 hours)	
Income of family	.3305*
(dollars)	
Square feet	.2356*
Age of house	−.0465*
(years)	
Mortgage duration	.4063*
(years)	
Lot size	.0917*
(square feet)	
School quality index	−.0729*
(1 = highest, 4 = lowest)	
Incidental expenses of house	.0361*
(dollars)	
Distance to CBD	.0321
(miles)	
Distance to Lake Michigan	−.0202*
(tenths of miles)	
Median income level of community	.1216*
area, 1966 (dollars)	
Frame house dummy	−0810*
Detached house dummy	.1004*
Neighborhood crime rate	−.0296*
(index with base = mean rate for city)	
R^2	.771

Source: Anderson and Crocker (1970).
*Indicates the coefficient is significant at the 95% level.
[a]All variables are in natural log form.

study by Bednarz (1975) also included an analysis of data aggregated to the census tract level. The results reported by Anderson and Crocker (1970) for a sample of houses appraised by FHA in 1967 are shown in Table 3.5. The results show that house value was significantly reduced by particulate pollution, but that the high correlation of the measures of particulates and sulfur dioxide prevented Anderson and Crocker from obtaining a reliable estimate of the effect of the latter.[6] Since the regression was run in double-log form, the numerical results are interpreted as elasticities. Bednarz (1975)

---

[6] The measures of air pollution are interpolations of the measures made by the Chicago Air Pollution Control District.

used the same sample of 275 single-family houses sold during 1970–1972 that was analyzed extensively in the previous section. Bednarz (1975) used measures of particulates and sulfur dioxide generated by a computer model of air pollution in use at Argonne National Laboratories. In none of the regression analyses performed with all of the independent variables listed in Table 3.2 included does either pollution measure have a significant negative effect on house value. Indeed, the signs of the coefficients of pollution are not consistently negative. When distance to the CBD is dropped from the equation, the signs of the coefficients of pollution are negative, as expected. These results point up the high correlation of distance to the CBD with the measure of sulfur dioxide ($-.40$) and particulates ($-.74$). The study by Tolley and Cohen (1976) also showed that there is a high negative correlation between distance to the CBD and measures of various polutants.[7] These high correlations will allow air pollution to be added to a model of the urban housing market relatively easily.

Bednarz (1975) also analyzed the data that consists of 231 census tracts or tract groups that were studied by Berry (1976). The description of the data is given in the previous section and Berry's results are shown in Table 3.1. For these data the simple correlations of the measures of sulfur dioxide and particulates with distance to the CBD are $-.48$ and $-.29$, respectively. As is shown in Table 3.1, the measure of particulate pollution had a significant negative effect on mean house value. When the measure of particulate pollution was replaced by the measure of sulfur dioxide, this new coefficient was also significant and negative in sign. Bednarz (1975) did not report any results in which both pollution measures were used as independent variables. As Bednarz (1975, pp. 96–98) pointed out, it might be appropriate to discount the results obtained with the sample of 275 individual houses because it is not representative of the entire SMSA. However, while it is true that selling price data for individual transactions contains a great deal of "noise," it is not correct to argue, as Bednarz (1975) did, that "the effect of air pollution may be masked by this unexplainable component of the selling price [p. 97]." The effect would be masked only if pollution were highly correlated with the unexplainable component of selling price.

A recent study by Smith (1978) has examined the impact of several externalities on the prices of lots upon which new houses were built in the Chicago SMSA in 1971–1972. The data were taken from the same properties used in the study of housing supply by Smith (1976) that is discussed in Chapter 4. Lot value was appraised by the mortgage lender. It is important

---

[7] The exception to this statement involves the pollution generated by the Gary, Indiana, area. These pollutants may have a significant effect on property values in the southeastern part of the Chicago SMSA.

to remember that the focus of Smith's study (1978) is *only* lots on which new construction occurred. This means that no properties were included in the sample from the area within four miles of the CBD and that very few observations were obtained from nonwhite neighborhoods. Smith's study is thus not a general study of the pattern of land values in the Chicago SMSA, but some useful results were obtained.

Smith (1978) argued that the appropriate measure of the amenity value of a lot is based upon the relationship

$$PL_i = PL_j + PREM_{ij}/(LS_i), \tag{2}$$

where PL_i is the price per square foot for lot i, LS_i is the size of lot i, and $PREM_{ij}$ is the premium paid for the ith location over the jth location. Solving for $PREM_{ij}$, we have

$$PREM_{ij} = (PL_i - PL_j)LS_i. \tag{3}$$

Assume PL_j is the minimum price of land in the urban area. This equation implies that the amenity premium depends upon the lot size selected.[8] The above formulation ignores the fact that the demand curve for land has a negative slope, so a better approximation is

$$PREM_{ij} = (PL_i - PL_j)LS_i + \tfrac{1}{2}(PL_i - PL_j)(LS_j - LS_i). \tag{4}$$

From the definition of own-price elasticity, η,

$$LS_j - LS_i = \eta(PL_j - PL_i)LS_i/(PL_i), \text{ or} \tag{5}$$

$$PREM_{ij} = \{1 + [\tfrac{1}{2}\eta(PL_j - PL_i)/(PL_i)]\}(PL_i - PL_j)LS_i. \tag{6}$$

From Chapter 1,

$$\eta = -[(1 - a)\sigma - a\eta_h], \tag{7}$$

where a = the share of land, σ = the elasticity of substitution between land and capital in the production of housing, and η_h = the price elasticity of demand for housing. Smith (1976) has estimated that $a = .2$ and $\sigma = 1.2$, so $\eta = -1.16$ and

$$PREM_{ij} = \{1 + [0.58(PL_j - PL_i)/(PL_i)]\}(PL_i - PL_j)LS_i. \tag{8}$$

This formulation for $PREM_{ij}$ was used by Smith (1978) as the dependent variable.

The regression results obtained by Smith (1978) are shown in Table 3.6. We see that the externalities air pollution (particulates), crime, and land use in the neighborhood similar to the lot in question are all significant with

---

[8] This simply repeats the argument made in Chapter 1.

TABLE 3.6
Smith's Regression Analysis of Amenity Premiums[a]

Variable	
Distance to O'Hare airport (miles)	−60.0
	(2.29)
Distance to CBD (miles)	−284.5
	(6.19)
Distance to major commuter	−309.9
transportation (miles)	(2.68)
Land use in neighborhood similar to	2785.3
lot in question	(6.18)
Public water and sewer available	1306.6
	(3.34)
Property tax rate (%)	−1471.3
	(2.86)
School expenditures per pupil ($)	9.99
	(4.83)
Crime per 1000 people in 1971	−138.2
	(4.83)
Average air pollution rate	−42.9
(micrograms of particulates)	(4.64)
Percentage nonwhite population in	−23.4
census tract	(1.20)
R^2	.555

Source: Smith (1978).
[a] t values are in parentheses.

the correct signs. All the distance measures (distance to O'Hare Airport, CBD, and major commuter transportation) have negative and significant signs. The public sector variables (property tax rate, public water and sewer available, and school expenditures per pupil) are also significant with the proper signs. However, percentage nonwhite is not a significant determinant of amenity premiums in the sample studied. This variable is significant with a negative sign for the lower income subsample (Smith, 1978, p. 385). These results confirm the results obtained by Bednarz (1975) and Anderson and Crocker (1970) discussed above. Additional discussion of the public sector variables is provided below.

The studies by Diamond (1978a,b) that were discussed in detail in Chapter 1 included a measure of particulate pollution as one of the amenities that influences the demand for a site in the Chicago suburbs in 1969–1971. At the point of means, the marginal value of a unit of air quality was estimated to be $225, a statistically significant result. A unit of air quality is defined as a reduction of one microgram in the average annual air particulate count. Diamond also found that a reduction in distance to the CBD of one mile was worth $302, a location closer to a commuter rail station was worth $460, a reduction of one in crimes per thousand in the municipality was worth $1665, and a location within 5 miles of Lake Michigan was worth $21,475.[9] Hilliness was found to be a disamenity. To summarize the results for air pollution, it can be concluded that air pollution lowers property values in Chicago, and that air pollution is strongly negatively correlated with distance to the CBD.[10] The effects of individual pollutants are less certain.

Recently urban crime has received a considerable amount of attention in urban housing studies. The hedonic study by Thaler (1978) of Rochester in 1971 indicated that a reduction in property crimes per capita of one standard deviation would have increased house value by an average of $430. The results reported by Kain and Quigley (1975), however, did not indicate that crime significantly effected property values or rents in St. Louis. The three studies for Chicago by Anderson and Crocker (1970), Smith (1978), and Diamond (1978a,b) all show that crime exercises a significant negative impact on property values. In Table 3.5, we see that Anderson and Crocker have estimated the elasticity of house value with respect to crime to be only −.03. On the other hand, Smith (1978) and Diamond (1978a,b) have estimated that a reduction of one in crimes per thousand people was worth $138 and $1665, respectively, in lot value. While the correlation has not been calculated, it is reasonable to assume that there is a negative correlation between crime and distance to the CBD in the Chicago SMSA.

Table 3.7 has been prepared as a preliminary examination of the spatial variation in crime rates over time. Using the number of offenses known to the police from the Uniform Crime Reports for the United States (published by the FBI), it is possible to construct time series data on crime rates for seven types of major crimes for the municipalities of Chicago, Berwyn, Cicero, Evanston, and Oak Park. These last four municipalities are older suburbs that are (except for Berwyn) contiguous to Chicago. Table 3.7 shows the crime rates for the city of Chicago and the means for the four suburbs for 1940, 1950, 1960, and 1970. Except for petty larceny, all crime rates in all years were higher in the city of Chicago than in the suburbs. Furthermore, except for the murder rate, all crime experienced sharp increases from 1950 to 1960 in the city of Chicago. Crime rates except murder also increased in the suburbs during this period, but the increases in the

---

[9] The estimated value of proximity of Lake Michigan seems to be too large. Proximity of Lake Michigan may be highly correlated with omitted neighborhood variables such as school quality and neighborhood income.

[10] The simulation study by Tolley and Cohen (1976) suggested that sulfur dioxide pollution lowers property values by up to 5% in the city of Chicago, by up to 2% in the rest of Cook County, and by negligible amounts in the rest of the SMSA.

TABLE 3.7
Central City and Suburban Crime Rates Over Time

	1940	1950	1960	1970
Murder and nonnegligent manslaughter per 1000 pop.				
Chicago	.068	.071	.103	.241
Four suburbs[a]	.012	.012	.011	.034
Robbery per 1000 pop.				
Chicago	1.708	1.514	3.756	6.890
Four suburbs	.678	.422	.523	1.202
Aggravated assault per 1000 pop.				
Chicago	.442	1.198	2.064	3.465
Four suburbs	.110	.480	.777	.763
Burglary per 1000 pop.				
Chicago	3.220	3.447	8.654	10.451
Four suburbs	2.592	2.582	3.644	6.603
Larceny ($50 or more) per 1000 pop.				
Chicago	1.130	2.245	6.023	4.894
Four suburbs	.759	1.563	2.890	4.561
Larceny (less than $50) per 1000 pop.				
Chicago	3.529	3.017	9.125	25.425
Four suburbs	5.241	4.664	6.875	16.702
Auto theft per 1000 pop.				
Chicago	.847	1.439	6.547	11.663
Four suburbs	.527	.836	2.405	5.042

Source: Federal Bureau of Investigation (1941, 1951, 1961, 1971).
[a]The four suburbs are Berwyn, Cicero, Evanston, and Oak Park.

suburbs were all smaller than the increases experienced in the city. If we assume that people care about the change in the probability of being a victim of crime, then the spatial pattern of increases in crime rates leads to the conclusion that, ceteris paribus, the attractiveness of the city of Chicago fell relative to the attractiveness of the surburbs during the period from 1950 to 1960. The sharp increase in crime rates in the city continued from 1960 to 1970 in the cases of murder, robbery, aggravated assault, petty larceny, and auto theft. These increases in the city exceeded the increases in the suburbs in these five categories.[11] Combining the results in Table 3.7 with those of Smith (1978) and Diamond (1978a,b), it seems quite likely that the rise in crime in the city of Chicago since 1950 has significantly depressed the demand for central city land relative to suburban locations.

[11] Furthermore, it is likely that the greatest increases in crime rates occurred in the inner areas of the city of Chicago. It is reasonable to assume that the crime rates in Evanston, Oak Park, and Cicero are roughly representative of crime rates in nearby areas within the city of Chicago.

Another externality that has received a great deal of attention in the literature is neighborhood income. The recent studies for Chicago that are reported in this study consistently show that neighborhood income positively effects the value of an individual property. The reasons for this are reasonably clear; higher income people create a neighborhood that looks better, are less prone to crime and other antisocial behavior, and attract higher quality businesses and other services. Furthermore, for the city of Chicago in 1970, there is a positive correlation between neighborhood income and distance to the CBD of .21 reported by Bednarz (1975, p. 62) for the census tract and tract group data examined above. The positive correlation of income and distance would undoubtedly be higher if the entire SMSA were examined.

Other studies, such as Kain and Quigley (1975), have attempted to quantify the effect on the value of an individual house of variations in the physical quality and appearance of neighboring houses. Kain and Quigley (1975) had particular success in determining the importance of the quality of the block of houses in which a house is located. However, this result occurs at a level of spatial detail that is too fine to allow its inclusion in the model to be developed in this study. Other studies such as Maser *et al.* (1977) and Davies (1974) have examined in detail the effects on house values of various kinds of neighboring land use. While these efforts have met with mixed success, nearby visible industrial land use clearly reduced house values in both studies. However, this sort of factor also occurs at a level of spatial detail that is too difficult to capture in the model developed in this study.

To summarize this section, it is clear that at least the three externalities of air pollution, crime, and neighborhood income significantly influence property values in the Chicago SMSA and are strongly correlated with distance to the CBD. Recognition of these results is made in the model presented in Chapter 8.

3   The Local Public Sector and the Demand for Housing

In this section we consider the impacts of both the local property tax and local government expenditures on the demand for housing. The recent theoretical literature began with the proposition introduced by Tiebout (1956) that people can move from one local jurisdiction to another to adjust their consumption of local public services. Next, Mieszkowski (1969, 1972) pointed out that at least part of the variations across jurisdictions in the property tax rate will be capitalized into property values. See Henderson (1977, Chapter 9) for a compact discussion of these models. If both of these hypotheses are correct, then it is interjurisdictional variations in public sector expenditures net of property taxes that will tend to be capitalized into property values. Hamilton (1976) has presented a model in which both the interjurisdictional and intrajurisdictional "fiscal surplus" lead to capitalization. Hamilton (1976) considered a world in which households have free mobility among many local jurisdictions, each jurisdiction contains houses of high and low quality and households of high and low income, and the property tax is proportional to property value. For simplicity, assume that the per capita expenditures on local public services are equal in all jurisdictions. Because of free mobility, all low-income (high-income) households that consume low- (high-) quality housing will attain equal levels of utility. Low-income (high-income) households in a jurisdiction with a relatively large percentage of high-quality housing will occupy houses of low quality (high quality) that have relatively high capital values because the tax rate is relatively low. While Henderson (1977, p. 190) has pointed out that Hamilton has failed to indicate the long-run implications of the model in the absence of zoning regulations, Hamilton's approach seems to be a reasonable point of departure.

The empirical testing of these hypotheses began with the studies by Oates (1969) and Orr (1968). Using a cross section of 53 communities in New Jersey, Oates (1969) found that the effective property tax rate and school expenditures per pupil influenced house values in the negative and positive directions, respectively. Oates (1969) used two-stage least squares as the estimation technique because the tax rate and expenditures depend upon the tax base. The Oates study generated a discussion over technical matters. Pollakowski (1973) pointed out that the results were sensitive to alternative specifications of the control variables and the public service variables. Edel and Sclar (1974) argued that adjustments in the supply of public services would tend to eliminate the capitalization effect. However, their argument is based upon an unnecessarily simple theory that, when made slightly more complex, vindicates Oates' study. Edel and Sclar (1974) assumed that each community possesses the same perfectly elastic long run marginal cost curve for a public service. Then the property tax will be exactly a marginal benefits tax if all households pay the same tax, which equals average and marginal cost. Thus the fiscal surplus equals zero for all households and no capitalization will occur. However, Edel and Sclar (1974) have implicitly assumed that in long-run supply equilibrium

1. All households in all communities pay the same tax amount
2. There are not quality variations across communities in the public service

If these assumptions are relaxed, we obtain a model similar to the one studied by Hamilton (1976) and discussed above. The empirical tests conducted by Oates (1969) and Edel and Sclar (1974) themselves examined, for example, the effect of an increase in school expenditures per pupil holding the tax rate *constant*. Surely expenditures per pupil can vary across communities because the quality of the service varies, and the tax rate can remain constant across communities at the same time because the tax base per pupil varies across communities. This variation in school quality will be capitalized into property values.

Orr (1968) examined the effect of the property tax and local public services on rents paid for rental housing. For a sample of 31 communities in the Boston SMSA, Orr (1968) found that neither the tax rate nor the public services were significant determinants of rent. Heinberg and Oates (1970), in a critique of Orr's study, were unable to alter these conclusions for rental housing, but found significant capitalization of the property tax and expenditures per pupil into property values in the Boston SMSA. Orr's response (1970) to Heinberg and Oates (1970) conceded that he used the wrong dependent variable in his original study. A further empirical analysis pointed out the instability of the results with respect to alternative specifications of the independent variables.

Subsequent studies include the work done by Hyman and Pasour (1973a,b), Sabella (1974), and Gustely (1976). The studies by Hyman and Pasour (1973a,b) showed that the property tax differentials across municipalities in North Carolina significantly influenced rents but did not influence property values. The effects of variations in public services did not have large effects on either rents or property values. The study by Sabella (1974) examined the *change* in the value of individual houses as a function of *changes* in the tax bill and school expenditures per pupil. Sabella concluded that changes in property values were influenced by both types of changes in the expected directions. The recent studies by Gustely (1976) and Smith (1978) also confirmed the existence of tax and benefit capitalization. In summary, the empirical literature has, for the most part, confirmed the hypothesis that property values are influenced by the variations in the local property tax rate and public services.

Given that these hypotheses have been established, is it necessary to include the local public sector explicitly in a model of the Chicago housing market? Certainly the answer depends upon the purpose of the analysis. The procedure followed in Chapter 8 is to discount the importance of the local public sector per se because the model is not very detailed. The model is used to explain the basic patterns of population density and land values presented in Chapters 6 and 7. Most of the interesting features in these basic patterns occur within the city limits of Chicago, so the local taxes and public expenditures could not be a factor in determining these features. The local public sector would be more important if the focus of the analysis were on the suburbs. However, there is one aspect of local public services that is important to the model. The nature of the neighborhood in which services are provided may influence strongly the ultimate quality of those services. For example, it is known that the socioeconomic background of pupils influences the quality of the schools they attend. Researchers, such as King and Mieszkowski (1973), Grether and Mieszkowski (1974), and Kain and Quigley (1975) have found that school quality, as measured by the median achievement test score in the school, influenced property values and rents. The only study of the effect of school quality on property values in Chicago is Anderson and Crocker (1970), shown in Table 3.5 above. They did not indicate how the school quality index was measured, but it was a significant determinant of property values in 1967. Furthermore, it is plausible to assume that school quality within the city of Chicago is positively correlated with distance to the CBD.

A study by Burkhead (1967) of 39 public high schools in the city of Chicago for 1961–1962 confirms that the quality of a school is strongly influenced by the median family income of the neighborhood in which it is located and little else. School quality was measured by the dropout rate, average eleventh grade I.Q. scores, and eleventh grade reading scores. The simple correlations between these three variables and median family income were − .69, .90, and .91, respectively. However, Burkhead (1967) found some evidence that reading gains from ninth grade to eleventh grade were related to the median years of teacher experience in the school. Burkhead's examination of the relationships between school inputs and neighborhood income found no patterns except that higher income neighborhoods had more experienced teachers. This result reflects the fact that teachers last longer in more pleasant schools. Also, some experienced teachers were allowed to transfer to better schools. The studies by Walberg and Bargen (1974a,b) of elementary and secondary public schools in the city of Chicago for 1971 generally confirm Burkhead's conclusion that school system resources were evenly distributed except for teacher experience. The maps provided by Walberg and Bargen (1974a, p. 231) make it clear that teacher experience and education level in the elementary schools were positively correlated with distance to the CBD and negatively correlated with black and Latino enrollments. Other maps developed by Walberg and Bargen (1974b, p. 369) show that the percentage of first grade children considered "ready" for school was positively correlated with distance to the CBD and negatively correlated with minority enrollments. Average fourth grade reading achievement level is strongly positively correlated with distance to the CBD and negatively correlated with minority enrollment. An analysis of the factors related to reading achievement gains from grades 1 to 4, 4 to 6, 6 to 8, and 9 to 11 by Bargen and Walberg (1974) found that teacher quality (experience and education) consistently showed a strong positive effect and percentage black enrollment showed a negative effect. It is reasonable to assume that households are aware of these basic spatial patterns of school quality. Indeed, average achievement scores for each public school are published in the newspapers annually.

4 Conclusion

In this chapter we have identified several external effects that exert significant effects on the demand for housing at a particular location. In my judgment, the most important of these factors for white households in Chicago is race. Air pollution, crime, school quality, and neighborhood income are also important variables to consider. While the location pattern of the black households cannot be characterized simply, the other four variables are probably highly correlated with distance to the CBD. This means that the four externalities (air pollution, crime, school quality, and income) can easily be incorporated into an analytical model of the urban housing market by assuming simple exogenous relationships for each with distance to the CBD. However, the introduction of race into a formal model is difficult. Essentially, the model in Chapter 8 takes the pattern of black residence as given and does not attempt to explain it or even to describe it accurately. The introduction of race formally into a realistic general equilibrium model of the housing market is a topic that should have high priority in future research.

4

Models of the Supply
of Urban Housing

This chapter presents a reasonably complete survey of the models of urban housing supply that have been developed thus far. The traditional notions of market period, short-run, and long-run supply are maintained because these categories allow a particularly convenient method of categorization. Rather than begin with the most complex model as was done in Chapter 1, the models in this chapter begin very simply and become progressively more complex. We begin with the long-run supply model introduced by Muth (1969) and its recent extensions. Next, the market period models are examined. This model in a spatial context is equivalent to the assignment model developed by Koopmans and Beckmann (1957). In this model suppliers are assumed not to respond to input and output price changes. The use of the model in empirical studies such as Kain and Quigley (1975), King (1976, 1977), and Straszheim (1975) is examined in detail. Because market period models fail to provide an explanation of the existing configuration of housing supplied, the "putty–clay" vintage model is examined next. In this model the construction of housing at time t follows a simple long-run model, but the factor proportions are then fixed forever unless the housing is demolished. The works of Muth (1976) and Anas (1978) are emphasized. The chapter concludes with a survey of the widely varied short-run models. Included in this section are some discussions of the merits of models of "filtering" in the housing market. In addition. we examine the supply models built into the urban simulation models developed by de Leeuw and Struyk (1975) and Bradbury *et al.* (1977). The basic purpose of the survey of supply models is to identify the empirical tests that will lead to the rejection of a less complex model in favor of a richer model. As always, the question is to determine the necessary degree of complexity. The focus of this chapter is only on models of housing narrowly defined. The supplies of neighborhood amentities and public services are not considered. The next chapter on the operation of the housing market will include some discussion of neighborhood amenities that can be considered to be endogenous to the operation of the housing market.

1   Models of Long-Run Supply

Throughout this chapter the focus is on the individual supplier of housing who rents a unit of urban land and faces competitive input and output markets.[1] The amenities of the neighborhood and the activities of the public sector are exogenous. The simplest supply model was presented by Muth (1969) to mirror his demand model. The production function is

$$h = f(K, L), \tag{1}$$

where h is the total amount of housing services produced on the given amount of land L using the chosen amount of the variable factor of production, capital K. The production function is usually assumed to exhibit constant returns to scale and to have a constant elasticity of substitution (CES). The price of housing services, land, and capital are exogenous to the housing producer. Given these assumptions, the standard microeconomic theory of the firm in the short run can be directly applied. Since this standard model is so familiar to economists its implications will not be described in detail here. However, because the model is so familiar and can be used so easily in a wide variety of applications, one should consider very carefully proposals for its abandonment. The key relationship derived by Muth (1969, p. 55) is the price elasticity of the value of housing produced per unit of land, or

$$d \ln(ph/L)/d \ln p = 1 + \sigma(P_K/P_L), \tag{2}$$

where P_K is the share of capital, P_L is the share of land, and σ is the elas-

---

[1] Because constant returns to scale are normally assumed, the analysis can focus on the behavior of a producer who occupies one unit of space. If returns to scale are not constant, then the scale of the housing firm in terms of land area occupied becomes a variable to be determined, of course.

ticity of substitution.[2] The elasticity of land rent with respect to the price of housing is simply $d \ln R/d \ln p = 1/P_L$. It should be noted that, since the elasticity of substitution is not necessarily assumed to be equal to one, the shares of land and capital will vary with the price of housing. Thus, the supply elasticity is not a constant over space.

A considerable amount of research effort has been used to estimate the elasticity of substitution parameter. The key issue is whether σ is significantly different from 1.0. As is well known, the finding that $\sigma = 1.0$ means that the supply model can be based upon a Cobb–Douglas production function. These studies typically examined a measure of the intensity of land use for newly constructed housing as a function of land value. The first study to follow this procedure is by Muth (1971a), in which he estimated σ for single-family homes. The equation estimated is[3]

$$\ln[RL/(rK)] = a + (1 - \sigma)\ln(R/r). \tag{3}$$

Here the expenditure on land is the Federal Housing Authority (FHA) estimated market price of the site including street improvements, utilities, and landscaping. Muth's estimate of σ is .5, which turned out to be significantly less than 1.0. Another study, by Koenker (1972), examined only multifamily structures that were newly constructed. Assuming the price of capital is constant, Koenker's equation for estimation is

$$\ln[(ph - RL)/L] = a + \sigma \ln R. \tag{4}$$

He found $\sigma = .71$, which is also significantly less than 1.0.

Using data collected on rental housing for the housing supply experiment in Brown County, Wisconsin, Rydell (1976) has also estimated σ to be 0.5. Rydell's approach was to regress a measure of $\ln(K/L)$ on $\ln R$. The measure of K is the difference between total property value and the value of land divided by an index of the price of capital improvements on the site. The price of capital improvements equals $1 minus the present value of future maintenance and insurance costs (based on the age of the unit and other factors). Another study of new multifamily housing, by Fountain (1977), found an estimate of $\sigma = .57$, a figure that is significantly less than 1.0 but not significantly less than .71. Fountain (1977) also tested for nonconstant returns to scale, but could not reject the assumption that the production function exhibits constant returns to scale. However, some variation in σ was found to depend upon tenure choice (own or rent) and the

[2] Or, $d \ln(h/L)/d \ln p = \sigma(P_K/P_L)$.

[3] This equation can be derived directly from the definition of the elasticity of substitution, $\sigma = d \ln(K/L)/d \ln(R/r)$.

number of stories in the structure. No explanations for these variations were offered.

The possibility that the elasticity of substitution varies systematically with the capital–land ratio has been investigated by Sirmans et al. (forthcoming). There are many functional forms for a variable elasticity of substitution (VES) production function (Revankar, 1971), and Sirmans et al. (forthcoming) have chosen the function introduced by Revankar (1971) because of its relative simplicity and the ability to conduct a statistical test to discriminate the VES from the CES form. Revankar's VES function is specified by Sirmans et al. as

$$h = \gamma L^{\alpha(1-\delta\rho)}[K + (\rho - 1)L]^{\alpha\delta\rho}, \tag{5}$$

where α, δ, ρ, and γ are parameters.[4] This function includes the Cobb–Douglas function ($\rho = 1$) as a special case. The returns-to-scale parameter is α. It can be shown that the elasticity of substitution is

$$\sigma = 1 + \left(\frac{\rho - 1}{1 - \delta\rho}\right)\frac{L}{K}. \tag{6}$$

Assuming constant returns to scale ($\alpha = 1$) and competitive input and output markets so that the ratio of marginal products equals the ratio of factor prices, we obtain

$$K/L = G_0 + G_1(R/r), \tag{7}$$

where $G_0 = (1 - \rho)/(1 - \delta\rho)$ and $G_1 = \delta\rho/(1 - \delta\rho)$, or

$$rK/L = rG_0 + G_1R, \tag{8}$$

where r, the price of capital, is assumed to be constant at all locations. Estimation of this equation by ordinary least squares produces an estimate of rG_0, which is related to the elasticity of substitution according to

$$\sigma = 1 - rG_0[L/(rK)]. \tag{9}$$

Sirmans et al. have used the data provided by Wendt and Goldner (1966) to estimate both the CES and VES forms of the production function. According to Wendt and Goldner (1966, p. 199), the value of improvements on a lot rK was determined by deducting the estimated land value from the

---

[4] The function requires that $\gamma > 0$, $\alpha > 0$, $0 < \delta < 1$, $0 \leq \delta p \leq 1$, and $K/L > (1 - \rho)/(1 - \delta\rho)$. The marginal products of land and capital are

$$\partial h/\partial L = \alpha(1 - \delta\rho)h/L + \alpha\delta\rho(\rho - 1)h/[K + (\rho - 1)L]$$

and

$$\partial h/\partial K = \alpha\delta\rho h/[K + (\rho - 1)L].$$

sale price of the property. Using the Koenker (1972) approach discussed above, Sirmans *et al.* (forthcoming) have estimated the elasticity of substitution for the CES function to be .77. The estimate of rG_0 for the VES function is .323, implying an elasticity of substitution at the mean value of $L/(rK)$ of .83. The range of $L/(rK)$ in the data is .23 to 1.04, so the estimated elasticity of substitution varies from .925 to .664.

Since the distinction between the CES and VES cases reduces to the choice of functional form in a simple regression of rK/L on R, Sirmans *et al.* (forthcoming) performed the Box–Cox test to determine the best functional form for the relationship. Box and Cox (1964) suggested writing the relationship as

$$[(rK/L)^\lambda - 1]/\lambda = b_0 + b_1[(R^\lambda - 1)/\lambda] + u_1, \qquad (10)$$

where λ is the crucial functional form parameter and u is the disturbance term. As λ approaches 0 the function approaches the CES (logarithmic), and if $\lambda = 1$ the function is VES (linear). The value of λ is chosen to maximize the value of the likelihood function. Sirmans *et al.* (forthcoming) found the best value for λ to be .7, with a 95% confidence interval of .2 to 1.1. The CES function is thus rejected. However, the unbiasedness of the results of Sirmans *et al.* (forthcoming), as well as the results of Koenker (1972), Muth (1971a), Rydell (1976), and Fountain (1977), can be questioned on the basis of measurement error in R. This point is discussed below.

A different complication has been introduced by Smith (1976), who drew the distinction between the supply of housing density and the supply of housing quality. The housing producer must decide on the number and quality of housing units to supply on the site in question. The quality of a unit is assumed to depend upon the amounts of land and capital used in that unit, or

$$Q = f(K, L), \qquad (11)$$

where Q is the unobserved index of quality. The supply of housing on the site in question is UQ, where U is the number of units each with quality level Q. The total land available on the site $\bar{L} = UL$. The objective of Smith's model is to estimate separate supply elasticities for U and Q in order to determine whether there is a unique solution for U and Q at each level of R, land rent.

The estimating equation used by Smith (1976) is derived as follows. Since $R = PQU - rKU$ (assuming zero profits in the long run) and $E = PQU$, where P is the price of a unit of housing quality and E is total revenue for the firm, total differentiation yields

$$dR = QU\,dP + PU\,dQ + PQ\,dU - rU\,dK - rK\,dU \qquad (12)$$

and

$$dE = UQ\,dP + PU\,dQ + PQ\,dU. \tag{13}$$

The first-order conditions for profit maximization and the assumption of zero profits in the long run imply that there exists a function $g(U, Q, P) = 0$, or in differential form,

$$dP = \frac{\partial P}{\partial Q}\,dQ + \frac{\partial P}{\partial U}\,dU. \tag{14}$$

The production function can be written in differential form as

$$dQ = Q_L\,dL + Q_K\,dK, \tag{15}$$

where Q_i is the marginal product of the ith factor in the production of housing quality. Substitution for dP and dK into the expression for dR yields

$$dR = QU\frac{\partial P}{\partial Q}\,dQ + QU\frac{\partial P}{\partial U}\,dU + PU\,dQ + PQ\,dU - \frac{rU}{Q_K}\,dQ$$

$$+ \frac{rQ_LU}{Q_K}\,dL - rK\,dU. \tag{16}$$

Since $L = 1/U$, $dL = L^2\,dU$ and $Q_L = -Q_U L^{-2}$, or $Q_L\,dL = Q_U\,dU$. Grouping terms, the equation becomes

$$dR = QU\frac{\partial P}{\partial Q}\,dQ + QU\frac{\partial P}{\partial U}\,dU + U\,dQ\left(P - \frac{r}{Q_K}\right)$$

$$+ dU\left(PQ + \frac{rUQ_U}{Q_K} - rK\right). \tag{17}$$

From the first-order conditions for profit maximization, $P = r/Q_K$ and $PQ = rK - (rUQ_U/Q_K)$,[5] so

---

[5] Since $U = 1/L$, the production function can be written $Q = g(K,U)$. The Lagrangian of the constrained maximization problem is

$$L = PQU - rKU - R - \lambda[g(K,U) - Q].$$

The first-order conditions are

$$PQ - rK - \lambda Q_U = 0,$$
$$PU + \lambda = 0,$$

and

$$-rU - \lambda Q_K = 0.$$

These can be rewritten as

$$PQ = rK - U(Q_U/Q_K) \quad \text{and} \quad P = r/Q_K.$$

$$\frac{dR}{R} = \frac{QUP}{R\varepsilon_Q}\frac{dQ}{Q} + \frac{QUP}{R\varepsilon_U}\frac{dU}{U},\tag{18}$$

where ε_Q is the price elasticity of Q and ε_U is the price elasticity of the number of units. Also, $QUP/R = 1/P_L$, where P_L is the share of land.

Substitution of the expression for dP into the equation for dE yields

$$\frac{dE}{E} = \left(\frac{1 + \varepsilon_Q}{\varepsilon_Q}\right)\frac{dQ}{Q} + \left(\frac{1 + \varepsilon_U}{\varepsilon_U}\right)\frac{dU}{U}.\tag{19}$$

Solving this equation for dQ/Q and substitution into the equation for dR/R yields

$$\frac{dR}{R} = \frac{1}{P_L(\varepsilon_Q + 1)}\frac{dE}{E} + \frac{[1 - (1 + \varepsilon_U)/(1 + \varepsilon_Q)]}{P_L\varepsilon_U}\frac{dU}{U}.\tag{20}$$

The estimation of the equation

$$\ln R = \alpha_0 + \alpha_1 \ln E + \alpha_2 \ln U\tag{21}$$

allows the calculation of ε_Q and ε_U as

$$\varepsilon_Q = [1/(\alpha_1 P_L)] - 1\tag{22}$$

and

$$\varepsilon_U = [(1/P_L) - \alpha_1]/(\alpha_1 + \alpha_2).\tag{23}$$

Recall that E and U are expenditures and number of units per unit of land, respectively. Smith's (1976) estimates of α_1, α_2, and P_L for new single family houses are 1.18, .34, and .18, respectively, implying $\varepsilon_Q = 3.75$ and $\varepsilon_U = 5.26$. The hypothesis that $\varepsilon_Q = \varepsilon_U$ can be rejected at the 99% level. This test is conducted by dropping $\ln U$ from the regression and noting a significant drop in explanatory power. The elasticity of substitution in Smith's (1976) study is

$$\sigma = \varepsilon_U P_L/P_K = 1.15,[6]\tag{24}$$

which is not significantly greater than 1.0.

Smith's (1976) estimation procedure has the advantage that the quantity that is most subject to error, the rent or value of land, is used only as the dependent variable in the analysis. The other estimates of σ (Muth, 1971a; Koenker, 1972; Rydell, 1976; Fountain, 1977; Sirmans et al., forthcoming) all employ an estimated value of R as the crucial independent variable.

---

[6] This formula is derived from the equation for derived demand $d \ln L = -P_K d \ln R$. From this we have $\sigma = -(d \ln L/d \ln R)/P_K = \varepsilon_U P_L/P_K$ because $d \ln R = d \ln P/P_L$ and $\varepsilon_U = d \ln U/d \ln P = -d \ln L/d \ln P$.

Suppose the regression equation used by Koenker (1972),

$$\ln(rK/L) = \alpha + \sigma \ln R + u, \tag{25}$$

is estimated (u = the random normal error term), but that $V = Re^{\delta}$ and $i = re^{\gamma}$, where V and i are the measured prices of land and capital, respectively, and δ and γ are random normal error terms. Substitution for r and R yields

$$\ln(iK/L) = \alpha + \sigma \ln V + (u - \sigma\delta + \gamma). \tag{26}$$

Here δ and γ can be considered to be omitted variables, which means that the bias in the estimate of σ can be written

$$E\hat{\sigma} - \sigma = -\sigma\beta_{\delta} + \beta_{\gamma}, \tag{27}$$

where β_{δ} and β_{γ} are the regression coefficients obtained in regressions of δ and γ on $\ln V$.[7] We know that $\beta_{\delta} > 0$, so if r is measured without error, the estimate of σ will be biased downward. However, the measurement of rK is, in all studies examined in this section, determined as the residual of the sale price of the property minus the estimated value of land. Assuming the sale price is correct, this means that δ and γ are negatively correlated, and that $\beta_{\gamma} < 0$. This adds to the downward bias of $\hat{\sigma}$. This analysis of bias applies to the study by Rydell (1976), as Quigley (1976) pointed out.

The estimation procedure used by Muth (1971a) presents a slightly more difficult analysis of the possible biases. The true equation to be estimated is

$$\ln[RL/(rK)] = a + (1 - \sigma)\ln(R/r). \tag{28}$$

As before, assume measurement error in R and r, or $V = Re^{\delta}$ and $i = re^{\gamma}$. In addition, assume that K is measured with error, or $C = Ke^{\eta}$. This latter assumption is introduced because Muth used an independent estimate of r (the Boeckh index of brick residential structures). We are thus able to consider the possibility that r is measured without error, but that rK is measured with error. Assume that γ is uncorrelated with δ and η and that δ is negatively correlated with η because the value of capital is defined as total property value minus estimated land value. Substitution of the expressions for R, r, and K yields

$$\ln[VL/(rC)] = \alpha + (1 - \sigma)\ln(V/i) + [u + \delta\sigma + \gamma(1 - \sigma) - \eta]. \tag{29}$$

The bias in the estimate of $(1 - \sigma)$ becomes

$$E(1 - \hat{\sigma}) - (1 - \sigma) = \sigma\beta_{\delta} + (1 - \sigma)\beta_{\gamma} - \beta_{\eta}, \tag{30}$$

---

[7] See Johnston (1972, p. 169) for a derivation of this result.

where β_δ, β_γ, and β_η are the regression coefficients obtained in regressions of δ, γ, and η on $\ln(V/i)$. The assumptions made above imply that $\beta_\delta > 0$ because V is positively correlated with δ and i is uncorrelated with δ. Similarly, $\beta_\eta < 0$. Finally, $\beta_\gamma < 0$. Thus, if r is measured without error, $\sigma - E\hat{\sigma} > 0$ as above. If r is measured with error, then the bias in $\hat{\sigma}$ will still be negative unless $-\beta_\gamma(1 - \sigma) > \sigma\beta_\delta - \beta_\eta$, a condition that can hold only if $\sigma < 1$. These analyses of bias lead to the conclusion that, except for Smith (1976), the existing estimates of the elasticity of substitution are biased downward. The extent of the bias is unknown except for the existence of Smith's result that the elasticity of substitution is close to, and perhaps slightly greater than, one.

In order to examine further the matter of the elasticity of substitution of capital for land in the production of housing services, a study has been conducted of newly constructed housing in the city of Chicago. The data are a sample of 113 buildings that were newly built and sold in the period 1969–1971. All buildings are located in the city of Chicago. The Market Data Center of the Society of Real Estate Appraisers provided information on the size of the lot, the sale price of the property, and the dates of sale and construction. Front foot land values as estimated by an appraiser as of 1970 were recorded from Olcott (1971). As with any such estimates, measurement error may be present. This study differs from previous studies in that both single-family and multifamily buildings are included. Out of 113 buildings, 25 (22%) contain two or more housing units. Furthermore, by using data from the areas of the central city in which new construction occurred, a substantial variation in land values is observed. Land values range from $115 to $700 per front foot, with a mean of $302 and a standard deviation of $124. See Table 4.1 for a further description of the data.

Following the procedure introduced by Koenker (1972), the result is obtained that

$$\ln \frac{(PQ - RL)}{L} = -3.915 + 1.13 \ln R, \qquad (31)$$
$$\phantom{\ln \frac{(PQ - RL)}{L} = } (4.96) \quad (8.12)$$

with $R^2 = .373$. The t values are shown in parentheses.[8] The estimate of σ obtained, 1.13, is not significantly different from 1.0 because the standard error of $\hat{\sigma}$ is estimated to be .14. Following Fountain (1977) and Rydell (1976) the number of units was added as an independent variable but no impact on σ was observed. While the estimate of σ presented here may be as biased as the other estimates found in the literature, the figure 1.13 is

[8] Tests on the residuals indicate that the probability of rejecting the assumption of normality is only 56%.

TABLE 4.1
A Sample of Newly Constructed Housing in the City of Chicago: 1969-1971[a]

	Mean	Standard deviation
Selling price	$42,000	$20,673
Number of units	1.42	1.06
Lot size (square feet)	3193	1513
Front-foot land value	$302	$124
Value of capital per square foot of lot	$16.77	$17.26

[a]Sample size = 113.

close to the estimate provided by Smith (1976) and is based upon a wider range of data for land value and land use intensity than are some other studies.

One study by Bradbury *et al.* (1977) has provided estimates of a supply function for land areas larger than one "unit" of land area. In particular, they estimate the supply of new construction for 89 zones in the Boston SMSA (14 Boston Redevelopment Authority Districts and 75 surrounding suburban cities and towns). The own-price elasticity of housing is a function of the elasticity of supply of vacant land and the elasticity of substitution of capital and land σ.[9] In particular,

$$\frac{dh}{dp}\frac{p}{h} = \frac{P_K}{P_L}(\sigma + e_L),\tag{32}$$

where e_L is the elasticity of supply of vacant land with respect to the price of land R. Speculators in vacant land are assumed to place more land on the market as R increases. The change in housing supply is also a function of the change in the amount of other land use, the change in the housing vacancy rate, and the amount of open space in the area available for unrestricted use. The percentage increase in new housing units over the decade from 1960 to 1970 was found to depend significantly on the change in price over the decade times the percentage of residential acres vacant in 1960 and the change in the vacancy rate.

Bradbury *et al.* (1977) also attempted to estimate supply functions separately for single-family houses and apartments for the 89 zones. Pre-

---

[9] The equation is derived as follows [see Muth (1964)]. As was shown above, for a fixed land supply $d \ln h/d \ln p = \sigma P_K/P_L$. Define $e_L = d \ln L/d \ln R$, or $e_L = P_L d \ln L/d \ln P$ because $d \ln P/d \ln R = P_L$. Thus e_L/P_L is the elasticity of land supply with respect to P. The increase in land supply, assuming optimal K is added to the land, leads to an increase in h as shown. See Muth (1964) for a detailed derivation.

sumably, these supply functions should include a measure of the change in the price of housing, a measure of land value, and variables such as zoning, which constrain supply in some way. The functions estimated do not include all of these variables, so little confidence can be placed in them. However Bradbury *et al.* (1977) have made a valuable contribution by introducing the supply of land into the analysis of housing supply in the long run.

This section on long-run supply concludes with an examination of the well-known study of rental housing by de Leeuw and Ekanem (1971). The study is an attempt to use information on rent differences among 39 metropolitan areas to estimate the elasticity of supply of rental housing. The U.S. Bureau of Labor Statistics provided a survey of the rental cost of housing units of fixed specifications for the 39 metropolitan areas. The variations in rent are related to variations in demand and supply factors. The authors state (de Leeuw and Ekanem 1971) that

> Studying differences among cities amounts to studying how housing markets behave in the long-run, in the sense of having had ample time to adjust to basic market forces. The reason is that differences among cities in size, costs, tax rates, real income, and so on tend to persist for years or even decades. What we observe when we look at rent levels in different cities, therefore, is dominated by the cumulated effects of these long-term differences [p. 806].

The discussion of this study is included here because of the innovative model employed and because the empirical results are highly implausible. A closer examination of the model will reveal the implausible nature of the findings.

In their reply to Grieson, de Leeuw and Ekanem (1973) argue persuasively that their specification of the basic structural model is correct. Demand is a function of income and relative prices and supply is a function of input prices and output price. The demand function written in log form is

$$(S - H) = \alpha_1 + \beta_1 Y - \beta_2 (R - P). \tag{33}$$

The supply function in log form is written

$$R = \alpha_2 + \beta_3 C + \beta_4 O + \beta_5 (S - H) + \beta_6 H. \tag{34}$$

The symbols are defined as follows:

S = quantity of housing services;
H = number of households;
Y = real income per household;
R = rent per unit of housing services;
P = price level of nonhousing goods and services;
C = price of capital inputs;
O = price of operating inputs.

Note that the supply curve is overidentified in this model because two variables in the demand equation, Y and P, are excluded from the supply equation. Similarly, the demand curve is overidentified because C and O are excluded from the demand equation. The lack of data for S, the quantity of housing services, prevents the use of the standard techniques for the unbiased estimation of an overidentified equation.

Substitution of the demand equation into the supply equation yields the reduced form equation

$$R = \left(\frac{\alpha_2 + \beta_5 \alpha_1}{1 + \beta_2 \beta_5}\right) + \left(\frac{\beta_3}{1 + \beta_2 \beta_5}\right)C + \left(\frac{\beta_4}{1 + \beta_2 \beta_5}\right)O$$

$$+ \left(\frac{\beta_5 \beta_1}{1 + \beta_2 \beta_5}\right)Y + \left(\frac{\beta_5 \beta_2}{1 + \beta_2 \beta_5}\right)P + \left(\frac{\beta_6}{1 + \beta_2 \beta_5}\right)H. \qquad (35)$$

From this equation, it is clear that β_5 can be identified only if β_1 or β_2 is known a priori. At this point it is useful to examine the assertions made about this equation. If supply is perfectly elastic, $\beta_5 = 0$, then the coefficients of Y and P are zero. Also, it is true that "a positive partial relationship between the rental measure used in this study and the price level therefore is probably a reliable indication of a less-than-perfectly elastic supply [de Leeuw and Ekanem, 1971, p. 810]." However, it is possible to have $\beta_5 < 0$ and to have $\beta_5 \beta_2/(1 + \beta_2 \beta_5) > 0$. For example, if $\beta_2 = 1$, $\beta_5 \beta_2/(1 + \beta_2 \beta_5)$ is greater than zero when $\beta_5 < -1$. This case can be regarded as a backward bending supply curve.

The purpose of this section is twofold: to show that the assumptions made by de Leeuw and Ekanem to identify the supply elasticity are not consistent with their empirical results; and, given that these assumptions are relaxed, to demonstrate that the results imply a zero supply elasticity for rental housing.

Given that only the reduced form equation can be estimated, additional information must be added if an estimate of β_5 is to be found. The solution used by de Leeuw and Ekanem (1971), and later by Grieson (1973), is to assume that $\beta_1 = \beta_2 = 1.0$. These assumptions allow estimation in the form

$$R = \frac{(\alpha_2 + \alpha_1)}{1 + \beta_5} + \frac{(\beta_3)}{1 + \beta_5}C + \frac{(\beta_4)}{1 + \beta_5}O + \frac{(\beta_5)}{1 + \beta_5}(Y + P) + \left(\frac{\beta_6}{1 + \beta_5}\right)H. \quad (36)$$

The results of estimating this equation are given by de Leeuw and Ekanem (1971, p. 814). It should be noted that assuming $\beta_1 = \beta_2$ is not sufficient to identify β_5. A specific numerical magnitude must be assumed to use this technique. The results presented by de Leeuw and Ekanem are not very sensitive to the choice of this numerical magnitude. For example, de Leeuw

TABLE 4.2
De Leeuw and Ekanem's Estimates of Reduced Form[a]

	R^2
$R_1 = 2.72 + 1.13P + .55Y + 28C + .160 - .04H$	.71
(2.3) (2.9) (3.7) (3.3) (1.8) (−2.7)	
$R_2 = 2.50 + 1.26P + .60Y + .24C + .070 - .04H$	.60
(1.8) (2.6) (3.3) (2.4) (.7) (−2.4)	
$R_3 = 1.78 + 1.24P + .70Y + .14C - .090 + .004H$	.34
(.8) (1.6) (2.4) (.8) (−.5) (.2)	

Source: De Leeuw and Ekanem (1971).
[a] R_1, R_2, R_3 refer to low-, moderate-, and high-rent levels for the standard housing unit in the BLS study. Test of hypothesis that coefficient of $P = 1.0$; $t = .13/.39 = .33$, $t = .26/.48 = .54$, $t = .24/.78 = .31$. t values in parentheses.

(1971) suggests a range of .8 to 1.5 for β_1 and β_2. The choice of .8 implies supply elasticities of .27 to .53 and the choice of 1.5 implies supply elasticities of .5 to 1.0.[10]

On the other hand, one may be unwilling to assume that β_1 and β_2 are exactly equal. If the assumption that $\beta_1 = \beta_2$ is relaxed, then the reduced-form equation must be estimated rather than Eq. (36). The empirical estimates of the first reduced form equation can be used as a test of the hypothesis that $\beta_1 = \beta_2$. The ratio of the coefficient of Y to the coefficient of P in Eq. (35) equals β_1/β_2. These ratios are estimated to be .49, .48, and .56 (see de Leeuw and Ekanem, 1971, p. 811). As Grieson (1973, p. 435) points out for another set of their estimates, it is likely that the hypothesis that $\beta_1 = \beta_2$ can be rejected.

After this equation is estimated, outside estimates of β_1 and β_2 can be inserted and two estimates of β_5 will be produced for each set of β_1 and β_2 values. It is hoped that these two estimates are roughly equal and not very sensitive to alternative assumptions for β_1 and β_2. Table 4.2 shows the estimates of the first reduced form equation for low-, moderate-, and high-rent units.

First, consider the coefficient of P in the estimates of this equation (designate this coefficient R_P). From the equation, $R_P = \beta_2\beta_5/(1 + \beta_2\beta_5)$. Solving this expression for the supply elasticity, we have

$$1/\beta_5 = (\beta_2/R_P) - \beta_2 = \beta_2[(1/R_P) - 1]. \tag{37}$$

From Table 4.2 we see that R_P is estimated to be 1.13 to 1.26. Remembering that $\beta_2 > 0$, the results imply a backward bending supply curve. For ex-

[10] The coefficients of $(Y + P)$ for low-, middle-, and high-rent units are .593, .653, and .745, respectively.

ample, if $\beta_2 = .8$ and $R_P = 1.2$, then supply elasticity is $-.13$. Supply elasticity is zero if $R_P = 1$. Examining Table 4.2, we see that the hypothesis that $R_P = 1$ cannot be rejected. One may wish to regard these results as implausible, but it should be noted that de Leeuw and Ekanem, in their discussion of possible errors in variables (1971, p. 810), express some preference for the estimates of R_P as guides to the supply elasticity. Similarly, the coefficients of Y in Table 4.2 (designated R_Y) can be used to compute estimates of the supply elasticity. From the first reduced form equation we have

$$1/\beta_5 = (\beta_1/R_Y) - \beta_2. \tag{38}$$

Given that β_1 and β_2 can range from .8 to 1.5 and R_Y ranges from .55 to .70, the estimate of the supply elasticity ranges from $-.36$ to $+1.93$. Supply elasticity is zero if $\beta_1/\beta_2 = R_Y$. The estimates of β_1/β_2 range from .48 to .56, as indicated above.

One further result in Table 4.2 is of interest. The coefficient of H is negative and significant in two out of three cases. Since this coefficient is $\beta_6/(1 + \beta_2\beta_5)$, we can see that it can be negative if $\beta_5 < 0$. Presumably $\beta_6 > 0$, so the coefficient is negative if $\beta_2\beta_5 < -1$. The estimates of β_5 calculated above indicate the possibility that $\beta_5 < -1.0$, so a negative coefficient for H is not necessarily contradictory of the rest of the results. However, if the elasticity of supply as defined above is zero, then the coefficient of H is zero, an assumption made by de Leeuw and Ekanem (1971, p. 812) when the first reduced form equation is refitted with H omitted.

The reinterpretation of the results obtained by de Leeuw and Ekanem (1971) has shown that the hypothesis of a zero elasticity of supply of rental housing, holding input prices constant, cannot be rejected. In the opinion of the author, the severe diseconomies of scale implied are implausible. For example, it is possible that the input price measures used do not capture fully the variation in input prices. Grieson (1973) emphasized the role of land prices in the capital cost measure. The procedures used to compute the average land price in each city should be explored more fully because of the importance of location in the determination of this price. It is clear that more empirical estimates of the elasticity of supply of rental housing were needed. The other studies discussed in this chapter have begun to provide more plausible estimates of supply elasticity in the long run.

2 Supply in the Market Period

For some purposes it is convenient to assume that the stock of housing is fixed in quantity, quality, and location, so that the task of a model of the housing market is to determine the assignment of households to the housing units and the rents earned by those units. Koopmans and Beckmann (1957) first examined models of this type as an integer programming problem. They showed that, if there are no locational interdependencies, there exists a set of competitive market prices that will sustain an optimal assignment of firms (or households in this case) to sites. However, if locational interdependencies exist in the form of "transportation costs," Koopmans and Beckmann (1957) suggest that no integer solution is optimal and that the price system cannot sustain any integer assignment. No competitive equilibrium exists![11] Recently, Heffley (1972, 1976) has shown that the Koopmans–Beckmann result depends upon their assumption that profits (or utility) of an individual economic unit net of transportation costs are independent of location. For an analysis of the housing market, the Koopmans–Beckmann assumption is inappropriate because the housing stock consists of widely varying units in terms of quality, so that households most certainly derive different utility levels from the services provided by different housing units. Given this change in assumption, Heffley (1972, 1976) showed the conditions necessary for an optimal assignment to be sustained by competitive prices. Essentially, it is necessary to have the households rank the houses differently. What is important for the present study is the possibility that, by introducing locational interdependencies, a competitive equilibrium may not exist. Is it necessary to introduce into a model of urban housing a locational interdependency (transportation cost) among households?

Empirical studies based upon the market period assumption have not assumed locational interdependencies among individual households. The typical assumption is that nonwork trips (e.g., shopping, social, recreational) are made to ubiquitous and substitutable destinations. Rather, the market period assumption is used in conjunction with the assumption that housing consists of several Lancastrian characteristics. For example, Kain and Quigley (1975) state

> Our alternative view of the housing market, which emphasizes the importance of stocks and the nonmarket production of many housing attributes, suggests, however, that many housing attributes are relatively fixed and earn quasi rents. Therefore, we expect the prices of housing attributes or bundles to exhibit irregular and quite complex patterns of spatial variation [p. 44].

This framework leads Quigley (1972), for example, to consider a fairly large number (18) of housing types based on residential density, age, and

[11] In a recent paper, Starrett (1978) has generalized the Koopmans–Beckmann result in some ways. Starrett (1978) points out that, if it is reasonable to assume that parcels of land (or housing units) can be occupied by only one household and that costs are positively related to the distance from other households, then there is always an incentive to move to another site in an attempt to reduce those costs.

quality. The cost of conversion of one housing type to another is assumed to be relatively expensive and the demolition of old units and replacement by new structures rarely occurs. Kain and Quigley (1975, pp. 49–55) more formally derived the implications of these assumptions. As was discussed in Chapter 1, King (1976, 1977) and Straszheim (1975) found that there was substantial variation over space in the prices of various housing goods and characteristics.[12] Straszheim (1975) summarized his results by stating that,

> The processes of metropolitan development typically produce large variations in the supply of housing with particular attributes at different locations. Since supply changes occur more slowly than demand changes, prices vary substantially across geographic submarkets. Because racial discrimination sharply limits access to the suburbs by black households and creates barriers between black and white submarkets, demand and supply conditions are often very different in the two types of submarket [p. 77].

However, we should recall that the primary use of these spatial price variations of Lancastrian characteristics was to estimate the demand functions for these characteristics. In Chapter 1 we concluded that, based upon the empirical evidence, it may not be necessary to specify a complex set of Lancastrian characteristics. Furthermore, a recent article by Murray (1978) suggests that differences in hedonic prices within a given market will not necessarily be eliminated in the long run. However, the models of Kain and Quigley (1975) and Straszheim (1975) assume otherwise. But, Murray (1978) notes that

> More strongly, if housing characteristics are jointly produced (as seems likely), I conjecture that if housing characteristics and their hedonic prices are to show the demand properties of traditional goods and prices, the structure of technology and preferences must be formally equivalent to a traditional structure *which permits the construction of a single composite good, 'housing services'* [p. 190].

The proof of this conjecture is presented in the appendix to this chapter. Thus it appears that there is no reason to tie the use of a market period supply model to the assumption of several Lancastrian characteristics.

The use of a market period model in conjunction with a single composite good, "housing services," leads naturally to the construction of vintage models of the housing market based upon the "putty–clay" assumption of Johansen (1959). Anas (1978), for example, assumes that housing services are produced according to a Cobb–Douglas production function with the services of land, capital, and labor. New housing is constructed assuming myopic expectations concerning the future prices of housing capital and labor. Once constructed, the housing stock is perfectly durable. Muth (1976)

[12] In an hedonic study by Ball and Kirwan (1977), the subdivision of the housing market into neighborhood groupings to allow the prices of attributes to vary by neighborhood did not significantly improve the explanation of house prices. They reject the submarkets hypothesis on this basis. A study by Schnare and Struyk (1976) leads to the same conclusion.

has developed a similar model of production except that a constant percentage rate of depreciation of capital is assumed. In another paper, Anas (1976) has considered the conditions under which the demolition of housing capital will take place. Hufbauer and Severn (1974) have presented a simple analysis of the economic demolition of old buildings. Assume the production function for housing services

$$h = f(K, L) \qquad (39)$$

with constant returns to scale, competitive input and output markets, myopic expectations, and perfectly durable capital. Ignoring demolition costs and scrap value, the building will be demolished and a new one constructed if

$$ph^n - rC > ph^o, \qquad (40)$$

where h^n is the output of the new building, h^o is the output of the old building, and C is the construction cost of the new building. Here rC is simply the annual capital charge of constructing the new building. However, since $ph^n = R^n + rC$ (where $R^n =$ the new rental rate on land), the basic condition reduces to

$$R^n > ph^o, \qquad (41)$$

which states that the new land rent must exceed the old total revenue. This feature can easily be incorporated into vintage models of housing supply to provide for some limited flexibility in the use of land that has previously been occupied by structures.

The data on 275 single-family houses used in Chapter 3 to examine the relationship between race and housing prices can be used to provide a test of the vintage model of housing supply. These data include the sale price, lot dimensions, and age for a sample of houses sold during 1970–1972. Land value estimates were added from Olcott (1971). Estimation of Koenker's equation (Koenker, 1972) produces

$$\ln[(ph - RL)/L] = 1.281 + .237 \ln R, \qquad (42)$$
$$(26.06) \quad (3.59)$$

with $R^2 = .045$. The t values are shown in parentheses. This result of .24 for the elasticity of substitution is clearly far below all of the estimates found using samples of new housing. If capital were instantly malleable, the estimates of the elasticity of substitution obtained from samples of "older" housing should not be lower, or the omission of the age of the house from the regression analysis should not bias the estimate of the elasticity of substitution. To test this hypothesis, the estimate of σ is allowed to depend upon the age of the house by the addition of an interaction term between ln R and the age of the house. The result obtained is that

$$\ln[(ph - RL)/L] = 1.274 + .855 \ln R - .018 \ln R(\text{Age}),\qquad (43)$$
$$\quad\quad\quad\quad (28.78)\quad (8.76)\quad\quad (7.98)$$

with $R^2 = .228$. The t values are shown in parentheses. The addition of the interaction term has substantially increased the R^2 and the t value of the estimate of the coefficient of ln R. The estimated equation implies that $\sigma = .86$ for new housing (Age = 0), and that the estimate of σ declines .018 per year as the sample ages.[13] In other words, if the sample consisted only of houses that are 47.5 years of age, the estimate of the elasticity of substitution would be zero. Given that much of the housing stock in the city of Chicago was constructed before 1930, it is likely that in many areas there is very little correlation between current land value and the value of housing capital per square foot of land. The results of these tests reject the assumption of perfectly malleable capital and strongly suggest that a vintage model is more appropriate.

3 Supply in the Short Run

In this section we consider models in which the quantity of housing services supplied by an existing structure can be varied (without abandonment, of course). The systematic study of models of this kind probably begins with Lowry (1960), who was concerned with the notion of filtering in the housing market. His objective was to evaluate the notion that the quality of housing consumed by low-income households is increased by a policy that adds to the stock units of high quality intended for occupancy by high-income households. Lowry (1960) summarizes the argument for filtering by stating

> When such (high-income) households decide in favor of new construction the dwellings vacated by them form a price-depressing surplus which causes a filtering-down of all units in the inventory and a subsequent shift in occupancy as prices decline so that the income distribution shifts upward relative to the quality scale. . . . The effectiveness of filtering as a means of raising housing standards thus hinges on the speed of value decline relative to quality decline [p. 363].

Quality decline for housing consists of technological obsolescence and physical deterioration, with physical deterioration the more important component. Lowry assumes that physical deterioration can be reduced to zero by "normal" maintenance expenditures. Lowry divides the landlord's

---

[13] The value for σ of .86 is not significantly different from 1.0.

expenses into three categories: fixed costs (costs incurred if the unit were vacant such as taxes, insurance, interest); user costs (heat, power, janitorial service); and maintenance costs that can offset physical deterioration and technological obsolescence. If the price per unit of housing services commanded by the unit falls below marginal cost in the short run (marginal user and maintenance costs), the landlord has an incentive to cut back on these expenditures. If user costs are fixed if the unit is occupied (an assumption examined in detail below), then the landlord of a "filtering" unit will purchase less than the "normal" maintenance and the quality of the unit will decline. The landlord has thus adjusted downward the quantity of housing supplied by the unit.

Dildine and Massey (1974) have criticized Lowry (1960) on the grounds that the model does not treat symmetrically the possibility of quality improvement as well as quality decline and that the future, or anticipated, trends in the housing market are not included. Decisions in the Lowry model are myopic in that current prices and production technology are expected to continue indefinitely. Dildine and Massey (1974) set out to correct these defects by developing a dynamic, optimal control model of housing maintenance decisions. The structure of their model is set forth here in order to clarify the assumptions made in the empirical studies discussed below. Dildine and Massey (1974) considered a single existing dwelling structure that occupies a unit of land. The problem is to maximize net returns over the remaining life of the building;

$$V = \int_0^T Y(t)e^{-\rho t} \, dt + Se^{-\rho T}, \tag{44}$$

where T is the remaining life of the building, ρ is the rate of time discount, and S is the terminal value, which is assumed to be simply the value of the site at time T discounted to the present. Net returns $Y(t)$ are the difference between gross rent and expenditures on current costs (user costs) and maintenance, or

$$Y(t) = p(t)h(t) - C(t) - I(t), \tag{45}$$

where $p(t)$ and $h(t)$ are defined as before, $C(t)$ is current costs assumed proportional to $h(t)$, and $I(t)$ is maintenance expenditures, which equal $q(t)M(t)$, or price times quantity. By assumption, current costs cannot be shifted to the tenant, so define $\hat{p} = p - c/h$ as the market price of a unit of housing services net of unshifted current costs. The objective function may now be written

$$V = \int_0^T [\hat{p}(t)h(t) - q(t)M(t)]e^{-\rho t} \, dt + Se^{-\rho T}. \tag{46}$$

The change in the output of housing services depends upon the quantity of maintenance and the rate of depreciation, or

$$\dot{h}(t) = D[M(t), \bar{h}] - \delta(t)h(t), \tag{47}$$

where $\dot{h}(t)$ is the time derivative of $h(t)$, $\bar{h}$ is the output of the dwelling at the time of its construction, $\delta(t)$ is the rate of depreciation, and $D[M(t), \bar{h}]$ is the production function describing the relationship between maintenance and additional units of output. The problem is to find the optimal path $M^*(t)$ and the optimal economic life T^* by maximizing the objective function subject to the differential equation for $\dot{h}(t)$ and the condition that $M(t) \geq 0$.

Applying Pontryagin's principle for maximization leads to the rule for maintenance that the marginal benefits, or discounted value of all future rents derived from the marginal unit of $M(t)$, must equal marginal cost, or the discounted value of the price of maintenance. The optimal T^* is the time at which

$$Y^*(T) = pS, \tag{48}$$

or the net returns equal the current rent on land. Comparative static analyses indicate that a higher (lower) $\hat{p}$ will lead to an increase (decrease) in the optimal amount of maintenance over the life of the building. An increase (decrease) in S will shorten (lengthen) T^* and thus reduce (increase) the optimal amount of maintenance over the life of the building. It should be noted that the model requires perfect information about the time paths of $\hat{p}$ and q as well as S. One issue to examine is the degree to which the requirements for information about the future can be reduced and simplified.

Studies have been conducted to estimate empirically the extent to which user costs (or operating inputs) and additional maintenance expenditures contribute to the output of housing services from existing buildings. Some attempt has also been made to estimate the rate of depreciation of the building. In the opinion of this writer, the most important studies are Ingram and Oron (1977), de Leeuw and Struyk (1975), and Rydell (1976). In addition, Bradbury et al. (1977) have estimated conversion supply equations. Since the focus of this study is on empirical tests, simulation models such as Ingram et al. (1972) and Ohls (1975), which did not estimate supply functions, are not discussed. The analytical models of commodity hierarchies by Sweeney (1974) are also not discussed.

A useful place to begin is with the supply model embedded in the Urban Institute model of the urban housing market as presented by de Leeuw and Struyk (1975). The model deals with 10-year time periods, so whether the model is a "short-run" model might be questioned. The production function of housing services for an existing structure is assumed to be

$$h_j = \{\beta_1 + [2\beta_2(X_j/h_o)]^{.5}\}h_0, \tag{49}$$

where h_o is the output of the structure 10 years ago, X_j is capital added during the intervening 10 years measured on a flow basis, and β_1 and β_2 are parameters. Citing a study by Muth (1971b), operating costs are assumed to be proportional to h_j and thus do not enter the production function directly. Note also that the production function does not include land. Setting $X_j = 0$, we see that the rate of depreciation is $1 - \beta_1$. The marginal product of additional capital is $\frac{1}{2}(2\beta_2 h_o)^{.5}/X_j^{.5}$, which is a positive and declining function of X_j. The task is to estimate β_1 and β_2. The strategy followed is to run the simulation model under alternative assumptions about β_1 and β_2 and compare the results for variables that are easily observed with their actual magnitudes for 1960–1970 for six metropolitan areas. In order to conduct the simulation experiments, the production function must be transformed into a supply function that depicts the behavior of housing suppliers. Explicit assumptions must be introduced to capture how suppliers view the future. Current profits are

$$\pi = h_j(P_j - P_o) - P_C X_j - F_j, \tag{50}$$

where P_o = the price of operating inputs per unit of output, P_C = the price of X_j, and F_j is fixed cost. A longer time horizon is introduced by introducing a rate of discount r and a "rate (λ) at which rent less operating costs is expected to decay over time [de Leeuw and Struyk, 1975, p. 28]." Expected profits are thus the sum of profits earned in the current and future decades, or

$$
\begin{aligned}
\pi_e = \; & h_j(P_j - P_o) - P_C X_j - F_j \\
& + [1/(1 + r)][\lambda\beta_1 h_j(P_j - P_o) - P_C X_j - F_j] \\
& + [1/(1 + r)]^2[\lambda^2\beta_1^2 h_j(P_j - P_o) - P_C X_j - F_j] + \cdots,
\end{aligned}
$$

or

$$\pi_e = [(1 + r)/(1 + r - \beta_1\lambda)](P_j - P_o)h_j - [(1 + r)/r](P_C X_j + F_j). \tag{51}$$

It is further assumed that $r/(1 + r - \beta_1\lambda) = \frac{2}{3}$. The supply curve is derived by maximizing π_e with respect to h_j and X_j subject to the production function. The two first-order conditions are

$$[(1 + r)/(1 + r - \beta_1\lambda)](P_j - P_o) - \eta = 0, \tag{52}$$

and

$$-[(1 + r)/r]P_C + \eta[\tfrac{1}{2}(2\beta_2 h_o)^{.5}/X_j^{.5}] = 0. \tag{53}$$

The latter condition is consistent with the prescription provided by Dildine and Massey (1974). Solving these two equations for h_j gives

$$h_j = h_o\{\beta_1 + \tfrac{2}{3}\beta_2[(P_j - P_o)/P_C]\}. \tag{54}$$

One serious problem with this procedure is the implicit assumption that λ, the decadal rate of decay of rent less operating costs, is a positive number. We might expect that P_o, the price of operating inputs, will increase in real terms, but P_j might also be expected to increase if the construction cost of new units increases or if demand is expected to grow. By assuming that $r/(1 + r - \beta_1\lambda) = \tfrac{2}{3}$, we assume

$$\lambda = (1/\beta_1)(1 - \tfrac{1}{2}r). \tag{55}$$

In other words, $\lambda > 0$ if $1 - (r/2) > 0$, where r is the decadal rate of discount. This implies that λ can be negative only if $r > 2$, or if the annual rate of discount is slightly less than 12%. While this may seem plausible, it is not clear why the rates of "decay" and discount should be tied together in this manner. The general problem with the procedure is the indirect nature of the estimation technique. The validity of the estimates obtained depends upon the validity of all of the assumptions made in constructing the simulation model. Many of these assumptions, such as the relationship between λ, r, and β_1, have not been tested empirically. It would seem that a preferable procedure is to estimate the production function for h_j directly with sample data. The results of the simulations for six metropolitan areas indicate a range for β_1 of .4 to .7 (or 3.5 to 5.5% on an annual basis) and .4 to .9 for β_2. The implied range for supply elasticity is .42 to 1.10. While these figures seem to be plausible, no further evaluation of their accuracy is possible.

The assumption that operating inputs are proportional to output is relaxed in the study by Rydell (1976). He introduces the CES production function with three inputs

$$h = \alpha[\delta_L L^{(\sigma-1)/\sigma} + \delta_K K^{(\sigma-1)/\sigma} + \delta_S S^{(\sigma-1)/\sigma}]^{\sigma/(\sigma-1)}, \tag{56}$$

where δ_i is the distribution parameter of the i input, S is the input of "services," and σ is the partial elasticity of substitution between any two inputs. Rydell (1976, p. 38) acknowledges that the assumption concerning the partial elasticities of substitution is strong. In Rydell's model, maintenance and depreciation add to and subtract from K, respectively. Expenditures on service inputs ($E_S = P_S S$) were measured by survey, and the quantity of service inputs found by using "the well-known fact that the unit cost of providing services goes down as the size of the property increases [Rydell, 1976, p. 38]." Rydell (1971) found in a study of public housing in New York City that $P_S = kS^{-.09}$. Since $S = E_S/P_S$, $P_S = kE_S^{-.1}$, and $S = E_S^{.9}/k$, it is important to recognize that S and P_S were not measured independently. Efficient production with competitive markets leads to the conditions

$$S/L = (\delta_S/\delta_L)^\sigma (R/P_S)^\sigma \qquad (57)$$

and

$$K/L = (\delta_K/\delta_L)^\sigma (R/r)^\sigma. \qquad (58)$$

The estimation of the latter equation is discussed above. The estimation of the former equation gave an estimate of σ of 0.5. However, there may be measurement errors in R, S, and P_S. Define $V = Re^\delta$, $S = \hat{S}e^\gamma$, and $\hat{P}_S = P_S e^\lambda$, where V, $\hat{S}$, and $\hat{P}_S$ are the measured values of R, S, and P_S, respectively, and δ, γ, and λ are random normal error terms. Substitution for R, S and P_S yields

$$\ln(\hat{S}/L) = a + \sigma \ln(V/\hat{P}_S) + (u + \gamma - \sigma\delta + \sigma\lambda). \qquad (59)$$

Here γ, δ, and λ are the omitted variables, which means that the bias in the estimate of σ can be written

$$E\hat{\sigma} - \sigma = \beta_\gamma - \sigma\beta_\delta + \sigma\beta_\lambda \qquad (60)$$

where β_γ, β_δ, and β_λ are the regression coefficients obtained in regressions of γ, δ, and λ on $\ln(V/\hat{P}_S)$. We know that $\beta_\delta > 0$ because V is positively correlated with δ and $\hat{P}_S$ is (by assumption) uncorrelated with δ. Also, β_λ is positive because λ is positively correlated with $\hat{P}_S$ (and uncorrelated with V). Furthermore, because γ and λ are negatively correlated, $\beta_\gamma > 0$. The direction of the bias is thus indeterminate. However, the bias is positive if the error introduced by Rydell's formula for the calculation of S and P_S is relatively large. There is no way to judge the importance of this problem. My conclusion is that we can at least state that the "services" or operating inputs can substitute for other inputs to some degree. It remains to be seen how important it is to add this complication.

The study by Ingram and Oron (1977) is, among other things, another attempt to estimate the elasticity of substitution between operating inputs and capital. This possibility for substitution is embedded in a model in which housing services are produced by land, capital, and operating inputs. Capital is divided into two components: "structure capital" of infinite durability and "quality capital" of limited durability. A minimum amount of structure capital is required to produce housing of a particular structure type (high-rise building, small multiple unit building, etc.). Once this requirement is met, it is assumed that quality capital and operating inputs produce structure quality according to a CES production function. The equation to be estimated is

$$\ln(Q/S) = a + \sigma \ln(P_S/P_Q), \qquad (61)$$

where Q is units of structure quality, P_Q is the price of a unit of structure quality, and S and P_S are defined as before. The data for the study are annual time series information for 1953–1969 on 29 apartment buildings in the Boston area. Expenditures on operating inputs and total rents are the available data. P_S was measured as a price index for utilities and fuel, and S is operating expenditures divided by this index. P_Q was measured as the price index for rents in Boston provided by the Bureau of Labor Statistics, and Q is total rent divided by this index. Assuming these measures of P_Q and P_S are accurate, estimates of the price and quantity of housing services have been obtained. As Ingram and Oron (1977, p. 311) recognized, these are not the same as the price and quantity of structure quality (see Chapter 1). Housing services are also produced by land and structure capital. Thus the estimate of σ cannot be taken seriously. While the coefficient of (P_S/P_Q) is positive and significant, the only conclusion that can be reached from the data is that higher prices of operating inputs cause higher rents.

The study Bradbury et al. (1977) contains some tests of the factors related to the conversion of the use of existing structures. For example, the increase in multifamily units per acre (other than through new construction) for the 89 zones in the Boston SMSA is significantly positively related to the existing number of old single-family units and negatively related to the change in the vacancy rate, the number of deteriorating multifamily units per acre, and the amount of new construction per vacant acre. Unfortunately, the dependent variable in the analysis does not distinguish between abandonment and demolition for the purpose of replacement. However, the results suggest that the availability of old single-family units leads to the conversion to multifamily units. This says nothing about the supply of housing services per se, but does indicate that it might be prudent to include the assumption that the number of units, and thus population density, can be varied in the context of an existing housing stock.

4 Conclusions

The supply of housing services is a topic that involves a great deal of complexity. This chapter is a highly critical review of existing studies. The central question to be answered simply involves the necessity of assuming a production function more complex than

$$h = aK^\alpha L^{1-\alpha}, \tag{62}$$

where h is housing services, K is capital services, L is land services, and α is a constant. Studies of long-run supply suggest that it is probably *not* necessary to introduce a more complex model. However, this functional form may not be adequate for the construction of putty–clay vintage models. In the context of a vintage model, it is useful to include operating inputs to the production function because the study by Rydell (1976) suggests that they substitute for capital and land. Furthermore, a more realistic theory of housing abandonment is generated. Without operating inputs, housing is abandoned when rent becomes *negative*. With operating inputs, housing is abandoned when rents fail to cover operating costs. Finally, it may be useful to assume that existing units can depreciate or can be augmented by additional capital inputs (maintenance). The study by de Leeuw and Struyk (1975) assumes that the marginal product of additional capital is related positively to the initial size of the structure measured by the original *h* and declines as more additional capital is added. The empirical tests discussed in this chapter indirectly confirm these two hypotheses because the marginal product of capital is seen to depend upon the amount of *land* used (land input is fixed for existing structures) and the marginal product of capital declines with the amount of capital employed in all of the studies cited.

Appendix   Murray's Analysis of the Composite Good Housing

The article by Murray (1978) contains a theoretical demonstration of the point made in the text that for housing characteristics and their hedonic prices to show the traditional demand properties, it is possible to collapse the analysis to the case of a single composite good called *housing*. Otherwise, variation in the price of a housing characteristic over space, for example, has no particular theoretical meaning. To prove his main result, Murray (1978) assumed linear homogeneous joint production of housing characteristics and homothetic preferences. The utility function $U(q)$ is maximized subject to a budget constraint

$$y = \sum p_i x_i \qquad (A1)$$

and a joint production function

$$0 = h(\mathbf{q}, \mathbf{x}), \qquad (A2)$$

where $\mathbf{q}$ is the vector of housing characteristics, $\mathbf{x}$ is the vector of goods, and $\mathbf{p}$ is the price vector for $\mathbf{x}$. The joint production function is assumed to have concave production possibility frontiers for $\mathbf{q}$ given $\mathbf{x}$ and convex isoquants for $\mathbf{x}$ given $\mathbf{q}$. As shown by Muellbauer (1974), the linear homogeneity and homotheticity assumptions allow the demands for the q_i's to be written

$$q_i = y\phi_i(\pi),$$ (A3)

where π is the vector of shadow prices associated with $\mathbf{q}$. These shadow prices are functions of $\mathbf{p}$ alone. This property of the demand functions for the q_i's permits the construction of a composite characteristic Q, with composite shadow price π_c,

$$Q = f(\mathbf{q}),$$ (A4)

and

$$\pi_c = \pi_j/[\partial f(\phi_1, \ldots, \phi_m)/\partial q_j] \quad \text{for all} \quad j,$$ (A5)

where π_c is evaluated at the optimal $\mathbf{q}$ vector. I find that this proposition is intuitive; a formal proof is provided by Katzner (1970, pp. 142–143). Furthermore, since the composite characteristic Q can be constructed, the traditional analysis of the demand for "inputs" can be applied to the analysis of the demand for $\mathbf{x}$, the vector of goods. It is important to remember that Murray's (1978) analysis is a long-run argument.

5

Analytical Models of the Urban Housing Market

The contention in this study is that an altered version of the standard monocentric long-run competitive model first introduced by Muth (1969, pp. 71–77) can be used to explain the basic observed facts in the Chicago housing market. The facts to be explained are presented in detail in Chapters 6 and 7. In this chapter careful consideration is given to Muth's basic supply and demand model and its numerous extensions. In Chapters 6 and 7 we will see that Muth's basic model cannot explain some of the salient facts for Chicago in recent periods. Which extension of the model should we then choose? An answer to this question is provided in Chapter 8, the concluding chapter.

In the first section of this chapter we briefly develop Muth's original model. Subsequent sections consider the implications of various extensions of the model. For easy reference Table 5.1 lists all of the assumptions made to develop Muth's original model and indicates the theoretical studies (if any) in which that assumption has been relaxed. The book by Henderson (1977) is an examination of many of these extensions of the basic monocentric model.

1 Muth's Standard Model and Minor Extensions[1]

Muth (1969, pp. 71–77) assumed the existence of a central business district (CBD) of constant size at which all employment except widely

[1] Some points of clarification in Mills (1972b, pp. 78–85) are included.

TABLE 5.1

The Assumptions of the Standard Long-Run Competitive Monocentric Model

Assumption	Example of a model in which the assumption is altered
1. Monocentricity	M. White (1976), Papageorgiou (1971), Papageorgiou and Casetti (1971)
2. Perfectly malleable capital	Anas (1976, 1978), Fisch (1977), Evans (1975), Muth (1976)
3. Cobb–Douglas production function for housing	Kau and Lee (1976a), Muth (1975)
4. Equal full income for all households	Solow (1972, 1973), Beckmann (1969, 1974), Mills (1972b), MacRae and Struyk (1977)
5. Constant marginal commuting cost	Amson (1972), Henderson (1977)
6. Price elasticity of demand for housing equals -1.0	Mills (1972b), Kau and Lee (1976b)
7. Homogeneous tastes for housing and other goods	Blackburn (1971)
8. Absence of public goods and taxes	Polinsky and Rubinfeld (1978), Beckmann (1974), LeRoy (1976), Epple *et al.* (1978)
9. Absence of neighborhood effects and other externalities	Polinsky and Shavell (1976), Richardson (1977b), Henderson (1977)
10. No distinction on grounds of race	Rose-Ackerman (1975, 1977), Courant (1973), Courant and Yinger (1976)
11. Absence of zoning restrictions	Courant (1976), White (1975), Moss (1977)
12. Constant proportion of land used for housing at all distances (except for central business district)	Mills (1967) and many others
13. Each household contains one worker	White (1977a), Madden (1977)
14. No distinction between owners and renters	MacRae and Struyk (1977), Muth (1969, 1975)
15. Utility is a function only of housing, leisure, and other goods	Polinsky and Shavell (1976), Polinsky and Rubinfeld (1978)
16. Housing is produced only by the services of land and capital	Anas (1976, 1978)
17. Closed city (constant population in current period)	Wheaton (1974) and many others
18. No competition among land uses (CBD has a constant size)	Mills (1967) and many others
19. Land owned by absentee landlords	None

scattered local employment is located. The rest of the city is located on a featureless plain with transportation equally costly in all directions. Housing occupies ϕ radians of the circle at each distance beyond the CBD. The remaining $2\pi - \phi$ radians are unavailable for urban land use or are occupied by other uses such as local employment and transportation facilities. The value of ϕ is constant. Each household contains one worker who earns a fixed amount if the workplace is the CBD. CBD workers make a fixed number of trips to the CBD per time period. Locally employed workers earn a wage that depends upon distance to the CBD.[2] All households have the same tastes for housing, leisure, and other goods. Racial distinctions among households are ignored. All households rent their housing and the number of households is fixed at N. For each household, the demand function for housing is written

$$h(u) = A/p(u) \qquad (1)$$

where u is distance to the CBD, A is a constant, and the price elasticity of demand for housing is -1.[3] Household locational equilibrium for CBD workers is

$$h(u)p'(u) + t = 0, \qquad (2)$$

where t is the constant marginal transportation cost. Households with a locally employed person satisfy the condition

$$h(u)p'(u) + w'(u) = 0, \qquad (3)$$

where $w'(u)$ is the rate at which earnings change with distance to the CBD.

On the supply side, housing is produced with services of land and perfectly malleable capital according to the function $h(u) = aL(u)^{\alpha}K(u)^{1-\alpha}$. No zoning restrictions are present. All externalities, public goods, and taxes are absent. Housing is produced in a competitive market, meaning that

$$R(u) = \alpha p(u)h(u)/L(u) \qquad (4)$$

and

$$r = (1 - \alpha)p(u)h(u)/K(u), \qquad (5)$$

where r is the price of capital services, which is invariant over space. Land rent at the fringe of the urban area $\bar{u}$ is $R(\bar{u}) = \bar{R}$. Solving the last three

---

[2] See Brueckner (1978a) for a further development of a model with noncentral employment.

[3] The assumption of a constant A is inconsistent with a constant income for a CBD worker. The demand for housing at distance u is a function of tastes, prices of housing and other goods, and income net of the cost of obtaining that income (transportation costs).

equations for $p(u)$ as a function of r and $R(u)$ yields

$$p(u) = [a\alpha^{\alpha}(1 - \alpha)^{1-\alpha}]^{-1}r^{1-\alpha}R(u)^{\alpha}. \tag{6}$$

The elasticity of $p(u)$ with respect to $R(u)$ is α. The derivative of this expression with respect to u is

$$p'(u) = a^{-1}[\alpha r/(1 - \alpha)]^{1-\alpha}R(u)^{-(1-\alpha)}R'(u). \tag{7}$$

Now, from the demand function, substitute for $h(u)$ in the condition for locational equilibrium for CBD workers,[4] or

$$p'(u)A/p(u) + t = 0. \tag{8}$$

Substitution from the supply side equations for $p(u)$ and $p'(u)$ yields

$$A\alpha[R'(u)/R(u)] + t = 0. \tag{9}$$

The solution to this differential equation is simply

$$R(u) = \bar{R}e^{A\alpha t(\bar{u}-u)}. \tag{10}$$

Population density at distance u is defined as the total housing supplied per unit of area at distance u divided by the housing consumed per household at distance u. The supply of housing per unit area is

$$\frac{h_s(u)}{L(u)} = a\left(\frac{1 - \alpha}{\alpha r}\right)^{1-\alpha} R(u)^{1-\alpha}, \tag{11}$$

and the amount of housing consumed per household as a function of $R(u)$ is

$$h(u) = A[a\alpha^{\alpha}(1 - \alpha)^{1-\alpha}]r^{1-\alpha}R(u)^{\alpha}. \tag{12}$$

Population density is thus proportional to $R(u)$, or

$$D(u) = R(u)/(\alpha A) = \bar{R}e^{A\alpha t(\bar{u}-u)}/\alpha A. \tag{13}$$

The basic results are that population density is a constant times land rent and a negative exponential function of distance and that the elasticity of the price of housing with respect to land value is a constant equal to the share of land.

A number of relatively simple extensions of this model have been introduced. See McDonald and Bowman (1976) for a summary of several extensions of the kind discussed here. Amson (1972) introduced alternative nonconstant functional forms for marginal commuting cost and derived additional land rent and density functions. For example, if commuting costs

---

[4] For locally employed workers $w'(u)$ plays the role of t and, for equilibrium, $t = w'(u)$.

are a quadratic function of distance, then $t(u) = c + du$, where c and d are constants. In this case

$$D(u) = \bar{R}e^{A\alpha[\bar{u}c + u(ud - c) - du^2]}/\alpha A,$$

a normal distribution. Kau and Lee (1976a) have used the CES function to describe the production of housing services. The functional forms for land rent and density as a function of u are complex, but the general result is that land rent is negatively and density positively related to the elasticity of substitution. Density remains a positive function of land rent, but is no longer the simple negative exponential function of distance. Muth (1975) has used numerical solutions for this case. Furthermore, Mills (1972b) has relaxed the assumption that the price elasticity of demand for housing equals -1. Allowing this price elasticity to assume any value θ, Mills (1972b, p. 83) derives

$$R(u) = [\bar{R}^\beta + \beta t E(\bar{u} - u)]^{1/\beta}, \tag{14}$$

where $\beta = \alpha(1 + \theta)$ and

$$E^{-1} = \alpha A[a\alpha^\alpha(1 - \alpha)^{1-\alpha}]^{-(1+\theta)}r^{(1-\alpha)(1+\theta)}.$$

Also, $D(u) = ER(u)^{1-\beta}$. The density function implied is a binomial function

$$D(u) = E[\bar{R}^\beta + \beta t E(\bar{u} - u)]^{(1-\beta)/\beta}, \tag{15}$$

which, assuming $\bar{R} = 0$, can be simplified to

$$D(u) = E[\beta t E(\bar{u} - u)]^{(1-\beta)/\beta}. \tag{16}$$

   Given the possibility of introducing any or all of the three minor complications discussed in the preceding paragraph, there exists an unlimited number of functional forms that can be derived to describe how land rent and population density decline with distance to the CBD. A number of studies (Casetti, 1969; Kau and Lee, 1976b; McDonald and Bowman, 1976) have attempted to determine empirically the best functional form for the population density function.[5] Significant deviations from the simple negative exponential were found for a number of metropolitan areas, but it would be wrong to "explain" this deviation as caused by the alteration of one assumption in the standard model. For example, Kau and Lee (1976b), following Mills (1972b, p. 83), relax the assumption that the price elasticity of demand for housing is -1.0 and rewrite the density function above as

$$[D^\lambda(u) - 1]/\lambda = D_0 - \gamma u, \tag{17}$$

----

[5] A study by Kau and Sirmans (1979) examined land values in Chicago. This study is discussed in Chapter 7.

where

$$\gamma = (1 - \beta)tE^{1/(1-\beta)},$$

$$D_0 = \frac{[E\bar{R}^{1/(1-\beta)}]^\lambda - 1}{\lambda} + \gamma\bar{u},$$

and

$$\lambda = \beta/(1 - \beta).$$

Here $\beta = \alpha(1 + \theta)$ as above. This is a version of the Box–Cox transformation (Box and Cox, 1964), where the function approaches a negative exponential if λ approaches 0 and is linear if $\lambda = 1$. The optimal λ was estimated for 49 U.S. metropolitan areas by the maximum likelihood technique. In 23 cases out of 49 the optimum value for λ exceeded 0, implying that the density function is between exponential and linear in almost 50% of the cases examined. Kau and Lee (1976b) concluded that "Evidence also suggests that where the exponential function is inappropriate and the λ value positive, the price elasticity of demand for housing is less than minus one (inelastic) [p. 197]." This is so because

$$\beta = \lambda/(1 + \lambda) = \alpha(1 + \theta) \tag{18}$$

and $\lambda > 0$. However, Kau and Lee (1976b) did not suggest why the price elasticity of demand for housing should vary across metropolitan areas. More importantly, other assumptions could lead to the Kau–Lee functional form. The Kau–Lee function implies that density declines less steeply and then more steeply with distance than the negative exponential. This same result could occur if marginal transportation cost increases and, beyond some point, decreases with distance. In principle, the Kau–Lee function could also be generated by alterations in many of the assumptions listed in Table 5.1. In general, empirical density functions and changes in them over time are facts to be explained by theory, but the estimation of density functions does not provide a powerful test of alternative theories. In the case of Chicago, the results presented by Muth (1969) for 1950 and by Kau and Lee (1976b) for 1960 indicate that the negative exponential is the appropriate functional form.[6]

2 Major Extensions of the Standard Model

In this section we examine some of the most important major extensions of the standard analytical model. These extensions are included in

---

[6] Muth's conclusion is based upon the statistical insignificance of a quadratic distance term added to the exponential function. Kau and Lee used the Box–Cox test.

Table 5.1. One of these extensions stands prior to nearly all of the others. Wheaton (1974) introduced the distinction between the "closed" and the "open" city. In the closed city population is assumed to remain constant during the time period in question, but with the open city model migration is assumed to be instantaneous and costless so that the level of utility of households in the city remains constant throughout the analysis. For example, if there is an improvement in the transportation system so that transport costs are lower, population will immediately increase via in-migration and drive up housing prices so that no resident of the city experiences an increase in utility. This device greatly simplifies the analysis of some of the extensions of the model. For example, although he did not explicitly indicate it, Mills (1972b, pp. 85–88) utilized the assumption of an open city in his analysis of a model with two income classes. Other theorists followed Wheaton (1974) by carrying out their analyses for closed and open cities for purposes of comparison.

Since one of the key issues concerns the method to be used to relax the assumption of a perfectly malleable capital stock, it is worthwhile to examine closely the work of Anas (1978), Evans (1975), and Muth (1976) in which "vintage" models are developed. Of particular interest, of course, are the theoretical devices used to capture the behavior of housing suppliers. As a purely arbitrary point of departure, the model by Anas (1978) will be examined first and the other models will be compared to his. He assumed that the housing stock is perfectly durable and that all decisions of households and suppliers are myopic, or based upon current prices, incomes, technologies, etc. This assumption of myopia may not be appropriate, but a vintage model requires that some assumption must be made concerning how decision makers view the future. Instead of myopia, one could assume perfect foresight or posit probability distributions for future variables and assume that consumers maximize expected utility and that suppliers maximize expected profits. Anas (1978) assumed that a ring of housing structures is added to the city in each time period as population and income grow, and that this new construction exhibits a capital–land ratio that reflects the contemporaneous market conditions. However, a key issue is the nature of the mechanism assumed to generate payments to the factors of production embodied in the housing constructed in earlier periods. Since both capital and land are perfectly durable, they cannot be adjusted to reflect their marginal productivities in time periods after the construction date. Anas assumed that a unit of capital continues to receive the *same* payment for all time that it recieved when the structure was new. Land receives the residual, or total revenue minus the payments to capital. Furthermore, Anas assumed that, once constructed, the structures in a ring will either house a constant number of households or will be abandoned. Thus, because incomes grow and the households are constrained to consume a fixed amount of housing or move elsewhere, the inner rings of a city will eventually be abandoned as households choose to move to the suburbs to be able to consume more housing and incur larger transportation cost.[7] The housing is abandoned when the residual payment to land falls to zero. In the Anas (1978) world, the abandoned structures in the inner ring last forever. Land is not recycled by demolition and new construction, although Anas (1976, pp. 271–273) carried out an extension to relax this assumption.

The formulation of the supply side in Muth's model (1976) is based on the production function

$$h_\tau(t) = e^{-a\delta(t-\tau)}k_\tau^a l_\tau^b m(t)^c, \tag{19}$$

where $h_\tau(t)$ is the output at time t of housing built at time τ, δ is the rate of depreciation of capital k_τ, l_τ is land, and $m(t)$ represents maintenance inputs at time t. Here $a + b + c = 1$. This formulation would allow suppliers to adjust the supply of housing to changing market conditions with maintenance expenditures, but at a diminishing rate of marginal productivity. Also, the capital may depreciate to an amount approaching zero. Muth (1976) assumed perfect foresight and a constant percentage growth for land rent per unit area. The capital is purchased at the time of construction and receives no further payments. The housing supplier thus makes a living by buying capital, renting land, deciding upon maintenance, and receiving the residual of total revenue. Muth closed the model by assuming constant percentage growth rates for land supply, population, and income. The spatial dimension was ignored.

The model developed by Evans (1975) is helpful in its formulation of the theory of land rent received by land on which structures built in previous periods are located. Evans (1975) studied a city with a fixed area and no locational factors that had entered a "golden age," in which all relevant variables grow at constant rates. He solved for the golden age distribution of housing vintages given a constant rate of population growth. He showed that a golden age equilibrium is possible in which the age of the buildings demolished, their economic life, remains constant as the city grows. He worked out the model alternatively assuming myopic expectations or perfect foresight. A key element in the model is the assumption that landlords rent land to developers and that developers can be thrown off the land at any time in order to have the site redeveloped at the most profitable density. With myopic expectations, for example, this means that the developer who currently occupies the site must pay the landlord a rent equal to the amount a new developer would pay, which is equal to the new developer's total revenue minus the cost of capital for the period in question. An adjustment for

---

[7] Anas (1978) worked out the model for both closed and open cities.

demolition cost and site preparation costs could easily be added to the model. This mechanism generates demolition along the lines suggested by Hufbauer and Severn (1974) and discussed in Chapter 4. Except for the work by Anas (1976, 1978) and Brueckner (1978b), I am aware of no other analytical versions of the standard urban model that incorporate supply models for housing other than the simple long-run models as discussed in Chapter 4.

Next, let us consider major extensions which have been introduced on the demand side. Beckmann (1969) introduced a continuous distribution of income to a standard urban model.[8] Assuming a Pareto distribution for income, it was shown that an analytical solution exists. However, in a later paper, Beckmann (1974) illustrated the conditions under which the distribution of income is irrelevant for the determination of the land rent function and the pattern of the intensity of land use measured as the capital–land ratio. In particular, we assume that everyone has the same Cobb–Douglas utility function

$$u = a_0 \log X + a_1 \log h + a_2 \log t, \qquad (20)$$

where X is the composite good, h is housing, and t is leisure time. Further assume that commuting to the CBD involves only time cost and that housing services are produced by the usual Cobb–Douglas function of land and malleable capital. It is easy to see that households of all income levels are indifferent to all locations in equilibrium. As distance to the CBD increases, each household is compensated exactly for the loss of leisure time by the reduction in the price of housing. As Beckmann (1974, p. 104) pointed out, this situation is disturbed if money costs of commuting are added to the model. In this case, higher income households will live at greater distances to the CBD because of the assumption that purchasing power has a declining marginal utility. The situation of all income classes indifferent to location is also disturbed if tastes vary by income. Taste variations can easily be incorporated into the model by allowing a_0, a_1, and a_2 to vary by income level.[9] To summarize these arguments, higher income households

---

[8] Delson (1970) and Montesano (1972) corrected some mathematical difficulties in the Beckmann (1969) model.

[9] The model developed by Blackburn (1971) incorporates specific assumptions for the distributions of parameters in the utility function. In particular, $U = a_1 s - a_2 x - sp(x)$, where s is units of land, x is distance to the CBD, $p(x)$ is the price of a unit of land, and a_1 and a_2 were assumed to have independent negative exponential and gamma distributions, respectively. Blackburn's city is closed, the value of nonurban land is zero, and incomes are all equal. Using the joint density function for a_1 and a_2 and the first-order conditions $a_1 = p(x)$ and $a_2 = sp'(x)$, Blackburn (1971) was able to solve for the joint density function for s and x by the change of variable technique. Using the market clearing condition, the joint density function for $p(x)$, or $p(x) = (1/u) \log[2\pi\lambda x/(Nku)]$, where N is total population and u, λ, and

will live at greater distances from the CBD if the income elasticity of demand for housing is greater than the income elasticity of commuting costs. Empirical evidence presented by Wheaton (1977a) that was based on household data for the San Francisco area indicate that these two elasticities are very similar. Wheaton (1977a) concluded that the spatial income pattern probably cannot be explained using the standard urban model, and suggested that the suburbanization of the middle and upper income groups can be explained by "housing market externalities and the fiscal incentives of municipal fragmentation [p. 631]."

While externalities and municipal government have not been added to a model in which incomes vary, some interesting models have been developed in these areas. Polinsky and Shavell (1976) have added "amenities" to the standard models for both the open and closed city. Amenities are exogenously determined at each location and costlessly supplied, and the wage rate for all workers is fixed. If the city (or neighborhood) is small and open, the equilibrium land rent patterns include the demand schedule for amenities in that city (or location). This is an extremely useful result. The model developed by Henderson (1977) is somewhat different in that the disamenity of air pollution is assumed to be generated by the industrial activity in the CBD. Assuming that the cloud of pollution diffuses and dissipates, the level of the disamenity in the residential annuli declines with distance to the CBD. This means that an increase in distance to the CBD is associated with a disamenity, increased travel cost, and an "amenity," reduced air pollution. The change in the value of residential land with increasing distance to the CBD will thus be the net outcome of these two opposing effects. The shape of the land value function is not known without further information about the shape of the transportation and pollution cost functions. Henderson (1977) assumes that transportation cost is an increasing function of distance to the CBD and that the pollution cost function exhibits smaller marginal declines as distance to the CBD increases.[10] These two cost functions imply

---

k are parameters in the joint density function for a_1 and a_2. Substituting for $p(x)$ in the joint density function for s and x and solving for the conditional distribution of s given x yields

$$h(s|x) = \frac{(\lambda/uk)}{\Gamma(k)} s^{k-1} e^{-(\lambda/ux)s},$$

which is simply a gamma function with parameters k and $\lambda/(ux)$. In other words, the consumption of s varies at a given distance, but the distribution of s shifts with distance x. Blackburn (1971) also pointed out that $h(s|x)$ in this formulation does not depend upon N, the total population.

[10] Henderson (1977) assumes transportation costs consist only of foregone leisure, implying that marginal transportation cost rises with distance to the CBD. This formulation is consistent with the model in Chapter 2.

that residential land value may actually increase with distance to the CBD over a range of distance near the CBD, and then decline with distance to the CBD at greater distances. This pattern would exist because, next to the CBD, a marginal increase in distance to the CBD is associated with a relatively small increase in commuting cost and a relatively large decrease in pollution. The article by Richardson (1977b) is similar to Henderson (1977) in both its assumptions and conclusions.

Polinsky and Rubinfeld (1978) have added both local public services and a residential property tax to the standard model of the open city. Labor, as well as capital and an export good, are perfectly mobile among cities. The same tax rate and level of public services apply to all households in the city, but business property is untaxed. Polinsky and Rubinfeld (1978) proved, for example, that an increase in the tax rate lowers land rents everywhere and increases the money wage paid to all workers in the city, and that an increase in public services will increase land rents everywhere in the city and lower the money wage. In contrast, Henderson (1977) has developed a model of an open city in which labor is not perfectly mobile. Henderson's analysis of the property tax includes the assumption that business property is taxed. The effects of an increase in the property tax in this model are to lower both money wages and land rents. It is interesting to note that both Polinsky and Rubinfeld (1978) and Henderson (1977) conclude that an increase in the property tax lowers land values, but differ on the conclusion regarding money wages. Both Beckmann (1974) and LeRoy (1976) have also added a property tax to the standard urban model. However, the effects of variations in the property tax rate within a metropolitan area have not been examined in a spatial context. The results of Polinsky and Shavell (1976) cited above can be applied to variations in public services across space in a metropolitan area.

The question of how to incorporate racial prejudice and/or racial discrimination in an urban model has received a great deal of attention. One point of departure is the original border model posited by Bailey (1959) in which one group (whites) prefers to live away from the other group (blacks).[11] The blacks may prefer to live near whites or be indifferent to the race of their neighbors. Courant (1973) and Rose-Ackerman (1975) have added the assumption of white prejudice to standard models of the closed city in which blacks are assumed to occupy the central residential area of the city. The results about urban structure implied by such models have been summarized by Courant and Yinger (1977):

1. The housing price–distance function for whites is flatter when whites

---

[11] Another model of white prejudice has been developed by Yinger (1976). In his formulation, the utility levels of whites are influenced by the proportion of the population residing at the same distance to the CBD that is black.

are prejudicial and may be positively sloped near the black–white border.
2. Blacks pay less for housing and live at lower densities when whites are prejudiced.
3. Whites who are not near the black–white border pay more for housing and live at higher densities if they are prejudiced.
4. The land rent at the black–white border may fall below the non-residential land rent and create a buffer area of nonresidential land use.
5. A closed city with white prejudice is larger than it would be without prejudice.

These conclusions hold if all households have the same income level or if we use Beckmann's model (1974) as described above in which income does not influence location choice. However, as Courant and Yinger (1977) have pointed out, matters get much more complex if we allow income to vary and to influence the choice of location. High-income blacks may bid more than whites for the land at the edge of the city, for example. For the purposes of this analysis, I shall assume that income per se does not influence location choice.

An alternative formulation is to assume that whites can collude and discriminate against blacks. Rose-Ackerman (1977) has included this assumption in a standard urban model. Starting with the model with prejudiced whites described above, Rose-Ackerman (1977, pp. 154–158) assumed a cartel of white landlords near the black–white border that may resist the movement of the border in the face of rising black demand. The cartel bases its decisions on whether total rents in its area will be higher or lower if blacks are allowed to enter previously white areas. Rents will rise in the areas of new black occupancy but will fall in nearby white areas because of the prejudice of white tenants. If the cartel decides to exclude blacks, then black rents and population density will be greater than otherwise.

Another extension of the standard model that is of potential importance is the analyses of subsidies to homeowners by Muth (1969, 1975) and MacRae and Struyk (1977). As discussed in Chapter 1, homeowners receive a subsidy because mortgage interest and property taxes may be deducted in the calculation of the federal income tax and they need not report as income the implicit rental value of the home and implicit return on their equity. Also, the Federal Housing Adminstration (FHA) has provided insurance programs for homeowners. The early work of Muth (1969, pp. 314–321) examined both factors in a preliminary manner. In later work, Muth (1975) examined the effects of tax advantages and MacRae and Struyk (1977) have analyzed the effects of FHA on residential land use. Muth (1975) assumed that all households have the same income level and that the outer annulus of the city is occupied by homeowners. Assuming homeowners receive a tax saving of 20% of housing expenditures, the land area of the city expands and density declines in the homeowner sector as homeowners consume more housing than without the subsidy. MacRae and Struyk (1977) argued that the cost of capital decreases with household income because of lower depreciation and lower risk for lenders. Their model is an open city with three income classes. They showed that the inner annulus is occupied by the lowest income group, the middle annulus by the middle income group, and the outer annulus by the upper income group. The primary effect of FHA, according to MacRae and Struyk (1977), is to lower the cost of capital to the middle income group. This change causes the middle annulus of the city to expand, forcing lower income groups to live closer to the CBD at higher densities and upper income groups to live at greater distances to the CBD at higher densities. The effect on the lower income renter group is a new implication brought out by the MacRae–Struyk model.

A simple model can easily be constructed to demonstrate the point made in Chapter 1 that, holding income constant, homeowners live at lower population densities than renters because of the income tax advantages of homeownership. Returning to what has been noted above as Muth's standard model, let us add the assumption that some households are homeowners and others are renters because some households (homeowners) have a long expected length of tenure and others (renters) have a short expected length of tenure. As was shown in Chapter 1, those households that choose to be homeowners face a price per unit of housing services that is lower than the rental price.

Consider homeowners and renters with the same income level who reside at the same distance u to the CBD. Write the demand for housing of homeowners as

$$h_o(u) = A/p_o(u), \tag{21}$$

and the renters' demand function as

$$h_R(u) = A/p_R(u). \tag{22}$$

On the supply side, we maintain the assumption that housing is produced by the services of land and perfectly malleable capital according to the function $h(u) = aL(u)^b K(u)^{1-b}$. For the land market at distance u to be in equilibrium, the rent on land must be the same whether occupied by homeowners or renters. Using Eq. (4), this condition implies that

$$bp_o(u)h_o(u)/L(u) = bp_R(u)h_R(u)/L(u), \tag{23}$$

or that

$$p_o(u)/p_R(u) = h_R(u)/h_o(u). \tag{24}$$

Population density is defined as the total housing supplied per unit of land divided by housing consumed per household. Since land rent does not depend upon type of tenure, total housing supplied per unit of land at distance u also does not depend upon type of tenure.[12] The ratio of the population density of homeowners to the population density of renters is simply

$$D_o(u)/D_R(u) = h_R(u)/h_o(u) = p_o(u)/p_R(u), \tag{25}$$

which is less than 1.0.

Another potentially important influence on the patterns of population density and land value is zoning. Ohls, *et al.* (1974) have distinguished externality zoning from fiscal zoning. Externality zoning is defined as the efficient separation of land uses, while fiscal zoing is defined as restrictions on land use for objectives other than economic efficiency. For example, a suburban community might zone vacant land for large lots in the hope that only high-income households will occupy such land and pay local taxes in excess of the cost of providing them with local public services. Courant (1976) has examined the effects of fiscal zoning in a closed urban model. Zoning places a ceiling on the capital–land ratio, and may be applied to the entire metropolitan area or only to a small area. In the former case, land near the CBD is restricted and some of its inhabitants will move to the unzoned sector, thus increasing city size and increasing housing prices and density in the unzoned sector. In the latter case, restrictive zoning in small areas restricted to residential use will lower land value. An empirical test of this proposition for the city of Chicago is provided in Chapter 7. White (1975) examined the effects of restrictive zoning in all "suburbs" beyond some specified distance to the CBD assuming the central city remains unzoned. The effects are to drive up land values and population densities in the central city and, perhaps, to expand the area of the entire metropolitan area. This latter effect is reversed if enough people are induced to move back into the central city. The value of suburban land may rise or fall depending upon the direction of the population movement.[13]

Stull (1974) has incorporated an analysis of externality zoning in an open city model in which "manufacturing" that produces a negative ex-

---

[12] We assume that the cost of capital is the same for owners and renters because income is held constant.

[13] The results of Moss (1977) are generally consistent with the results obtained by Courant (1976) and White (1975).

ternality occupies the central annulus of the city. The utility of households depends, in part, upon distance from the zoning boundary. The effects of moving the zoning boundary on the wage rate and employment level in the city were examined and compared with the case in which the negative externality does not exist.

The assumption of monocentricity has been dropped by Papageorgiou (1971), Papageorgiou and Casetti (1971), and White (1976). Papageorgiou (1971) and Papageorgiou and Casetti (1971) have shown that the analysis of population density and land values in a multicenter setting is relatively easy if an open city is assumed. Land value functions are derived from each employment center and residential land is allocated to the worker who bids the most. Depending upon the locations of the employment centers, land values and population density patterns can assume virtually any form. White (1976), on the other hand, has worked with a closed city in which employment is located at the CBD and along a circumferential highway. Analytical solutions for the land value and population density functions are possible in this case. White (1977a, 1978a) has pursued this approach to examine a model in which the household contains more than two workers (one works at the CBD and the other at the employment ring), or a model in which the effects of job suburbanization on central city workers in the presence of suburban fiscal zoning are of concern.

The final extension examined here relaxes the assumption that other urban land uses do not compete for residential space. Muth (1969) assumed both that the CBD is of constant size and that the proportion of land available for residential use is constant at all distances outside the CBD. Remarkably, in his initial paper on the subject, Mills (1967) relaxed both of these assumptions. In this model the production of goods occurs in the CBD, and land outside the CBD is used for transportation and housing. Indeed, a substantial proportion of the analytical work in normative urban economics has been concerned with the optimal allocation of land to transportation in the presence of congestion externalities.[14] From the perspective of positive economics, however, the relaxation of these assumptions about the supply of residential land is not very important if we know that very little net conversion of land use from residential to other urban uses has taken place in Chicago over the time period of interest. Harrison and Kain (1974, p. 97) have presented time series data for land use in the city of Chicago for the period from 1850 to 1961 derived from a master plan of residential land use. These data are presented in Table 5.2 and show that, from 1923 to 1961, the proportion of total land in use (not vacant) in the city of Chicago that was

---

[14] See Anas and Dendrinos (1976) and Richardson (1977a) for surveys of the "new urban economics."

ECONOMIC ANALYSIS OF AN URBAN HOUSING MARKET

TABLE 5.2
Historical Changes in Utilized Land by Various Uses: Chicago (1850-1961)

		1850	1870	1890	1923	1941	1956	1961
Utilized land	Acres	2,458	12,669	48,008	91,514	104,289	116,736	128,832
	Percentage	100	100	100	100	100	100	100
Residential	Acres	465	3,481	11,008	31,004	33,228	41,600	45,184
	Percentage	19	28	23	34	32	36	35
Industrial	Acres	185	2,703	10,647	16,577	19,696	19,712	19,712
	Percentage	8	21	22	18	19	17	15
Commercial	Acres	33	535	1,722	6,317	6,359	8,704	8,960
	Percentage	1	4	4	7	6	7	7
Roads	Acres	1,630	4,725	20,721	29,624	33,852	33,216	34,496
	Percentage	66	37	43	32	32	28	27
Other public	Acres	145	1,235	3,890	7,686	11,154	13,504	20,480
	Percentage	6	10	8	9	11	12	16

Source: Harrison and Kain (1974, p. 97).

residential changed very little. The proportion residential varied from 32 to 36%. While this is not conclusive evidence, it suggests that no model of land use conversion will be needed for the analysis of the housing market.[15]

In this section I have briefly described the major extensions of the standard model that might be considered for further use. In the next two chapters we examine the historical patterns of population density and land values and some of the empirical determinants of these patterns. In light of these empirical results, we shall return to these analytical models in the final chapter.

---

[15] The main exception to this statement is the conversion of land from residential to business use in areas near the CBD during the earlier part of the twentieth century.

Population Density in Chicago

This chapter presents the historical record of population density patterns in Chicago from 1870 to 1974 and contains a new study of the determinants of net residential density for 1970. Along with the data for Chicago presented by Muth (1969) and Harrison and Kain (1974) these studies constitute part of the phenomena that a model of the urban housing market should be able to explain. The history of population density in Chicago is presented in the first section, the studies by Muth (1969) and Harrison and Kain (1974) are discussed in the second section, and net density in 1970 is examined in the third section. A summary concludes the chapter.

1 Population Density in Chicago: The Historical Record

Table 6.1 contains the basic census data for the city of Chicago, Cook County, and the Chicago SMSA for the period 1870–1974. The land area of each unit is also listed. We note that the population of the city grew rapidly until 1930. The population of the city grew slightly during the 1940s (6.6%), probably because of the relatively low volume of new housing construction during World War II, but has declined steadily thereafter. Also, except for the O'Hare Airport site, the city of Chicago has been unable to annex new

117

TABLE 6.1
Basic Population Distribution Data for Chicago: 1870–1974

	City of Chicago		Cook County		Chicago SMSA	
Year	Population (1000s)	Area[a] (sq. mi.)	Population (1000s)	Area (sq. mi.)	Population[b] (1000s)	Area[b] (sq. mi.)
1870	279	35.15	350	954		
1880	503	35.15	608	954		
1890	1100	178.05	1192	954	1366	3103
1900	1699	189.52	1839	954	2056	3103
1910	2185	190.20	2405	954	2669	3103
1920	2702	198.27	3053	954	3361	3103
1930	3376	207.20	3982	954	4414	3103
1940	3397	207.25	4063	954	4532	3103
1950	3621	207.25	4509	954	5127	3103
1960	3550	218.80	5130	954	6221	3720
1970[c]	3363	218.80	5488	954	6975	3720
1974 (est.)	3173	218.80	5372	954	6971	3720

Sources: U.S. Census of Population, 1880–1970; Kitagawa and Taeuber (1963); Statistical Abstract of the U.S., 1977; and City and County Data Book, 1972.

[a]Net accretions from 1830 to 1933 were 5.62 square miles of Lake Michigan filled in. This area is not counted because it is not available for private use.

[b]Population and area listed for the Chicago SMSA prior to 1960 are for five counties (Cook, DuPage, Kane, Lake, and Will). McHenry County was included in 1960.

[c]In addition, the Chicago urbanized area consisted of 6,715,000 population and 1277 square miles in 1970.

territory since 1930. Most of the annexation occurred from 1887 to 1893 (Kitagawa and Taeuber, 1963). The growth of population in Cook County (in which Chicago is located) followed closely the growth of the city until 1940. During the 1940s, Cook County outside of the city grew 222,000. During the 1950s and 1960s, as the city declined in population, Cook County outside of the city grew by 692,000 and 545,000, respectively. From 1970 to 1974, as the city has lost an estimated 190,000 people the rest of Cook County has added 74,000 people. Population in the rest of the Chicago SMSA has shown steady growth, with the most rapid growth of 508,000 and 396,000 occuring in the 1950s and 1960s, respectively.[1]

A further analysis of population in the City of Chicago in Table 6.2 reveals that the loss of population since 1950 is concentrated in the area within approximately 4 miles of the CBD. From 1950 to 1960, the city lost 71,000 people and population within 4 miles of the CBD declined 127,000.

---

[1] The population of McHenry County is included in these calculations.

TABLE 6.2
Population in the City of Chicago: 1930–1970

Year	Population of city (1000s)	Population within 4 miles of CBD (1000s)[a]
1930	3376	748
1940	3397	696
1950	3621	748
1960	3550	621
1970	3363	508

[a]Population figures include population for community areas 7, 8, 24, 28, 31, 32, 33, 34, 35, 59, and 60. See Kitagawa and Taeuber (1963).

During the 1960s, the population of the city declined 187,000 and the area within four miles of the CBD lost 113,000 people, or 60% of the total loss.

The standard method for summarizing the information contained in Tables 6.1 and 6.2 is to calculate a negative exponential density function for each year. As was shown in Chapter 5, this functional form can be rationalized in the standard model. For the purposes of this exercise, let us assume that the gross population density for a small area is generated by the equation

$$D(k) = D_0 e^{-\gamma k + u}, \tag{1}$$

where k is distance to the CBD, γ is the density gradient, D_0 is the "central" density, and u is a random normal error term with mean zero and variance σ^2.[2] The conventional method of estimation is to convert to natural logs, or

$$D^*(k) = D_0^* - \gamma k + u \tag{2}$$

(where * indicates the natural log), and use ordinary least squares on a sample of small areas drawn from within the boudaries of the urbanized area. This method of estimation provides the best linear unbiased estimate for γ, $\ln D_0$, and σ^2. However, an unbiased estimate of D_0 is not obtained, and it is difficult to introduce corrections to eliminate the biases. This problem stems from the fact that for a random normal variable x, as shown by Parzen (1960, p. 348),

$$E(e^x) = \exp(m + s^2/2), \tag{3}$$

---

[2] We might assume that the error term enters additively rather than multiplicatively, or

$$D(k) = D_0 e^{-\gamma k} + u.$$

Tests by Greene and Barnbrock (1978) for Baltimore indicate that the equation in the text is more appropriate with respect to the criterion of homoskedasticity.

where m is the mean and s^2 the variance of x. The proof of this proposition follows from the definition of the moment generating function for a variable x, or $M(x) = E(e^{tx})$. Here we evaluate $m(x)$ at $t = 1$. The moment generating function for the normal distribution is $E[\exp(mt + s^2 t^2/2)]$, where m is the mean and s^2 the variance of x. If we wish to generate an estimate of D_0 by taking the antilog of $\hat{D}_0^*$, the estimate of D_0^*, we obtain

$$E[\exp(\hat{D}_0^*)] = \exp(D_0^* + S_0^2/2),\qquad (4)$$

where S_0^2 is the variance of $\hat{D}_0^*$. The variance S_0^2 is simply the variance of the constant term in a simple OLS regression, or

$$S_0^2 = \frac{\sigma^2 \sum k_i^2}{n \sum (k_i - \bar{k})^2},\qquad (5)$$

where n is the sample size and $\bar{k}$ is the mean distance in the sample. Thus, the correction for bias requires an estimate of σ^2, designated $\hat{\sigma}^2$. Unfortunately, the quantity $E[\exp(\hat{\sigma}^2/2)]$ is undefined. We know that $(n - 2)\hat{\sigma}^2/\sigma^2$ has a chi-square distribution with $n - 2$ degrees of freedom. The moment generating function for the chi-square is $M(X) = E[e^{tx}] = (1 - 2t)^{-r/2}$, where r is the number of degrees of freedom (see Brunk, 1965, pp. 230–232). This moment generating function is undefined for t greater than or equal to $1/2$, so we cannot find $E \exp \sigma^2/2$ analytically. We should note, however, that $E[\exp(\hat{D}_0^*)]$ provides a consistent estimate for D_0. However, it is possible to obtain an unbiased estimate of the constant term D_0. Using results obtained originally by Finney (1941), Goldberger (1968), and Heien (1968) have shown that an unbiased estimate can be written

$$\hat{D}_0 = \exp(\hat{D}_0^*)F(w; v, c)$$

where

$$F(w; v, c) = \sum_{j=0}^{\infty} f_j (cw)^j / j!.$$

Here

$$f_j = (v/2)^j \Gamma(v/2)/\Gamma(j + v/2),$$

$$w = nS_0^2,$$

$$v = n - 2,$$

$$c = -1/2n, \text{ and}$$

$$\Gamma(\ \ ) \text{ is the gamma distribution.}$$

Finney (1941) showed that $EF(w; v, c) = \exp(c\sigma^2)$, so the calculation of several terms of $F(w; v, c)$ produces the desired correction. None of the studies of population density has made use of this technique, so no further discussion of the problem is undertaken here. Goldberger (1968) found that, if S_0^2 is small and n is large, the calculation of $\exp(-S_0^2/2)$ using σ^2 produces a close approximation to $F(w; v, c)$.

Another method for estimating the negative exponential function was developed by Mills (1972a) and requires only two observations. The analysis of this method in the stochastic context was done by L. White (1977), and the following discussion draws from White's results. Suppose we know the population and land area of the central city and the entire SMSA. Assume both the central city and the SMSA can be represented as circles with $2\pi - \phi$ radians removed. Designate the radius of the central city k_c, the population of the central city N_c, and total population N. The number of people living in the central city can be found by integrating the density function by parts from 0 to k_c, or

$$E(N_c) = (1/\gamma^2)\phi D_0 \exp(\sigma^2/2)[1 - (1 + \gamma k_c)e^{-\gamma k_c}]. \tag{6}$$

Integrating to infinity, we get the total population N in the SMSA, or

$$E(N) = (1/\gamma^2)\phi D_0 \exp(\sigma^2/2).^3 \tag{7}$$

The Mills (1972a) method is to solve for γ in the equation

$$E(N_c)/E(N) = 1 - (1 + \gamma k_c)e^{-\gamma k_c}. \tag{8}$$

This equation is inherently nonlinear, so γ is estimated iteratively. L. White's Monte Carlo results (1977, p. 300) show that this estimate of γ contains little bias if the error term has been entered correctly into the density equation. The central density is then approximated as

$$D_0 \exp(\sigma^2/2) = \hat{\gamma}^2 N/\phi. \tag{9}$$

This estimate of D_0 is clearly biased upward, as White's Monte Carlo studies (1977, p. 300) confirm.

The data in Table 6.1 can be used to calculate two-point estimates of the density functions from 1870 to 1974. These estimates are shown in Table 6.3 along with the estimates for 1900 and 1940 reported by Clark (1951) and the OLS estimate for 1950 provided by Muth (1969).[4] Alternative two-point estimates are provided for 1920, 1930, and 1940 by using the population of

---

[3] To be more accurate, the integration should only include the distance up to k_m, the radius of the SMSA. However, inaccuracies introduced for Chicago by integrating to infinity turned out to be very small.

[4] The estimate provided by Muth (1969) is also subject to the sampling bias pointed out by Frankena (1978). Muth used census tract data, and the procedure used to designate census tract areas results in an underrepresentation in a sample of census tracts of areas of low density. The estimation procedure employed by Clark was not specified.

TABLE 6.3
Population Density Functions for Chicago: 1870–1974

Year	Data source	Central density (1000s)	Density gradient
1870	City–county	44.2	−.63
1880	City–county	86.9	−.67
1890	City–county[a]	60.4	−.41
1900	Clark (1951)	110.0	−.45
	City–county	88.7	−.40
1910	City–county	99.3	−.37
1920	City–county	106.4	−.34
	City–SMSA	79.5	−.28
1930	City–county	108.1	−.30
	City–SMSA	83.2	−.25
1940	Clark (1951)	120.0	−.30
	City–county	103.0	−.29
	City–SMSA	78.7	−.24
1950	Muth (1969)	60.0	−.18
	City–SMSA	74.8	−.22
1960	City–SMSA	54.2	−.17
1970	City–SMSA	41.2	−.14
	City–urbanized area	44.2	−.145
1974	City–SMSA	35.5	−.13

[a]Central density and gradient may be unreliable because a very large fraction of the total population was located in the central city. See L. White (1977).

Cook County or the population of the five-county metropolitan area as the total population. The results show that, except for the unreliable estimate for 1890, the density gradient has steadily moved closer to zero since 1880. The decline in the gradient was particularly rapid between 1880 and 1900 and after 1940. The central density appears to have increased until 1930, declined slightly from 1930 to 1950, and then declined rapidly after 1950. These conclusions about the central density must remain guarded because of the unknown extent of upward bias present in the estimates. However, these trends in the gradient and the central density are some of the basic facts that a model of the housing market should be able to explain.[5]

---

[5] Newling (1969) has used Clark's data (1951) for Chicago to estimate quadratic gross density functions for 1900 and 1940. His results for 1900 are

$$D = (29,000) \exp(.27k - .08k^2),$$

and for 1940

$$D = (9800) \exp(.575k - .06k^2),$$

where k is distance to the CBD. Unfortunately, Newling did not report t values for the coefficients, so we cannot tell whether the quadratic terms add to explanatory power. These two func-

2   Population Density in Chicago:
The Studies by Harrison and Kain, Muth, and Mills

The studies of population density by Harrison and Kain (1974) and Muth (1969, Chapter 9) contain a great deal of detailed information on the trends in and determinants of population density in Chicago. A study by Mills (1969) includes an analysis of land use intensity on residential land. In this section careful consideration is given to these studies both for their empirical contents and theoretical insights.

Harrison and Kain (1974) began with the assumption that housing is never demolished, implying that the density pattern at any point in time consists of "rings" of uniform density each constructed in previous time periods. Gross density in a ring is assumed to be simply a function of the percentage of housing units in that ring that are single-family homes. Using data on 40 large cities for 1960, this relationship was estimated to be $GD = 19,740 - 201SF$, where GD = gross density and SF = percentage single-family homes. No allowance is made for the possibility that other factors influence gross density. The percentage of single family homes in the incremental ring in a time period for 83 metropolitan areas was estimated as a function of the size of the metropolitan area at the beginning of the period and a time trend. Knowledge of the estimated incremental gross density and population growth allows the calculation of the area of the new development and the change in the radius of the urbanized area. Since the population density in each ring is assumed to remain fixed, the current density gradient was calculated from the data generated by the Harrison–Kain procedure.[6] For Chicago for 1960, the estimated gross density function is

$$D = (20,900)e^{-.07k}, \tag{10}$$

where k is distance to the CBD. The central density is smaller and the gradient much flatter than the estimates in Table 6.3. It is worth noting that the Harrison–Kain procedure, for example, assumes that Chicago to a radius of 4.9 miles was constructed prior to 1900 and that this area has experienced no change in gross density. The data in Table 6.2 clearly show this not to be the case.

Recognizing that their procedures have serious shortcomings, Harrison and Kain (1974, pp. 84–90) presented elaborations of the model applied to

---

tions imply a maximum density of 35,900 at a distance of 1.59 miles in 1900 and 36,000 at 4.57 miles in 1940. These results suggest an expansion of the nonresidential areas near the CBD and a trend toward an "emptying out" of the central area that is, in general, consistent with the data in Table 6.3.

[6] The initial time period was pre-1879, and incremental gross densities were calculated for each subsequent time period.

TABLE 6.4
Harrison and Kain's Estimates of the Density Function for Chicago: 1920-1960

	1920	1930	1945	1950	1960
	Central density (1000s)				
1. Basic procedure	17	19	20	20	21
2. Lot sizes and land use proportions vary	28	28	36	40	40
3. Family size, lot sizes, and land use proportions vary	28	28	36	34	29
	Density gradient				
1. Basic procedure	−.03	−.05	−.06	−.06	−.07
2. Lot sizes and land use proportions vary	−.05	−.05	−.11	−.13	−.13
3. Family size, lot sizes and land use proportions vary	−.05	−.05	−.11	−.12	−.11

Source: Harrison and Kain (1974, p. 87).

Chicago. In these elaborations, lot sizes were allowed to vary over time according to information obtained on typical lots in each time period, the percentage of land used for residential purposes in each ring was allowed to vary over time, and the average population per dwelling unit was allowed to vary by distance and time period (for the period 1940–1960). The first two factors are refinements of the estimate of incremental gross density. The third factor allows gross density to vary over time in rings that were previously constructed. One of Harrison and Kain's (1974, p. 91) major findings is that average population per dwelling unit declined from 1940 to 1960. This implies that the amount of area developed in the time periods since 1940 were larger than Harrison and Kain had previously estimated. The results of introducing these elaborations are shown in Table 6.4. Allowing lot sizes and land use proportations to vary clearly tends to increase the central density and make the gradient steeper. This happened because lot sizes for all types of structures increased by about $2\frac{1}{2}$ times from 1910 to 1960. The introduction of the correction for population per dwelling unit, however, leads to lower central densities and slightly flatter gradients. This exercise is useful in pointing to some factors that influence the density function. However, the Harrison–Kain study cannot be considered to be a test of the vintage model of the housing stock. The data were constructed assuming the model is correct. Furthermore, as White (1977b) has pointed out, some of the empirical results obtained are implausible. For example, the results in Table 6.4

TABLE 6.5
Average Population Per Dwelling Unit by Distance from the CBD, City of Chicago:
1940-1960

Distance (miles)	1940	1950	1960
0-1	2.41	2.45	2.05
1-2	3.07	2.93	2.70
2-3	3.20	2.93	2.81
3-4	3.22	2.89	2.60
4-5	3.13	2.89	2.80
5-6	3.35	3.28	3.02
6-7	3.17	3.32	3.15
7-8	3.64	3.38	3.15
City of Chicago	3.6	2.9	2.6
Suburbs	3.9	3.4	3.3

Source: Harrison and Kain (1974, p. 91).

show that the gradient was getting steeper over time in the modern (post-1920) period. While these criticisms of the Harrison–Kain study are strong, they have uncovered an important fact that a model of the housing market should attempt to explain. The average population per dwelling unit increases with distance to the CBD and has declined over time. Table 6.5 shows these facts as presented by Harrison and Kain (1974, p. 91).

The chapter in Muth (1969) entitled "Population Density and Its Components on the South Side of Chicago" has two objectives. First, Muth was interested in examining the factors, other than distance to the CBD, that influence gross and net density. Second, Muth examined the components of density, expressed as

$$D = (P/U)(ph/L)[U/(ph)],$$ (11)

or population per housing unit (P/U) times the value of housing output per unit of land (ph/L) times the inverse of housing expenditures per unit or household [$U/(ph)$]. Detailed regression results were presented for 1950 and 1960 for a sample of 67 census tracts on the South Side.

The better measure of population density is net density, or population per unit of residential land. Because there are some significant differences in the results obtained by Muth in the regression analyses of gross and net density and because Muth (1969, p. 218) prefers the net density measure, this discussion will focus on the determinants of net density in 1950 and 1960. Muth's results are shown in Table 6.6. The results show a clear tendency for net density to decline with distance even after several other potential determinants of net density have been included in the analysis. Muth has used

TABLE 6.6
Muth's Analysis of Net Density in Chicago: 1950 and 1960

	1950	1960	1960	1960[a]
Distance to CBD (k)	−.11*	−.14*	−.061*	−.057
Within one mile of important transit route (T)	−.32	−.27	−.22	−.19
$k \times T$	.073	.067	.025	.027
In tract in square mile containing eight manufacturing firms	−.23	−.28	−.03	−.009
In tract in square mile containing from one to seven manufacturing firms	−.007	−.30*	−.19	−.16
In tract within one mile of major retail center	.14	.18	.055	.034
In tract within one mile of minor retail center	.25	.01	.01	.062
Percentage of units in tract built before 1920 (1940)	.76*	.35	.09	.023
Median income in tract	−.51	.11	−.068	−.059
Black population 80% or more in tract	.35	.25	.30	.29
Black population 5–80% in tract	−.007	.10	.30*	.21
Percentage of units in tract substandard	.063	.28*	.07	.13
Percentage of units with more than one person per room	—	—	−.005	−.15
R^2	.77	.71	.79	—
N	67	67	67	67

Source: Muth (1969, pp. 217, 224, 272).
*Significant at the 95% level.
[a]Two-stage least squares estimates treating percentage substandard units, income, percentage units with more than one person per room, and density as simultaneously determined. Dependent variable is in natural log form.

distance to the CBD rather than measures of potential access to manufacturing and retail employment because of the high correlation between distance to the CBD and measures of these potentials (−.84 and −.98, respectively). Some negative relationship between net density and the presence of nearby manufacturing seems to exist, especially in 1960. A positive relationship between net density and substandard housing was uncovered, especially for 1960. In 1960 density was higher in tracts with 5 to 80% black population. In 1950 there was a positive sign on the variable for the percentage of units built before 1920, but the percentage of units built before 1940 had a negative and insignificant sign in 1960 in two out of the three regressions reported. Muth's results indicate that net density was not significantly related to distance to an important transit route, presence of nearby retail centers, and income. While the pattern of results is somewhat inconsistent, a few potentially important facts seem to have emerged. First, population density may be higher in black areas, especially areas that are in the process of turning from white to black occupancy. Density may also be higher in areas with more substandard units (1960) or with more very old (pre-1920) units (1950). Finally, density should be negatively related to income of the neighborhood, but this result was not significant in Muth's results.

The analysis of the components of gross density was first performed for a sample of 16 cities (Muth, 1969, Chapter 8). In that analysis, Muth (1969, p. 89) found a clear tendency for the population per household to increase with distance to the CBD. Curiously, this same test was not performed for Chicago. In the analysis of the 16 cities, Muth (1969, Chapter 8) also found that the decline in density with distance to the CBD results both from the increase in the value of housing consumed per household and the decrease in the value of housing produced per unit of land. Muth (1969, Chapter 9) examines these two propositions in detail for the south side of Chicago for 1950 and 1960. In regression analyses that control for many other determinants of the value of housing consumed per household, Muth (1969, pp. 219, 226) found that distance to the CBD was a positive, but insignificant, factor in the determination of housing expenditures. The presence of nearby manufacturing and a higher proportion of older housing units leads to lower housing expenditures in both years. Housing expenditures in both years were higher in tracts with higher income levels, with a black population in excess of 80%, or with a larger proportion of elderly people (over 65). Finally, housing expenditures in both years were negatively related to the proportion of people who lived in the same location 5 years prior to the year in question.

The value of housing output per unit of land used for residential purposes was significantly negatively related to distance to the CBD in both years. In addition, the value of housing output per unit of land in both years was lowered by the presence of nearby manufacturing and was higher in tracts with black population in excess of 80%. A positive effect for nearby retail centers was found in 1950, and for the percentage substandard housing in 1960. These results suggest clearly that the decline in net density with distance to the CBD primarily stems from the decline in the value of housing output per unit of land as the standard model predicts. The result for the black areas should also be noted.

The study by Mills (1969, pp. 250–252) contains a brief examination of floor space per acre of residential land for 1959 as a function of distance to the CBD. The results are, for example,

$$\ln F = 4.931 - .229k, \qquad (12)$$
$$(4.98)$$

where F is floor space per acre, k is distance, and the t value is in parentheses. The R^2 for the regression is .58. The sample consisted of 20 districts from throughout the SMSA which ranged in size from 1 to 16.5 square miles. This result is consistent with either a malleable capital model or a vintage model.

3   Population Density in Chicago: 1970

Many empirical tests have been conducted for the received theory of the urban housing market developed and popularized by Muth (1969) and Mills (1972b). Most of the tests have confirmed the theory. This section reports on data for Chicago that fail to confirm an important aspect of the theory. The essential features of the model are that a unit of housing services can be produced by the services of land and capital inputs in varying proportions, and that perfect competition prevails in the input and output markets. One of the most important implications of the theory is that intensity of land use is a positive function of land rent (or value). Intensity of land use can be measured by population density, by the value of housing services produced per unit of land, by the rental value of capital per unit of land, or by the ratio of factor shares at a location. Most empirical tests have examined population density, although Muth (1969) and others have used the second approach. Koenker (1972), Fountain (1977), Rydell (1976), and Sirmans et al. (forthcoming) have followed the third approach, and Muth (1971a) has used the fourth measure. The purpose of this section is to examine net population density in the city of Chicago as a function of land value and other variables as derived from the model. Despite the large number of studies of urban population density, this approach has not previously been followed.

Most of the studies of population density have involved estimating gross population density (population per unit of land, including all uses of land) as a function of independent variables. It is clear that the theory pertains to net population density (population per unit of land used for housing), so the use of gross density will bias the results if any of the independent variables and the percentage of land used for housing are correlated. Furthermore, no study of net population density has examined population as a function of land value. Muth (1969, pp. 206–40) examined net population density in Chicago. Instead of using land value directly as a determinant of population density, he included several variables that determine the accessibility of the site. These variables determine land value in part. The study by Martin (1973) is similar to Muth's work in that land value is not used directly as a determinant of net population density. Thus both Muth and Martin have estimated equations for net density that do not permit the identification of the impact of land value on density. However, the two studies differ in that Martin found median income in the census tract to be a significant determinant of density and Muth did not. The sign of the coefficient of income was negative in Martin's study.

The standard theoretical rationale is developed below. In order to conduct this test, data on land values are needed. The data source is Olcott's (1971) land value book for Chicago. This source has been used many times [for example, Bednarz (1975), Berry (1976), Mills (1969), Rothenberg (1967), Yeates (1965), and McDonald and Bowman (1979)]. However, the reader should bear in mind that these data are only estimates made by an appraiser. The data are more fully described below. The empirical results indicate that some implications of the received theory are confirmed, but land value is not a significant determinant of net population density in Chicago. Given that the intensity of land use for new construction, measured as the value of capital per unit of land, *is* sensitive to land value as measured by Olcott 1971, Chapter 4), a vintage capital model of housing supply is suggested. Another preliminary test of this notion is presented.

The model to be tested is the received theory of the urban housing market developed by Muth (1969) and Mills (1972b). The model presented here follows the development in Mills (1972b, pp. 79–85), but is somewhat more general.

The basic model of population density assumes perfectly competitive input and output markets. All actual or potential housing producers have identical production functions in which housing services are produced by the services of land and capital. Each firm operates in a region where its production function is homogenous of degree one. The production function for the firm can be written

$$X_S = f(K, L), \tag{13}$$

where X_S is output supplied, K is capital services, and L is land services. Now consider housing production on a fixed area of land with exogenously fixed accessibility and other amenities. Assume that the land market contains many sites with identical characteristics, so that competition in the land market fixes the land rent (and value) of the site in question. The rental price of capital is also exogenous to the site and the producer (or producers) who occupy the site. Given that input prices and the quantity of land are fixed, only one level of output is consistent with short-run and long-run equilibrium. This output can be produced and sold because competition in the output market establishes the exogenously fixed price of housing services (given the accessibility and other amenities of the site).

Now assume a change that increases the land rent on the site in question. For example, an improvement in accessibility or some other amenity will produce the desired result. The change in land rent and resulting change in the price of housing have predictable impacts on population density. Because the site in question is a minute fraction of the total urban land supply, none of these changes has any impact on the rest of the housing and land markets.

Assume initially that the production function is Cobb–Douglas, so that

$$X_S(\mathbf{u}) = AL(\mathbf{u})^\alpha K(\mathbf{u})^{1-\alpha}, \qquad (14)$$

where $X_S(\mathbf{u})$ is the output of housing at location $\mathbf{u}$ and A and α are constants. The share of land is α. In the model $\mathbf{u}$ is a vector of locational information that includes distance to the CBD as one element. Assuming perfectly competitive input and output markets,

$$X_S(\mathbf{u})/L(\mathbf{u}) = A[(1-\alpha)/\alpha]^{1-\alpha} R(\mathbf{u})^{1-\alpha} r(\mathbf{u})^{\alpha-1}, \qquad (15)$$

where $R(\mathbf{u})$ is the rental rate on land and $r(\mathbf{u})$ is the rental rate on capital at location $\mathbf{u}$. Assuming efficient production in a competitive market, we set the value of the marginal product for each input equal to the factor price and derive

$$p(\mathbf{u}) = [A\alpha^\alpha(1-\alpha)^{1-\alpha}]^{-1} r(\mathbf{u})^{1-\alpha} R(\mathbf{u})^\alpha, \qquad (16)$$

the cost function that is the dual to the production function (14).

The demand for housing by an individual household at location $\mathbf{u}$ can be written as

$$X_D(\mathbf{u}) = B[y - T(\mathbf{u})]^{\theta_1} p(\mathbf{u})^{\theta_2} N^{\theta_3}, \qquad (17)$$

where $X_D(\mathbf{u})$ is quantity demanded, y is income, $T(\mathbf{u})$ is the commuting cost at location $\mathbf{u}$, $p(\mathbf{u})$ is the price of housing, N is household size, and θ_1, θ_2, and θ_3 are constants. Additional demographic characteristics besides household size could have been added to Eq. (17), but it is assumed that this specification captures the primary determinants of housing demand. Population density $D(\mathbf{u})$ at location $\mathbf{u}$ can be written as

$$D(\mathbf{u}) = N(\mathbf{u})[X_s(\mathbf{u})/L(\mathbf{u})]X_D(\mathbf{u}),$$

or

$$D(\mathbf{u}) = E(y(\mathbf{u}) - T(\mathbf{u}))^{-\theta_1} N(\mathbf{u})^{1-\theta_3} R(\mathbf{u})^{1-\alpha(1+\theta_2)} r(\mathbf{u})^{(\alpha-1)(1+\theta_2)}, \qquad (18)$$

where $E = [A(1-\alpha)^{1-\alpha}\alpha^\alpha]^{(1+\theta_2)/(\alpha B)}$, a constant term, $y(\mathbf{u})$ is the mean income of the households at location $\mathbf{u}$, and $N(\mathbf{u})$ is the mean number of persons per household at location $\mathbf{u}$. Equation (18) can be written in log form for purposes of empirical estimation as

$$\ln D(\mathbf{u}) = \ln E - \theta_1 \ln[y(\mathbf{u}) - T(\mathbf{u})] + (1 - \theta_3) \ln N(\mathbf{u})$$
$$+ [1 - \alpha(1 + \theta_2)] \ln R(\mathbf{u})$$
$$+ [(\alpha - 1)(1 + \theta_2)] \ln r(\mathbf{u}) + e, \tag{19}$$

where e is a normal error term. Note that the coefficient of $\ln(y)$ is the negative of the income elasticity of housing demand. Because θ_2, the price elasticity of housing demand, is less than 0 and α is between 0 and 1, the coefficient of $\ln R(\mathbf{u})$ must be positive and exceed $1 - \alpha$, the share of capital. The coefficient of $\ln r(\mathbf{u})$ must exceed $\alpha - 1$, and thus can be either positive or negative. Note that the coefficient of $\ln R(\mathbf{u})$ can be written as $(1 - \alpha) - \theta_2\alpha$, where $1 - \alpha$ and α are the shares of capital and land, respectively.

Thus far the model has included the assumption that the elasticity of substitution between the capital and land inputs is 1.0. Recent empirical investigations by Koenker (1972), Muth (1971a), Rydell (1976), and Fountain (1977) indicate that the elasticity of substitution ranges from about .5 to .75, meaning that the increase in the use of capital is less than proportional to the increase in land rent. The model should be altered to take this possibility into account. Kau and Lee (1976a) have revised the Mills (1972b) model to include a CES production function. Unfortunately, the relationship derived by Kau and Lee (1976a, p. 86) indicates a very complex nonlinear relationship between density and factor prices. Their approach does not provide a clear picture of how the expected value of the coefficient of $\ln R(\mathbf{u})$ in Eq. (19) should be revised in order to take into account an elasticity of substitution different from 1.0. However, the approach developed by Muth (1964, 1971a) can be used to derive an approximation that is easily interpreted.

The elasticity of population density with respect to land rent may be written

$$\frac{d \ln D(\mathbf{u})}{d \ln R(\mathbf{u})} = \frac{d \ln X_s(\mathbf{u})}{d \ln K(\mathbf{u})} \frac{d \ln K(\mathbf{u})}{d \ln R(\mathbf{u})} - \frac{d \ln X_D(\mathbf{u})}{d \ln p(\mathbf{u})} \frac{d \ln p(\mathbf{u})}{d \ln R(\mathbf{u})}. \tag{20}$$

For small changes in $K(\mathbf{u})$, the first term in Eq. (20) can be derived from the total derivative

$$d \ln X_s(\mathbf{u}) = [K(\mathbf{u})f_K/X_s] d \ln K(\mathbf{u}) + [L(\mathbf{u})f_L/X_s(\mathbf{u})] d \ln L(\mathbf{u})$$
$$= (1 - \alpha) d \ln K(\mathbf{u}) + \alpha d \ln L(\mathbf{u}), \tag{21}$$

where f_K and f_L are marginal products. The last result follows because $f_K = r(\mathbf{u})/p(\mathbf{u})$ and $f_L = R(\mathbf{u})/p(\mathbf{u})$. Thus $d \ln X_s(\mathbf{u})/d \ln K(\mathbf{u}) = 1 - \alpha$. The second term in Eq. (20) is the elasticity of substitution σ. The third term is simply the price elasticity of demand θ_2. The fourth term, $d \ln p(\mathbf{u})/d \ln R(\mathbf{u})$, is simply equal to α, the share of land. This can be seen from Eq. (16). However, this result holds only approximately for finite changes in input prices if the elasticity of substitution is not equal to 1.0 and thus factor shares do not remain constant.

Substitution of all of these results into Eq. (20) gives

$$\frac{d \ln D(\mathbf{u})}{d \ln R(\mathbf{u})} = \sigma(1 - \alpha) - \theta_2 \alpha > 0. \tag{22}$$

Remember that σ is defined to be a positive number and θ_2 is a negative number. This result indicates that the effect of changes in $R(\mathbf{u})$ on $D(\mathbf{u})$ is composed of two effects, one operating through the capital–land ratio $\sigma(1 - \alpha)$ and the other operating through the impact of the change in price on the quantity of housing consumed by the average household on the site $- \theta_2 \alpha$. Assuming $\sigma = .5$, $\theta_2 = -.4$, and $\alpha = .2$ yields an expected coefficient of $\ln R(\mathbf{u})$ of .48. Thus the coefficient of $\ln R(\mathbf{u})$ is sensitive to the value of the elasticity of substitution, but .48 is probably an approximate lower bound.

Commuting costs at distance $\mathbf{u}$ are based upon the results of the previous study of commuters in the Chicago area in 1972 (Chapter 2). In that study, one estimate of the value of commuting time measured in cents per minute was found to be $.13t + .04y$, where t is commuting time and y is measured in units of $1000. Assuming an average speed of 20 miles per hour and monetary costs of 90¢ per day (public transit fare), the annual dollar commuting cost for 250 work days can be written

$$T(\mathbf{u}) = \$225 + 1500\mathbf{u}(.39\mathbf{u} + .04y)/100. \tag{23}$$

Median income is adjusted accordingly in the empirical estimates presented below.

Furthermore, it may be necessary to control for the possible influence of racial segregation on population density. Discrimination against blacks in the housing market may lead, ceteris paribus, to increased black population density. On the other hand, the aversion of whites to living near blacks may cause lower black population density, ceteris paribus. Thus the effect of segregation may be of either sign. Also, it may be the case that the income and price elasticities of demand for housing are different for blacks and whites. Explorations of these possibilities are presented below in the empirical results.

It must be noted that the model does not assume the presence of external effects in the urban land market. It is clear that the basic model views land value as being determined by the accessibility of the site and underlying constants in the demand and supply functions. Thus, actual land value is exogenous in Eq. (19) and is treated as such in this section. Also, it is assumed that $r(\mathbf{u})$ is constant at all locations, so that the coefficient of $r(\mathbf{u})$ can be included in the constant term.

The data used in this study are a stratified random sample of census blocks in the city of Chicago for 1970. The study was restricted to the city of Chicago because, as Martin (1973) has shown, population density can be influenced by central city or suburban location. About 1000 blocks were selected by a computer program that randomly identified census tracts and block numbers. Every fourth observation was selected from this list. This procedure results in underrepresentation of an area within 2 miles of the CBD, so all other observations on the list of 1000 that lay within a 2-mile radius of the CBD were added to the sample. Excluded from the sample were nonresidential blocks and residential blocks that contain more than one residential zoning category. The resulting sample size is 190. Land value data were recorded from Olcott (1971). A computer program calculated the area of the block and the square-foot land value from the front foot value provided in Olcott. Census block data include total population, black population, and mean household size. Census tract data were used for median income of families and unrelated individuals. Block data for this variable are preferable, of course, but not available. Distance to the CBD was calculated by a computer program that converted the address of the block (e.g., 2400 North, 3200 West) into a distance to the corner of State and Madison.

The estimates of Eq. (19) found using land value as reported in Olcott are presented in Table 6.7. In column 1 only land value, median income less commuting costs, and mean household size are used as independent variables. The estimate of the income elasticity of demand for housing is reasonable for aggregated data (1.26) and highly significant. The net effect of household size is also highly significant and equal to $-.90$, indicating that $\theta_3 = -1.90$. However, the coefficient of land value is actually negative $(-.17)$, which is the wrong sign, and significant at the 90% level for a two-tail test. In column 2 the variable proportion of black residents in the block is added to the specification, but this variable is not statistically significant. However, column 3 includes an interaction effect between income minus commuting costs and proportion black residents. In this regression both the proportion black and the interaction term are highly significant. A comparison of the sums of squared residuals for the regressions in columns 1 and 3 indicates that the addition of the two race variables adds significantly to explanatory power ($F = 3.1$ for 2 and 186 degrees of freedom, which is

134

ECONOMIC ANALYSIS OF AN URBAN HOUSING MARKET

TABLE 6.7
Net Population Density Functions[a]

	1	2	3	4	5
Constant	17.696	17.381	20.442	15.610	17.191
	(13.49)	(12.65)	(10.88)	(9.81)	(7.20)
Land value	−.172	−.155	−.066	−.155	−.052
(natural log)	(1.78)	(1.56)	(.63)	(1.62)	(.50)
Income less commuting	−1.255	−1.221	−1.569	−1.067	−1.252
costs (natural log)	(8.45)	(7.86)	(7.36)	(6.32)	(4.88)
Household size	−.903	−.925	−.872	−.838	−.839
(natural log)	(4.78)	(4.84)	(4.59)	(4.43)	(4.44)
Proportion of black	—	.106	−7.981	—	−5.898
residents		(.78)	(2.32)		(1.67)
Proportion black ×	—	—	.904	—	.683
ln(income)			(2.36)		(1.74)
Proportion of housing	—	—	—	.467	.488
units built before				(2.26)	(2.18)
1940					
R^2 (adjusted)	.380	.379	.394	.394	.406

[a]Dependent variable is in natural log form. t values are in parentheses.

significant at the 95% level). The coefficient of the interaction term indicates that the income elasticity of demand is less for blacks (.67) than for whites (1.57). This finding is plausible because the choice of housing is more limited for blacks than for whites. The income elasticity thus appears lower for blacks, but might be more similar to the income elasticity for whites if the limitations on black housing choice were removed. The coefficients indicate that population density is greater in black areas if income exceeds $6850. An additional interaction term for proportion black and land value was added to the specification in column 3, but the additional coefficient was not significant.

Column 3 thus becomes the final specification. The coefficient of the natural log of land value is −.07 with t = .63, or close to zero, insignificant, and with the wrong sign. On the other hand, the other variables in the equation are significant with plausible coefficient values.

The reason for this failure of the theory can be described empirically. When the natural log of net population density is estimated as a function only of linear distance to the CBD, the result is

$$\ln(\text{density}) = 6.045 - .091(\text{distance}), \qquad (24)$$
$$(50.58) \quad (6.795)$$

where the $R^2 = .194$ and t values are in parentheses. The addition of quadratic and higher order distance terms does not add to the explanatory power of the regression, so the usual population density gradient indicates a decline of population density of 9.1% per mile. However, a study of land values for Chicago in 1970 (McDonald and Bowman, 1979) indicated that land value *rises* with distant to the CBD over the range of 4 to 10 miles. Thus, over this distance range, population density falls while land value rises.

Rather than assume that housing capital is perfectly malleable, it is more reasonable to assume that capital remains fixed on the land unless it is demolished. Following Hufbauer and Severn (1974), private demolition will occur if the land rent on the new land exceeds the value of housing services produced by the old building plus the annual capital charge for demolition and site preparation. Otherwise, population density in the older housing areas will reflect the structure of the housing market from previous periods. In particular, because commuting costs were relatively high in the previous periods, the price of land relative to the price of capital was higher in the previous periods than is the case in the current period. This suggests that older housing exhibits a relatively high ratio of capital to land and, therefore, older housing areas have a greater population density. Furthermore, land values in these areas may be depressed by high demolition and site preparation costs.

As a preliminary test of the vintage approach, a measure of the age of the housing stock on a block has been added to the specification of the equation for net population density, Eq. (19). The variable used is percent of housing units on the block constructed before 1940, as indicated by the Census of Housing. The results of regressions including this variable are in columns 4 and 5 of Table 6.7. In column 4 the two race variables (proportion black and the black income interaction term) are omitted. The housing vintage variable is highly significant in column 4, and its coefficient indicates that population density increases by 47% as the proportion of houses built before 1940 increases from 0 to 100%. Comparing column 4 with column 1, we see that the coefficients of the other variables are not changed appreciably by the addition of the housing vintage variable. The two race variables are included in the estimated equation shown in column 5. The housing vintage variable is highly significant, but the coefficient values and levels of statistical significance for the two race variables are reduced compared to the results in column 3 in which the housing variable is omitted from the specification. It might be expected that race will be a less significant factor once a control has been introduced for the age of the housing stock. While the housing vintage variable used here is not ideal, the results strongly suggest that the vintage capital approach has a high potential to lead to an improved understanding of the operation of the urban housing market.

A further refinement of the analysis of net population density is to include the percentage of households in a block that own the home. The models developed in Chapters 1 and 5 that pertain to this factor indicate that homeowners face lower prices for housing services than renters and, consequently, consume more housing and live at lower net population densities than renters. As indicated in Chapter 1, the benefits for a household from homeownership are greater the greater is the demand for housing. From Eq. (17), this suggests that the probability of homeownership is positively related to $y - T(\mathbf{u})$, income net of commuting costs, and N, household size. These hypotheses have been confirmed by Kain and Quigley (1975), McDonald (1974), and many others who have studied the determinants of homeownership. These results mean that part of the impacts of income and household size on net population density operate through the homeownership variable. A test of these hypotheses is provided here.

Table 6.8 contains the results obtained after the proportion of homeowners in the census block has been added to the analysis reported in Table 6.7. The sample size is slightly smaller in Table 6.8 (182 rather than 190) because homeownership was not reported in the census for eight blocks in the original sample. Column 1 in Table 6.8 is a replication of the specification used in column 3 of Table 6.7 using the smaller sample. The results in these two columns are similar, although the effect of household size is somewhat closer to zero in column 1 of Table 6.8. In column 2 of Table 6.8 we find the result of adding to the specification in column 1 the variable proportion of

TABLE 6.8
Net Population Density Functions Including Homeownership[a]

	1	2	3
Constant	18.804	10.010	10.301
	(11.11)	(5.01)	(4.86)
Land value (natural log)	.030	.003	−.002
	(.30)	(.30)	(.02)
Income less cummuting costs	−1.440	−.464	−.488
(natural log)	(7.47)	(2.06)	(2.10)
Household size (natural log)	−.450	.126	.133
	(2.08)	(.59)	(.62)
Proportion of black residents	−6.434	−3.681	−3.927
	(2.12)	(1.34)	(1.40)
Proportion black × ln(income)	.727	.418	.443
	(2.15)	(1.36)	(1.42)
Proportion of homeowners	—	−1.316	−1.352
		(6.74)	(6.33)
Proportion of housing units	—	—	−.084
built before 1940			(.42)
R^2 (adjusted)	.355	.484	.482

[a]Dependent variable is in natural log form. t values are in parentheses.

homeowners. This variable is highly statistically significant ($t = 6.74$), and the coefficient of -1.32 means that increasing the proportion of homeowners by 1% reduces net population density by 1.32%. Comparing columns 1 and 2 in Table 6.8, we see that, after controlling for homeownership, the effect of income has been considerably reduced and the net effect of household size has been driven to zero. These results confirm the hypotheses that the effects of income and household size on density partly operate through the home-ownership decision. Finally, column 3 in Table 6.8 contains the result of adding to the specification the proportion of housing units built before 1940. The results show that, controlling for homeownership, the age of housing stock variable does not add significantly to the explanatory power of the regression equation. The simple correlation between proportion of home-owners and proportion of housing units built before 1940 is $-.604$, so it is clear that it is difficult to disentangle the homeownership effect from the housing vintage effect. The reason for this problem is also clear; more newer housing has been designed for owner occupancy by, for example, being con-structed as single-family houses. This type of construction may have been, in part, stimulated by the tax advantages of homeownership. These tax ad-vantages increased significantly after World War II as income tax rates increased. The results suggest that it would be fruitful to develop a vintage model of housing supply in the context of a significant increase in the tax advantages of homeownership.

In this section a new test of a popular theory of the urban housing market has been conducted. The theory implies that net population density in a small area is a function of the factor prices of land and capital, the income of the residents of that area, and the mean household size of the residents. For the city of Chicago in 1970 there is strong confirmation that income and household size influence density in the predicted manner. However, the influence of land value on density is zero. Also, holding income constant at a level greater than (less than) $6850, population density is higher (lower) in areas occupied by black people than in areas occupied by whites. This pattern of results suggested that a vintage capital approach to the study of housing supply would be fruitful. The preliminary empirical tests of this notion are encouraging. This set of results calls for additional tests in other cities and for the development and testing of more complex vintage models.

Appendix Age Structure of the Housing Stock in Chicago Over Time

Empirical tests reported in Chapters 4 and 6 support the use of a model that includes an explicit treatment of the vintage of the housing stock. The purpose of this appendix is to present a summary of the available information

TABLE 6.A1

Age Structure of Housing Units in the Chicago SMSA[a]

1940

	SMSA	Cook County	Chicago
pre-1900	309,894	278,710	258,599
1900–1909	230,021	212,122	190,645
1910–1919	241,510	225,873	189,503
1920–1929	401,651	368,385	288,874
1930–March 1940	66,780	49,583	27,689
Total reported	1,249,856	1,134,673	955,310
Age not reported	44,074	35,952	34,193

1950

	SMSA	Cook County	Chicago
pre-1920	826,725	744,430	665,680
1920–1929	423,825	381,990	305,295
1930–39	87,645	61,600	37,970
1940–March 1950	160,165	117,490	51,200
Total reported	1,498,060	1,305,510	1,060,145
Age not reported	65,657	55,853	45,974

1960

	SMSA	Cook County	Chicago
pre-1930	1,214,012	1,090,497	939,661
1930–1939	162,448	132,060	98,040
1940–1949	154,373	112,060	53,090
1950–March 1960	465,967	340,744	123,764
Total reported	1,996,800	1,675,883	1,214,555
Age not reported	589	529	403

1970

	SMSA	Cook County	Chicago
pre-1940	1,107,343	970,811	803,302
1940–1949	246,264	202,284	138,383
1950–1959	453,707	338,154	137,476
1960–March 1970	481,553	341,909	127,784
Total reported	2,288,867	1,853,158	1,206,945
Age not reported	0	0	0

[a]Data refer to the original date of construction of the structure in which the housing unit is located. Dates of conversion, remodeling, etc., are ignored.

138

on the age structure of the Chicago housing stock over time. These data are available in the Census of Housing for 1940 and the subsequent housing censuses. The data refer to the original date of construction of the structure in which a housing unit is located.

Table 6.A1 contains the basic information for 1940, 1950, 1960, and 1970. The first fact to note is that 3.4% and 4.2% of the units in the SMSA in 1940 and 1950, respectively, did not have an age reported. In 1960 this problem was eliminated. The building boom in the 1920s and the depression of the 1930s are evident in the figures for 1940. Also, in 1940, most of the housing units in the city of Chicago (66.9%) were located in structures built before 1920. In fact, 27.1% of the units in the city of Chicago were in structures built before 1900. These percentages are only slightly lower at the Cook County and SMSA levels. The figures for 1950 show that construction during the 1940s was much greater than during the 1930s, but still relatively low compared to the earlier decades of the twentieth century. Only 51,200 units, or 4.8% of the total with age reported, were added in the city of Chicago during the 1940s. The bulk of the units in the city of Chicago (62.8%) were still in structures built before 1920. The figures for 1960 show the building boom in the suburbs during the 1950s. Some 43.7% of all units in the SMSA outside the city of Chicago were constructed in the 1950s. Also, the number of units built in the city of Chicago during the 1950s is a substantial 10.2% of the total units in the city as of 1960. However, 77.4% of the units in the city in 1960 were in structures built before 1930. Finally, in 1970 we see the continuation of the suburban building boom into the 1960s. By 1970 61.9% of the units in the SMSA outside the city of Chicago were in structures built after 1949. The 1960s also included a substantial addition to the stock of units in the city of 10.6% of the 1970 total for the city. However, 66.6% of the units in the city in 1970 were in structures built before 1940.

Table 6.A2 presents a clearer picture of one aspect of the housing vintage effect by showing the percentage of units in structures built before

TABLE 6.A2
Percentage of Housing Units in Structures Built before 1940[a]

Year	SMSA	Cook County	Chicago
1940	100.0	100.0	100.0
1950	86.3	91.0	95.2
1960	68.9	73.0	85.4
1970	48.4	52.4	66.6

[a]The figures for 1940 assume that no construction occurred from January to March, 1940. The percentages are based upon the total number of units that reported the date of construction.

1940 for 1940, 1950, 1960, and 1970. Recall that very little construction occurred during the 1930s. The decadal decline in this percentage clearly increased, especially in the city of Chicago. The pre-1940 (really pre-1930) housing stock is being replaced, but the 1970 housing market in the city is still dominated by units in structures that are at least 30 years old. Many are over 50 years old.

Table 6.A3 shows the survival of units in structures built in the 1920s, 1930s, and 1940s. The problem of the failure to report the age of the structure in 1940 and 1950 should be remembered in examining Table 6.A3. Nevertheless, the striking tendency evident in this table is the increase in the number of units located in structures built during these three decades. In particular, the reported increase from 1960 to 1970 of units in structures built during the 1940s is not contaminated by the failure to report the age of the structure. One reasonably convincing explanation for this trend is the conversion of structures to increase the number of housing units in those structures.

The data presented in this appendix suggest two elements for a model of the housing market. First, the housing stock is replaced very slowly. In 1970 the housing in the city of Chicago was still dominated by units in structures built before 1930. Second, a model should allow for the subdivision of housing units into smaller units. A plausible assumption might be that a housing structure produces a fixed amount of housing services over time, but that the number of households in the structure is variable, at least in the positive direction.

TABLE 6.A3
Surviving Number of Units in Structures Built in Various Decades

Year	SMSA	Cook County	Chicago
	Units in structures built in the 1920s		
1940	401,651	368,385	288,874
1950	423,825	381,990	305,295
	Units in structures built in the 1930s		
1940	66,780[a]	49,583[a]	27,689[a]
1950	87,645	61,600	37,970
1960	162,448	132,060	98,040
	Units in structures built in the 1940s		
1950	160,165[b]	117,490[b]	51,200[b]
1960	154,373	112,582	53,090
1970	246,264	202,284	138,383

[a]Figures for 1940 assume that no construction occurred from January to March 1940.
[b]Figures for 1950 assume that no construction occurred from January to March 1950.

7

Land Values in Chicago

The spatial distribution of land values in Chicago has been studied more extensively than in any other metropolitan area in the world. The main modern studies are Berry (1976), Bednarz (1975), Kau and Sirmans (1979), Mills (1969), Smith (1978), Yeates (1965), and this chapter. The two chief sources of data on land values are Hoyt (1933) and Olcott's annual series (1907–present). Both data sources provide estimates of land values rather than records of market transactions and thus may be subject to error. However, since land value is the dependent variable in the analysis, random error does not produce biased estimates of the coefficients in question. The first section of the chapter reviews the evidence on the spatial distribution of land values from 1836 to 1970 presented by Berry (1976) Bednarz (1975), Mills (1969), Kau and Sirmans (1979), and Yeates (1965).[1] The second section contains new results from 1960 and 1970. The final section examines the question of whether the existence of the possibility that residential zoning constrains the intensity of land use will cause bias to appear in studies that fail to take this possible constraint into account. The conclusion of this study of zoning is that the omission of the variable to control properly for the zoning constraint does not cause serious bias.

[1] The study by Smith (1978) was discussed in Chapter 3.

1   A History of Land Values in Chicago

Table 7.1 contains the results obtained by Mills (1969)[2] using the data from Hoyt (1933). Each data point is the estimated average land value for a square mile; thus residential and nonresidential land uses are included. Nevertheless, the results probably give a good, if somewhat rough, idea of the historical pattern of land values. The only independent variable in the analysis is distance to the CBD. The constant term clearly increased over time, and the land value gradient clearly flattened over the period 1857–1928 (or 1836–1928).[3] However, the land value gradient in 1910 was identical to the one in 1873, and was steeper than the one found for 1892. In summary, the Hoyt data do not suggest an even decline in the slope of the land value gradient over time.

Table 7.2 contains the results obtained by Yeates (1965) in an analysis of front foot land value estimates in *Olcott's Land Values Blue Book of Chicago and Suburbs* (1911–1961). A sample of 484 blocks (about 3% of the blocks in the city of Chicago) was used. Both residential and nonresidential blocks were included in the sample. Yeates used as independent variables distance to CBD, nearest major shopping center, elevated subway system, and Lake Michigan. In addition, population density and percentage population nonwhite in the census tract were used. The results clearly indicate a flattening of the relationship between land value and distance to the CBD, although no flattening occurred from 1930 to 1950. The relationships between land value and distances to shopping, Lake Michigan, and the elevated subway system also have flattened over time. From 1930 on the effect of nonwhite population has been to decrease land values. The coefficient of $-.002$ for 1960 means that increasing nonwhite population from 0% to 100% decreased land values by 20%. Yeates (1965, p. 65) pointed out that race and income are highly correlated, so part of the racial effect should be attributed to low income. Finally, Yeates erroneously included gross population density in his regression analysis. Gross population density declined in many tracts near the CBD as business and commercial areas expanded, so that by 1950 there was a significant negative relationship between gross density and land value. However, the results should neither be construed as a test of the proposition that land values influence the intensity of residential land use nor as evidence of a disamenity associated with high net population density. Furthermore, Yeates (1965, p. 66) stated that there was a slight positive relationship between gross population density and distance to the

----

[2] The results for 1892 are from Kau and Sirmans (1979). The dependent variable is in natural log form.

[3] The results for 1836 are discounted because of the small size of the city at that time.

TABLE 7.1
Hoyt's Land Values in Chicago: 1836-1928[a]

Year	Constant	Distance	R^2
1836	5.799	−.399 (27.11)	.78
1857	8.792	−.487 (35.36)	.86
1873	10.05	−.330 (22.43)	.71
1892	10.04	−.246 (11.17)	.42
1910	10.84	−.328 (13.27)	.59
1928	11.85	−.218 (11.80)	.50

Sources: Mills (1969) and Kau and Sirmans (1979).
[a]Dependent variable is in natural log form. t values are in parentheses.

TABLE 7.2
Yeates' Analysis of Olcott's Land Value Data for Chicago: 1910-1960[a]

	1910	1920	1930	1940	1950	1960
Constant	4.745	4.826	4.107	3.387	3.562	3.356
Distance to CBD (log)	−.837*	−.673*	−.268*	−.275*	−.268*	−.173*
Distance to shopping center (log)	−.038	−.122*	−.156*	−.134*	−.081	−.092*
Distance to lake (log)	−.450*	−.414*	−.367*	−.285*	−.227*	−.146*
Distance to elevated (log)	−.248*	−.240*	−.214*	−.140*	−.152*	−.050
Population density (log)	.105*	−.008	.039	.044	−.116*	−.137*
Percentage nonwhite population	.005*	.001	−.003*	−.002*	−.002*	−.002*
R^2	.77	.65	.37	.34	.24	.18

Source: Yeates (1965).
*Significant at the 95% level.
[a]Dependent variable is in log form.

CBD in 1960. This result is at variance with all of the studies examined in Chapter 6.

One of the most interesting aspects of the Yeates study is the separate regression analysis done for six sectors of the city for 1960. The six sectors are the CBD (within $1\frac{1}{2}$ miles of the corner of State and Madison), the north side, northwest side, west side, southwest side, and the South Side. Yeates found

TABLE 7.3
Mills' Analysis of Olcott's Residential
Land Values: 1965[a]

Constant	4.294
Distance to CBD	−.0184
	(.8759)
Percentage not	.0094
dilapitated	(2.1258)
Ray 1 dummy	−.1778
	(1.3745)
Ray 2 dummy	−.2627
	(2.2627)
Ray 3 dummy	.0960
	(.7449)
Multiple family	.0381
zoning	(.2913)
Residential zoning	.0772
dominates block	(.7815)
R^2	.3022
N	51

Source: Mills (1969).
[a]Dependent variable is in natural log form.
t values are in parentheses.

that land values significantly *increased* with distance to the CBD on the north, northwest, and south sides. Except for the CBD, land values decreased with distance to the CBD only on the west side. Futhermore, the coefficient of distance on the west side is not statistically significant. The coefficients of the other variables in the sectoral analysis suggest some consistent patterns in that distance to Lake Michigan was important only on the north and south sides and that distance to the elevated subway system had a negative sign in all sectors. Also, percentage nonwhite population had a significant negative effect on the west and southwest sides. The effect of nonwhite population was negative and insignificant on the north and south sides and positive and insignificant on the northwest side. The sectoral analysis reveals effects of distance to the CBD that call for additional explanation.

The study by Mills (1969) includes an analysis of a small sample of 51 residential blocks drawn from Olcott (1966). Data were drawn at every mile along four rays from the CBD. The results of the regression analysis are shown in Table 7.3. Land values were not significantly related to distance to the CBD. Most of the explanatory power was provided by the percentage of residences in the census tract not dilapidated and the dummy for ray 2.

In an analysis of a larger sample ($N = 132$) from Olcott (1966), which included land uses of all types, Mills (1969) found that land values in 1965 declined significantly at the rate of 11% per mile from the CBD. These data were taken at 1-mile intervals along eight rays running along major streets

TABLE 7.4
Berry and Bednarz' Analysis of Mean
Lot Values: 1968–1972[a]

Constant	3026
Median family income	.06
	(1.00)
Mobility: percentage living in	−56
different house 1965 and 1970	(2.54)
Percentage of dwelling	204
units multifamily	(4.86)
Location in: white area adjacent to	−786
minorities[b]	(1.30)
Zone of black expansion	−1555
	(5.57)
Black neighborhood	−4363
	(7.09)
Zone of Latino expansion	−2495
	(3.60)
Spanish neighborhood	−2394
	(2.27)
Distance to CBD (miles)	378
	(4.06)
R^2	.35

Source: Berry (1976).
[a]Dependent variable in dollars.
t values are in parentheses.
[b]The omitted category is peripheral
white neighborhoods.

that pass near the CBD. Both samples from Olcott (1966) used by Mills (1969) included data from the suburbs as well as the city of Chicago.

The studies by Bednarz (1975) and Berry (1976) contain an analysis of Olcott's residential land values for 1968–1972. Some 30,000 single-family home transactions in the city of Chicago during 1968–1972 were identified and then arranged into 231 areal groupings (based upon census tract boundaries). While the central focus of these studies is on the sale prices of single-family houses, Olcott's land values were also recorded for the 30,000 houses. The dependent variable in the land value analysis is the mean dollar lot value of the houses sold in each of 231 areas. Table 7.4 contains representative regression results presented by Berry (1976, pp. 412–13). The results show that lot values in black and Latino areas were significantly below the values in peripheral white neighborhoods after controlling for neighborhood income, population mobility, extent of multifamily housing, and distance to the CBD.[4] Furthermore, lot values in the zones into which the black population was expanding were higher than in the older black neighborhoods.

[4] Further analysis suggested that the low lot values in Latino areas may stem from high pollution levels. See Berry (1976, p. 411).

However, the results indicate that lot value *increased* significantly with distance to the CBD after controlling for race, income, etc. The statistical significance of this effect was eliminated when the regression was run in double log form, but the positive sign remained (Berry, 1976, p. 413). One feature of the data to note is that very few observations were taken from the area within 4 miles of the CBD (Berry, 1976, p. 403), probably because relatively few single-family houses were sold (or, indeed, exist) in this area. As is explained below, this restriction on the data set provides one reason for the coefficient of distance to the CBD obtained.

2 Land Value Functions: A Reevaluation[5]

For many years land values were presumed to decline monotonically with distance from the central business district (CBD). Recent developments in both the theoretical and empirical literature have bought this characterization under attack. After reviewing the literature we conclude that there is ample reason to believe that actual residential land value functions can exhibit complex curvilinear shapes. We therefore address ourselves first to a general question: What is the most appropriate functional form in a simple model that does not explicitly take account of effects other than distance? Next, we consider several potential influences on residential land values other than distance in an attempt to explain the observed systematic variations. The study employs data on land values in the city of Chicago from Olcott.

The results suggest that the best choice of functional form relates the natural logarithm of residential land value to a fourth-degree polynomial of distance to the CBD. This particular configuration seems not to result from patterns of racial and income segregation in the housing market, nor easily measured aspects of the quality of the housing stock. The same functional form is found for nonresidential land. The full explanation for the fourth-degree function remains undiscovered. These investigations suggest that future empirical work on urban land and property values should allow for the possibility that the effect of distance to the CBD may only be captured properly with a complex functional form.

The static model of the monocentric urban land market in most common use (Chapter 5) includes the assumptions that there are no external effects in the land market and the capital is all of the same vintage and perfectly malleable and mobile. These models lead to the conclusion that land value is a declining function of distance to the CBD. Land value exhibits a constant

---

[5] H. Woods Bowman is coauthor of this section.

percentage decline per mile (negative exponential function) if it is assumed that location cost increases by a constant amount with distance from the CBD, the price elasticity of demand for housing is unitary, and housing production is a Cobb–Douglas function of capital and land inputs. Alteration of any of these assumptions (or other assumptions) will change the functional form of the relationship between land value and distance to the CBD.

Recently theorists have explored the implications of more complex versions of the basic model (see Chapter 5). These theoretical results suggest that the form of the function relating land value and distance to the CBD is not known a priori. It is not even necessarily true that land value always declines with distance to the CBD if some of the determinants of land values, other than transportation cost to the CBD, are related to distance. If these "other" determinants of land values (e.g., age of housing stock, accessibility of non-CBD employment centers, race, amenities such as lack of air pollution or congestion, and other neighborhood effects) are held constant, then land values decrease with distance to the CBD. However, the appropriate functional form is still unknown. Even more troublesome is the fact that the empirical researcher typically does not possess good measures of all "other" determinants of land values. The result of this lack of data is that the coefficient of distance to the CBD in a regression explaining land or property values can be of either sign. Furthermore, it is possible that the relationship between land values and distance contains some regions in which the value rises with distance and some regions in which value declines with distance. A very flexible functional form is suggested.

Several studies could be cited, but the point is clear. Out of necessity, researchers have used distance to the CBD as a proxy variable for a variety of influences on land values. Given that distance to the CBD must serve as a proxy for other variables in addition to accessibility to the CBD, it would seem that the functional relationship between land value and distance can assume many forms. The failure to use the appropriate functional form in a given study can lead to biased estimates of the coefficients of other variables. In this case, the proxy variable omitted may be the higher order terms of distance to the CBD. Also, restricting to distance variable to a linear form (or linear in the log form) may result in an incorrect impression about the relationship between land values and distance.

The data on land values used in this study are taken from *Olcott's Land Values Blue Book of Chicago and Suburbs* for 1960 to 1970. The reader should bear in mind that these data are only estimates made by an appraiser. Both measurement error and bias may be present. The presence of measurement error will not cause biased coefficients because land value is the dependent variable in the analysis. Some possible sources of bias in mind of the appraiser (race, neighborhood income, age of housing stock, and zoning category) are included in the analysis, so we believe that it is unlikely that our estimated relationship between land value and distance is the result of systematic error on the part of the appraiser.

About 1000 blocks in the city of Chicago were selected for the present study by a computer program that randomly identified census tracts and block numbers. Every fourth observation was then selected from the list. This procedure resulted in underrepresentation of an area within 2 miles of the CBD. All other observations on the list of 1000 that lay within a 2-mile radius of the CBD were added to the sample used in this analysis, resulting in an augmented sample of about 300 blocks. Land value and zoning data were recorded from Olcott. A computer program designed by the authors split the blocks into fragments that were homogeneous by zoning category and front foot land value and computed square-foot land values for each fragment that was zoned differently. Block fragments with different zoning characteristics were treated as different observations in subsequent analyses. After these operations, we had 400 sample points for 1960 and 407 for 1970. Census block data for 1970 were used for percentage of housing lacking some plumbing facilities and percentage black population. Census tract data for 1970 were used for median income of families and unrelated individuals and percentage of housing units constructed before 1939. Block data for these variables are preferable, of course, but not readily available.

Since all models emphasize residential land values, only residential sample points were used in our preliminary work on functional form. A scatter diagram of the data for both 1960 and 1970 strongly suggested a polynomial of the fourth degree because, as distance from the CBD increased, local minimum and local maximum points were clearly discernable before an asymptotic limit was reached at the edge of the city. Table 7.5 summarizes the results of stepwise regressions for both 1960 and 1970 using the natural log of land value as the dependent variable.

Before analyzing the alternative functional forms we observe two facts. First, the gradient of the negative exponential functions, so commonly used, turns positive in 1970 (with a t value of 1.33). The other striking fact is that the R^2 statistics deteriorate markedly between 1960 and 1970, especially for the negative exponential function.

Even the addition of a single second-order distance term in either equation improves its explanatory power markedly. These equations have a sign pattern that correctly predicts higher land values near the CBD and lower land values near the edge of the city. Furthermore, the coefficients of both distance terms in each equation can be measured with considerable precision.

The equation for each year with first-, second-, and third-order distance

TABLE 7.5
Log of Residential Land Values as a Function of Distance from the CBD[a]

Constant	D	D^2	D^3	D^4	R^2	F_n[b]
			1960 (N = 253)			
−.0517	−.042				.09	.99
(6.68)	(4.91)					
−1.110	.213	−.010			.19	.96
(8.62)	(6.73)	(5.59)				
−.0195	−.224	.045	−.002		.26	.99
(.89)	(2.37)	(3.95)	(4.88)			
1.400	−1.264	.253	−.018	.0004	.33	.98
(3.61)	(5.52)	(5.82)	(5.51)	(4.94)		
			1970 (N = 258)			
.272	.012				.00	1.00
(3.45)	(1.33)					
−.191	.149	−.008			.07	1.00
(1.44)	(4.47)	(4.26)				
.497	−.187	.035	−.002		.12	.98
(2.15)	(1.90)	(2.88)	(3.60)			
1.892	−1.121	.224	−.016	.0004	.18	.85
(4.82)	(4.75)	(4.93)	(4.74)	(4.74)		

[a]Land value is measured in dollars per square foot and distance is measured in miles.
[b]F_n = the probability that the error term is not normally distributed. Numbers in parentheses beneath regression coefficients are t values.

terms performs tolerably well. They each have the correct sign pattern, implying high land values near the CBD and low values near the edge of the city. The precision of the estimated coefficients is generally good, but the addition of the third-order distance term cut into the precision of the coefficients of the first- and second-order terms as estimated above.

Including distance terms of all four orders improves the results for each year. The R^2 statistics receive another boost and the precision of the estimated coefficients on the first- and second-order distance terms is restored. In fact, the t statistics on all coefficients in these equations are remarkably high. Additional higher order distance terms seriously affected the precision of the results by lowering t values and causing unstable coefficients. Results of further experiments in this direction are not reported.

There are other reasons for preferring the fourth-degree polynomial for explaining land values. Taking ratios between the R^2 statistics in the 1960 and 1970 equations for comparable equation forms, one discovers that relatively less explanatory power is lost over time with the fourth-degree polynomial than with the other equations. Moreover, tests for normality and homoskedasticity run on the residuals of each equation led us to reject both properties for all but the fourth-degree polynomial for the 1970 data. The lack of normality of the residuals for the 1960 regression (Table 7.5) is eliminated when zoning is included (Table 7.6).

It was hypothesized that zoning is nearly as important as distance from the CBD in determining land values. Although there may be some systematic variations in zoning with distance (lower density zoning as one moves toward the edge of the city), the inclusion of dummy variables to reflect zoning characteristics should have no profound effect upon the shape of the land value surface, nor upon the precision of the estimated coefficients of the distance terms. These hypotheses are confirmed by the results reported in Table 7.6. However, in both cases the R^2 statistics were boosted consider-

TABLE 7.6
Log of Residential Land Values as a Function of Distance from the CBD with Zoning

Coefficient	1960	1970
Constant	1.089	1.584
	(2.93)	(4.24)
D	−1.108	−0.998
	(5.08)	(4.44)
D^2	.226	.204
	(5.53)	(4.79)
D^3	−0.016	−0.015
	(5.29)	(4.63)
D^4	.0004	.0004
	(4.75)	(4.20)
Coefficient of residential zone		
R-1	.283	.253
	(1.60)	(1.36)
R-2	.001	−0.061
	(0.10)	(0.58)
R-3	−0.043	−0.028
	(0.57)	(0.35)
R-5	.029	.232
	(0.28)	(2.01)
R-6	.496	.349
	(2.01)	(1.28)
R-7	1.490	1.655
	(6.09)	(6.15)
R^2	.44	.31
$F_n{}^a$	.58	.68
Sample size	253	258

^aF_n = the probability that the error term is not normally distributed. t values are in parentheses.

ably. For the fourth-degree polynomial the R^2 became .44 in 1960 and .31 in 1970. Notice that the reduction in explanatory power between the two years is only about 25% compared with a loss of nearly 50% when zoning is not taken into consideration. Furthermore, the inclusion of zoning dummies in the fourth-degree function improves the normality properties of the residuals. Consequently, zoning variables were included in all subsequent analyses.

Residential zoning categories for the city of Chicago are R-1 through R-8. They differ in the kind and intensity of uses permitted on the land, with higher and more intense uses corresponding to higher numbers. There was no R-8 in our sample. The coefficients of dummy variables for R-1 through R-7 (except R-4, the omitted category) are shown in Table 7.6. The general pattern of the results is for higher land values to be associated with higher zoning categories. This pattern is broken by the lowest zoning class, R-1, but the sample size for R-1 is relatively small (nine observations). The results for R-5, R-6, and R-7 provide one important reason for the high land values on the north side near the lake. Table 7.7 contains a full description of the zoning regulations.

One additional result can be derived from Table 7.6. There appears to be no appreciable lateral shift in the land value profile between the years 1960 and 1970. The secondary trough and the secondary peak were located at about 4 miles and 10 miles, respectively, in both years.

Before considering alternative models to explain the curvilinear land value profile, we examine possible explanations that are unique to Chicago: O'Hare Airport and the Lake Calumet industrial area. Located at the extreme northwest corner of the city, O'Hare directly provides employment opportunities for 10,000 persons and has stimulated commercial real estate development, which indirectly provides employment opportunities for many more. On the southern lakefront, the steel mills and other heavy industry in the Calumet area provide another major employment subcenter. The possibility that they are the causes of the rise in residential land value with distance to the CBD in our sample was enhanced by the scatter diagram, which showed the local maximum located at the same distance from the CBD as the airport and the Lake Calumet area. See Figure 7.1 for a map of Chicago that illustrates selected geographic features. To test for the influence of these employment subcenters, the data were separated into three groups drawn from different areas. The area on the north side embraced a wedge from 0 to 135 degrees and included the Edens Expressway. The northern wedge took the area from 135 to 225 degrees and included the Eisenhower Expressway. Finally, a southern wedge was defined from 225 to 360 degrees that included the Stevenson, Dan Ryan, and Calumet expressways. The results of running a separate regression on each of these groups for 1970 are reported in Table 7.8. The west side is presumably not influenced by either employment subcenter.

TABLE 7.7
Residential Zoning Categories and Restrictions: City of Chicago Zoning Ordinance of 1957

Category	Permitted use	Lot area per unit (sq. ft.)	Floor-area ratio	Front yard	Side yard	Rear yard	Off-street parking
R-1	One family detached	6250	.5	20 ft. or 16% (whichever is less) plus 1 ft. for each 2 ft. of height over 25 ft.	One story – 5 ft. on each side; over one story – two sides sum to 15 ft., each side must be 5 ft. or more	30 ft. or 2/3 of height, whichever is greater	1 space per unit on lot
R-2	Same as R-1	5000	.5	Same as R-1	One story – 4 ft. on each side; over one story – two sides sum to 12 ft., each side must be 4 ft. or more	Same as R-1	Same as R-1
R-3	One-family Two-family	2500	.7	Same as R-1	Height ≤ 25 ft. – 5 ft. on each side; height > 25 ft. – 1/5 height on each side	Same as R-1	Same as R-1
R-4	R-3 plus apartment hotels	900	1.2	15 ft. or 12% (whichever is less)	10% of lot width on each side (not to exceed 20 ft.)	30% (may be 6 ft. above curb level)	1 space per unit but may be located 300 ft. away
R-5 R-6	Same as R-4 Same as R-4	400 200	2.2 4.4	Same as R-4 Same as R-4	Same as R-4 None required	Same as R-4 30 ft. (may be 18 ft. above curb level)	Same as R-4 1 space per unit up to 100 units 60% of additional units
R-7	Same as R-4	145	7.0	Same as R-4	Same as R-6	Same as R-6	1 space per unit up to 50, 55% of additional units
R-8	Same as R-4	115	10.0	Same as R-4	Same as R-6	Same as R-6	55% of units

Source: Municipal Code of Chicago, Chapter 194A (Chicago Zoning Ordinance), passed by the City Council of the City of Chicago on May 29, 1957.

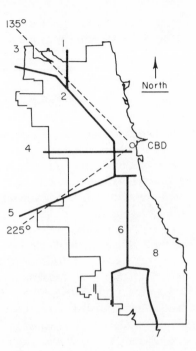

Figure 7.1. Map of Chicago.

1 Edens Expressway
2 John Fitzgerald Kennedy Expressway
3 O'Hare Airport (approximate site)
4 Dwight David Eisenhower Expressway
5 Adlai E. Stevenson II Expressway
6 Dan Ryan Expressway
7 Calumet Expressway
8 Lake Calumet industrial area

The results were not stable when the fourth-degree polynomial was fitted, but no appreciable explanatory power was lost by dropping the fourth power of distance (in fact the adjusted R^2 increased on the west side). The sign pattern for the third-degree functions in each case is such that a global maximum is predicted at the CBD and a global minimum is predicted

TABLE 7.8
Sectoral Analysis of Log of Land Value as a Function of Distance from the CBD: 1970[a]

	Constant[b]	D	D^2	D^3	R^2
North	.567	−.249	.052	−.002	0.46
(N = 58)	(1.21)	(.96)	(1.40)	(1.40)	
West	2.291	−1.358	.221	−.010	0.71
(N = 96)	(7.09)	(7.92)	(8.51)	(8.16)	
South	.534	−.215	.028	−.001	0.11
(N = 104)	(1.48)	(1.55)	(1.84)	(2.09)	

[a] t values are in parentheses.
[b] Full regression in each case included dummy variables for zoning characteristics. The constant term reported in this table assumes R-4 zoning.

at the urban fringe. Furthermore, the t statistics are strong on the west and south sides but somewhat weak on the north side.

The reason for the instability in the sectoral results can be seen when we realize that the distance from the CBD to the city limits is different for each of the three sectors. If the true function is indeed a fourth-degree polynomial, it would be difficult for data selected from the north and west sides to reveal that pattern because there is only a small amount of data from these areas that reaches beyond the secondary peak observed in the full sample plot (at 10 miles in both 1960 and 1970). Augmenting the sample by including observations drawn from suburban territory would introduce different property tax rates and public services provided by local governments. Because of the difficulties inherent in correcting for these effects, we decided to restrict the study to the city of Chicago. This restriction has been used in the other studies reviewed above, except for Mills (1969). Despite this shortcoming, the results in Table 7.8 reveal that, in all three sectors, land values rise over a range of distance to the CBD and then decline beyond a local maximum point. The local minima on the north, west, and south sides occur at approximately 3, $4\frac{1}{2}$, and $5\frac{1}{2}$ miles, respectively, for 1970. The increase in land values with distance to the CBD is largest on the west side and smallest on the south side. Because of the results for the west side, we conclude that the O'Hare and Calumet employment subcenters are not necessarily the cause of the increase in land values with distance to the CBD. In addition, the small rise in land values with distance to the CBD on the South Side indicates that the Calumet area may not be an important cause of the secondary peak in land values for the whole sample.

The nonresidential portion of the sample was examined in regression analyses similar to those reported in Table 7.6. The results of stepwise regression analysis including higher order distance terms for both 1960 and 1970 are summarized in Table 7.9. In 1960 the superiority of the fourth-degree polynomial function is clear: The R^2 is substantially larger than the R^2 for any other functional form and all t statistics are quite large. By contrast, the simple exponential (first-degree) function indicates a flat land value profile and explains a trivial amount of the total variance. In 1970 the superiority of the fourth-degree polynomial is less convincing, especially compared to the third-degree function. However, it is quite clear that the simple exponential function is inadequate; it even has a positive sign. For both years, land values rise with distance to the CBD over a range of distance. The employment changes documented in the appendix to Chapter 1 provide a tentative explanation for these results. Additional research might focus on this topic.

We now turn to the problem of explaining the undulations in the residential land value profile in terms of elements missing from the simple

TABLE 7.9
Log of Nonresidential Land Values as a Function of Distance from the CBD[a]

Constant[b]	D	D^2	D^3	D^4	R^2	F_n[c]
		1960 (N = 148)				
.111	−.008				.04	.36
(.95)	(.61)					
.135	−.018	.0007			.04	.42
(.88)	(.42)	(.24)				
.832	−.468	.069	−.003		.15	.78
(3.88)	(4.32)	(4.36)	(4.38)			
1.654	−1.215	.264	−.021	.0006	.23	.74
(5.44)	(5.29)	(4.78)	(4.20)	(3.67)		
		1970 (N = 150)				
.363	.013				.04	.95
(3.35)	(1.11)					
.228	.070	−.004			.06	1.00
(1.66)	(1.86)	(1.58)				
.527	−.118	.024	−.001		.09	1.00
(2.63)	(1.18)	(1.73)	(2.03)			
.680	−.255	.060	−.004	.0001	.09	.99
(2.27)	(1.14)	(1.12)	(.92)	(.69)		

[a] t values are in parentheses.
[b] Dummy variables were included for business and commercial zoning. The constant term reflects the value of land zoned for manufacturing.
[c] F_n = the probability that the error term is not normally distributed.

urban model of Muth and Mills. Each alternative considered involves un-evenness in the spatial distribution of amenities (disamenities) of a different kind. The first alternative considers the consequences of racial segregation, the second considers the effects of a deteriorating housing stock, and the third examines the effects of neighborhood income.

Model 1

In this model we explore the effects of racial segregation on land values. To the extent that there is a dual housing (and land) market, there will be systematic variations in land values. Racial concentrations will cause peaks and valleys to form on the land value profile. This is part of the view reflected in Rose-Ackerman's (1975) model mentioned in Chapter 5. The black population in the city of Chicago, unlike her model, is distributed along rays leading away from the CBD, primarily on the west and south sides of the city.

The results of including the percentage black population in the block in the basic equation for 1970 are summarized in Table 7.10. One of the most

TABLE 7.10
Log of Residential Land Values as a Function of Distance from the CBD, Racial Composition, and Housing Variables: 1970[a]

Constant[b]	D	D^2	D^3	D^4	Percentage Black population	Percentage Old units	Percentage Without plumbing	R^2
1.584	-.998	.204	-.015	.0004				.31
(4.24)	(4.44)	(4.79)	(4.63)	(4.20)				
2.112	-1.252	.248	-.018	.0004	-.799			.59
(5.79)	(5.95)	(6.33)	(5.95)	(5.22)	(11.60)			
1.586	-1.001	.205	-.015	.0004		.005		.31
(4.23)	(4.26)	(4.63)	(4.53)	(4.15)		(.03)		
2.113	-1.274	.253	-.018	.0004	-.790	.034		.59
(5.73)	(5.80)	(6.20)	(5.88)	(5.21)	(11.23)	(.25)		
2.200	-1.300	.255	-.018	.0004	-.781	.061	-.580	.59
(5.86)	(5.90)	(6.26)	(5.93)	(5.24)	(11.10)	(.44)	(1.21)	
.460	.004					-.135	-1.881	.19
(3.05)	(.33)					(.92)	(3.08)	

[a] t values are in parentheses.
[b] Full regression results in each case include dummy variables for zoning characteristics. The constant term reported in this table assumes R-4 zoning.

156

striking results is the increase in the R^2 statistic. For the city as a whole, it increases from .31 to .59. The coefficient of percentage black is $-.80$, which is highly statistically significant. This result implies that increasing percentage black from 0 to 100% reduces land value by 80%. The main effect on the functional form relating land values to distance is to increase the constant term and to reduce the magnitude of the coefficient on the first-order distance term. Coefficients on the higher order distance terms are only slightly affected. No change in the sign pattern is observed. We conclude that the racial composition variable is very important in determining land values, but its inclusion in a model that also includes a fourth-degree function of distance does not impair the fourth-degree function.

                                                                          ⌐

Model 2

In this model we recognize that the capital stock of a city is not perfectly malleable. The model contemplates urban growth radiating from the core outward in a series of discrete building booms. This has certainly been the case in Chicago, except that the process has been underway so long that many of the oldest structures near the core have been replaced. Thus, in Chicago at the present time the newest structures are concentrated in the core and on the fringe. Using census data on the percentage of housing units in a tract that were constructed before 1939, we explored the exact distribution of age of housing units throughout the city.[6] A fourth-degree polynomial function of distance fitted to the age data produced by the following result:

$$PCTOLD = -0.231 + 0.572D - 0.094D^2 + 0.005D^3 - 0.0001D^4,$$
$$(1.25) \quad (5.18) \quad (4.43) \quad (3.41) \quad (2.50)$$
$$R^2 = .41, \tag{1}$$

where $PCTOLD$ is the percentage of housing units built before 1939, D is the the distance to the CBD in miles, and the numbers in parentheses are the t statistics. The sign pattern indicates that its shape is exactly the mirror image of the land value function; the points closest to the core and to the fringe are minima and not maxima.

Rose-Ackerman (1975) suggested a mechanism by which the age of the housing units reduces their productivity in producing housing services. In her model land is not paid according to its marginal product, but instead receives a residual payment that is inversely related to the age of the housing stock at a given distance from the core. In the context of her model, the above empirical results suggest that controlling for age of the housing stock in the

---

[6] The tracts selected for analysis were those in which the blocks used in other analyses in this section are located. There are 228 tracts.

land value regression would diminish the effect of the higher order distance terms.

Table 7.10 reports the results of such regressions. When the age of housing stock variable is included, without any other explanatory variables except zoning and distance, there is hardly any impact on the coefficients attached to the distance terms, or on the various test statistics. Even when entered in conjunction with a racial composition variable, little additional effect is attributable to the age of housing stock variable.

We considered the possibility that the age of housing stock was an inadequate proxy for its condition. Since the idea was to measure housing quality, another variable was tried: the percentage of units without some or all plumbing facilities. The results of adding this variable are reported in Table 7.10. While the plumbing variable seemed to perform better than the age variable in terms of exerting a measurable influence on land value, its inclusion did not have any material effect on the coefficients attached to the distance terms or on the various test statistics.

Table 7.10 also shows the inability of a regression equation containing only a linear distance term and housing variables to perform as well as an equation with a linear distance term and three higher order distance terms with no housing variables. However, the housing variables are significant determinants of land value and have the correct signs in this specification. Coupled with the spatial distribution of the old housing described above, these results suggest that a model based upon the vintage of the housing stock provides additional explanatory power.

Model 3

In this model we hypothesize that the neighborhood effect of income (represented by the natural log of median income of families and unrelated individuals in dollars per year for the census tract) is the source of the shape of the land value profile. If neighborhood income and distance are positively correlated (in fact, the simple correlation is .85 in our sample), then the inclusion of income in the model may reduce the importance of the higher order distance terms and generate a monotonically declining land value–distance relationship. The results of this exercise are that income is a significant determinant of land values, but the fourth-degree function is not impaired. The full regression result for 1970, including percentage black and zoning, is shown in Table 7.11. This equation becomes our final specification. Comparing these results to those in Table 7.6, we observe that the addition of percentage black and income has boosted R^2 from .31 to .60 and increased the precision with which nearly all of the other coefficients are estimated (except the coefficient of zoning category R-1), including the higher order distance terms.

TABLE 7.11
Log of Residential Land Values as a Function of
Percent Black and Tract Income: 1970[a]

Constant	−.0600
	(.42)
D	−1.304
	(5.79)
D^2	.251
	(5.99)
D^3	−.017
	(5.62)
D^4	.0004
	(4.96)
Coefficient of residential zoning	
R-1	−.202
	(1.14)
R-2	−.209
	(1.99)
R-3	−.111
	(1.44)
R-5	.780
	(7.05)
R-6	.553
	(2.14)
R-7	1.540
	(6.03)
Percentage black	−.743
	(8.84)
Income	.321
(natural log)	(2.10)
R^2	.60

[a] t values are in parentheses.

3 Land Values and Zoning

Several empirical studies of zoning and land or property values have been completed since the mid-1960s. Several studies, such as Avrin (1977), Crecine et al. (1967), Rueter (1973) and Stull (1975), have examined the possible external effects resulting from the mixture of different types of land use. Other research, including the work by Avrin (1977), Hamilton (1978), Maser et al. (1977), and Stull (1975), have investigated the proposition that zoning influences land values by altering the aggregate supplies of land available for various uses in a city or metropolitan area. Recent theoretical work, however, has partly focused on the fact that residential zoning ordinances regulate in detail the intensity of land use. These theoretical contributions, such as the work of Courant (1976) and Orr (1975), are discussed below. One of the main points of this work is that zoning may lower the value of a site by restricting the intensity of land use. To my knowledge, only Orr (1975) has tested this hypothesis. His test used the minimum lot size as a measure of allowable land use intensity. This measure is deficient because theory has been developed to relate land value to the capital–land ratio. The establishment of a minimum lot size does not directly control the capital–land ratio. In this study of Chicago, the zoning variable is the maximum allowable floor–area ratio, the ratio of usable floor area to lot area. This variable is clearly a more direct control on the capital–land ratio. Furthermore, while Orr (1975) recognizes the fact that zoning effectively restricts the use of only some land parcels, he makes no effort to model the degree to which the zoning constraint is effective. An additional shortcoming of Orr's model is that the price of a unit of housing services is assumed to be constant over space.

The objective of this study is to develop and test a general model of the determination of land values that includes the zoning constraint as a possible influence on site value. Except for those noted above, studies of land and property values have not attempted to model the effects of zoning. This means that nearly all previous studies of land and property value suffer from a potential omitted variable bias.

The zoning system in Chicago is described above in Table 7.7, and the theory of zoning and land value is presented below. The models developed here all are based upon the assumption that housing capital is perfectly malleable and mobile. While this assumption is objectionable for some problems, I believe that it is acceptable for the problem under consideration. The current zoning categories were established in 1957, a time that is much later than the time of construction of most housing in Chicago. Thus, the zoning regulations really only affect the use of land in the long run. However, the land value also reflects the long-run prospects for the land parcel in question. In fact an appraisal of the value of land is needed primarily if the purchaser plans to redevelop the site. If redevelopment is the objective, then zoning becomes an important consideration. This is the central hypothesis of this section.

The current system of zoning in Chicago, which was enacted in 1957, contains a system for the zoning of residential land that, as Babcock (1957) described, was a departure from the older system. The older zoning ordinance classified residential districts by building types such as single-family, two-family, row houses, etc., minimum lot size, and building height. It was thought that such a system might, by being too restrictive, prevent some profitable redevelopment projects. In response to such criticism, the new

Chicago zoning system was formulated to control the intensity of land use while allowing the interspersal of buildings of different types. The crucial provision in the new ordinance controls the "floor–area ratio," which is the ratio of usable floor area to the area of the lot. As shown in Table 7.7, the floor–area ratio ranges from .5 for R-1 zoned land to 10.0 for R-8 zoned land. For example, R-8 zoning allows the construction of a 40-story building that occupies 25% of the lot. Table 7.7 also contains the other key provisions of the residential zoning system. Controls on minimum lot area per unit, minimum yard width, and minimum parking spaces are also indicated. The zoning ordinance also provides for variations and amendments (spot zoning), but such changes to the original zoning map are, according to Babcock (1957), more difficult to obtain than under the previous system.

What is important from a theoretical standpoint is the limitation on the floor–area ratio. This provision is very nearly a direct control on the ratio of capital–land inputs. Of course, structures of equal floor area can contain different capital inputs by variations in the quality of construction, number of bathrooms, etc. However, the building code places limitations on allowable variations of this kind. The analysis in this section will include the assumption that as a first-order approximation, the floor–area ratio is equal to the maximum allowable capital–land input ratio.

In this section a model of the effect of zoning on land values is presented. The model is based upon the recent theoretical work by Courant (1976) and Orr (1975). See Ohls *et al.* (1974), Stull (1974), and White (1975) for zoning models developed for other purposes. The basic model of the urban housing market assumes perfectly competitive input and output markets. All actual or potential housing producers have identical production functions in which housing services are produced by the services of land and capital. Each producer operates in a region where its production function is homogeneous of degree one. The production function for the firm can be written

$$H = f(K, L), \tag{2}$$

where H is output, K is capital services, and L is land services. Now consider housing production on a fixed area of land with exogenously fixed accessibility and other amenities. Assume that the land market contains many sites with identical characteristics, so that competition in the land market fixes the land rent (and value) of the site in question. The rental price of capital is also exogenous to the site and the producer (or producers) who occupy the site. Given that input prices and the quantity of land are fixed, only one level of output is consistent with short-run and long-run equilibrium. This output can be produced and sold because competition in the output market establishes the exogenously fixed price of housing services (given the accessibility and other amenities of the site). The value of the marginal product of land is simply

$$R(\mathbf{a}) = p(\mathbf{a})\frac{\partial H}{\partial L}, \qquad (3)$$

Where $R(\mathbf{a})$ is the rent on land, $p(\mathbf{a})$ is the price of housing services, and $\mathbf{a}$ is a vector of site amenities such as accessibility. The usual approach in land value studies is to make the observation that, since $p(\mathbf{a})$ and $k(\mathbf{a}) = K(\mathbf{a})/L(\mathbf{a})$ are both functions of $\mathbf{a}$, $p(\mathbf{a})$ and $\partial H/\partial L$ are perfectly correlated. One thus needs only to examine land rent as a function of the variables in the vector $\mathbf{a}$, or $R(\mathbf{a}) = f(\mathbf{a})$.

The introduction of zoning to regulate the floor–area ratio potentially breaks the perfect correlation between $p(\mathbf{a})$ and $\partial H/\partial L$. If the allowable capital–land ratio Z is less than the market determined capital–land ratio k^*, then $\partial H/\partial L$ is less than it otherwise would be, but $p(\mathbf{a})$ is unaffected. Now land rent can be expressed as

$$R(\mathbf{a}) = f(\mathbf{a})[g(k^*/Z)]^D, \qquad (4)$$

where $D = 1$ if k^*/Z is greater than one. In other words, land value is equal to $f(\mathbf{a})$ unless Z is less than k^*, in which case land value is less than $f(\mathbf{a})$ by an amount that is a function of the extent to which Z is less than k^*. This point can also be expressed in the language of nonlinear programming, or, for an individual land parcel,

$$\lambda(Z - k) = 0, \qquad (5)$$

where $\lambda = $ the shadow price of the zoning constraint (which equals 0 if Z is greater than k, where k is the actual capital–land ratio).

For purposes of empirical estimation, the zoning variable is relevant *only* if Z is less than k^*. Furthermore, the appropriate variable to use is k^*/Z, and *not* Z. These considerations may explain why Maser et al. (1977) failed to find any impact of residential zoning on property values. The appropriate equation to estimate is

$$\ln R(\mathbf{a}) = \ln f(\mathbf{a}) + D \ln g(k^*/Z) + U_1, \qquad (6)$$

where U_1 is the normal error term. Failure to include the term $D \ln g(k^*/Z)$ will lead to a potentially serious omitted variable bias in the coefficients of the $\ln f(\mathbf{a})$ function. Note that this criticism applies to most previous studies of land values. A part of the problem is to determine whether $D = 1$ or 0 for each parcel in the sample. One approach is to examine the actual floor–area ratio for recently constructed residential buildings. If $k = Z$ (or k is "almost" as large as Z), then $D = 1$. However, k^*/Z cannot be measured directly because k^* is not observed if Z is less than k^*. Furthermore, as is seen below, there are problems with determining D on the basis of a comparison of actual k and Z. One further point about Eq. (6) is of interest. If we assume that the production function for housing services has a constant elasticity of substitution (CES), then the functional form of the equation is simplified to

$$\ln R(\mathbf{a}) = \ln f(\mathbf{a}) - (D/\sigma)(\ln k^* - \ln Z) + U_1, \tag{7}$$

where σ is the elasticity of substitution. This follows because, by the definition of elasticity of substitution, $\sigma = \partial \ln k / \partial \ln R$.

The measurement of $\ln k^* - \ln Z$ can be formulated as a standard tobit problem (see Tobin, 1958). Suppose that

$$\ln k^* = h(\mathbf{a}) + U_2, \tag{8}$$

where U_2 is a normal error term. It is necessary to assume that the error terms U_1 and U_2 are positively correlated because unobserved factors that increase $R(\mathbf{a})$ also increase k^*. The value of the error term U_2 determines k^* and D, so both k^* and D are correlated with U_1 in Eq. (6). A solution to the problem is straightforward. From the definition of $\ln k^*$ above,

$$\ln k^* - \ln Z = h(\mathbf{a}) + U_2 - \ln Z. \tag{9}$$

We observe $\ln k - \ln Z$, where

$$\ln k - \ln Z = \begin{array}{ll} h(\mathbf{a}) + U_2 - \ln Z & \text{if RHS} < 0 \\ 0 & \text{if RHS} \geq 0. \end{array} \tag{10}$$

Estimation of this tobit model by the usual miximum likelihood methods provides an estimate of $h(\mathbf{a})$. Predicted values of $\ln k^* - \ln Z$ can thus be imputed for all parcels on the basis of the tobit index as $h(\mathbf{a}) - \ln Z$. This eliminates the correlation between $\ln k^* - \ln Z$ and U_1. Also, the correlation between D and U_1 can be eliminated by replacing D with the probability that $D = 1$. This probability is simply based on the estimates of $h(\mathbf{a})$ and the standard deviation of U_2, S_2, or

$$p(D = 1) = p(\ln Z - h(\mathbf{a}) < U_2). \tag{11}$$

The data are a sample of 113 buildings that were newly built and sold in the period 1969–1971. All buildings are located in the city of Chicago. The Market Data Center of the Society of Real Estate Appraisers provided information on the size of the building and its lot and the date of construction. Frontfoot land values as of 1970 were recorded from Olcott (1971). Census block data for 1970 were used for percentage black population, percentage housing units lacking some plumbing facilities, and percentage crowded units (more than 1.0 persons per room). Census tract data for 1970 were used for the median income of families and unrelated individuals and percentage of housing units constructed before 1939. Distance in miles to the CBD, the nearest expressway entrance, and Lake Michigan were measured on a map.

It is crucial to use newly constructed buildings in order to determine whether the use of the land parcel is being constrained by zoning. The floor–area ratio of older buildings may not be equal to the current market determined floor–area ratio in the case of unconstrained sites. Furthermore, the grandfather clause in the zoning ordinance allows buildings constructed before 1957 to violate the zoning regulations. However, it was discovered that a few newly constructed buildings apparently violate the zoning regulations. Buildings with a floor–area ratio that exceeded the zoning regulation by .3 or more were excluded from the sample on the grounds that a formal or "informal" zoning variance seems to have been granted. The resulting sample size is 106.

The results from estimating alternative versions of the model are presented in Table 7.12. In column 1 a land value function is estimated with

TABLE 7.12
Regression Analysis of Front Foot Land Values[a]

	1	2
Constant	9.562	9.724
	(3.50)	(3.53)
Distance to CBD (miles)	−.992	−1.010
	(4.40)	(4.42)
Distance to expressway (miles)	−.007	−.008
	(.19)	(.23)
Distance to lake (miles)	−.007	−.080
	(3.50)	(3.54)
Percentage black population	.139	.133
	(.50)	(.48)
Percentage units lacking some plumbing	−2.826	−2.809
	(2.45)	(2.43)
Percentage units crowded	−1.717	−1.712
	(2.84)	(2.83)
Percentage units built before 1939	.194	.189
	(.97)	(.94)
Median income (natural log)	−.217	−.225
	(.75)	(.78)
Distance to CBD squared	.150	.155
	(4.43)	(4.43)
Distance to CBD cubed	−.006	−.006
	(4.15)	(4.11)
Expected value of extent of zoning constraint		1.600
	—	(.61)
R^2 (adjusted)	.328	.323

[a] t values are in parentheses.

no attempt to account for the possible effects of residential zoning. Since the data are not a random sample of properties in Chicago, the results are not necessarily comparable to the results of other studies. Indeed, the data are drawn only from areas in which new private construction occurred; so the regression coefficients represent the effects of some standard determinants of land values in such areas. The results in column 1 indicate that the natural log of land value depends significantly upon distance to the CBD in linear, quadratic, and cubic form. This result is similar to the findings presented above. Land value falls, rises, and then falls again as distance to the CBD increases. Distance to Lake Michigan and the presence of substandard housing units (lacking some plumbing or crowded) also significantly influence land values. Percentage black population, percentage units built before 1939, and neighborhood income are not significant determinants of land values for the parcels in the sample. However, the sample contains only parcels in areas where one might suppose that these variables do not matter. New construction generally does not occur in poor predominantly black areas that have an old housing stock.

Column 2 contains the results of using the two-stage tobit procedure presented above. The variable added to the specification in column 1 is the expected value of the level of the zoning constraint estimated as a tobit function. This technique will avoid attributing increases in land value to increases in allowable density because the expected value of the level of the zoning constraint is only a function of the variables included in the model. As is discussed in detail above, the correlation between this new zoning variable and the error term U_1 has been removed in the first stage of the analysis. The results indicate that the appropriate zoning variable is not a significant determinant of land values ($t = .61$) and that the omitted variable biases in column 1 are minimal. The coefficient of the zoning variable is positive, but its lack of statistical significance makes this result less disturbing.

In this section an appropriate theoretical model has been developed for the purpose of examining the effect of zoning on the value of individual parcels of residential land. The correct zoning variable is the extent to which the zoning regulations actually constrain the use of the land to be less intensive than the market determined outcome. The empirical results for the city of Chicago for 1969–1971 indicate that this variable is not a significant determinant of land values, probably because the use of few land parcels is really constrained to any great extent.[7] It is probably safe to conclude that zoning

---

[7] An additional conjecture is that a land owner does not sell or redevelop land the use of which is constrained by zoning because he hopes to obtain a relaxation of the zoning constraint. If this argument is correct, then the examination of sites on which new construction has taken place will necessarily lead to the finding that zoning is not an effective constraint. However, this line of argument simply reinforces the point that zoning is not an effective constraint.

officials in Chicago, for the most part, do not wish to inhibit the possibilities for the redevelopment of sites.

It is interesting to note that, without the formal model developed in this paper, the researcher might not have reached this conclusion. The actual zoning regulation for a site is highly positively correlated with the site value. This is precisely the result one expects if zoning is endogenous. The fact that this actual zoning variable is highly significant in a multiple regression analysis of land values most likely simply indicates that there are variables omitted from the empirical specification.

The results in this section suggest that studies of land values in Chicago can proceed on the assumption that the omission of the appropriate zoning variable does not cause serious biases. However, this conclusion may not hold for other cities.

4 Conclusions

The studies of land values in Chicago are not comparable in many respects, but some general conclusions can be made. Prior to 1930, when Chicago was a fairly young city, a simple function of distance to the CBD, such as the negative exponential or a double log function, provided a high level of explanatory power. However, by 1930, Yeates (1965, p. 65) found that the log of distance to the CBD was no longer the most important determinant of the log of land value. By 1960 it was clear that land values did not decline monotonically with distance to the CBD. In fact, land values increase from 4 to 10 miles from the CBD. This result explains the similar finding of Bednarz (1975) and Berry (1976) for 1968–1972. The spatial pattern of new houses described above closely follows the same pattern, but does not fully explain the spatial pattern of land values. Combining the results of this chapter with the results in Chapter 3, several variables that measure various other neighborhood amenities consistently show significant effects. These variables include percentage black population (negative sign), income level (positive sign), distance to Lake Michigan (negative sign), crime (negative sign), measures of higher housing quality (positive sign), and air pollution (negative sign). The attempts to test the notion that access to non-CBD employment centers is important do not yield clear results. The study by Smith (1978) found that increasing distance to O'Hare Airport subtracts a small but significant amount from the amenity premium. Further research might focus on this issue. The study by Smith (1978) also has estimated the effects on land values of local taxes and public services. However, because the land value profile *within* the city of Chicago violates the conclusions of the standard monocentric model (Chapter 5), the activities of local governmental juristictions were not responsible for the failure of the standard model with no local government sector.[8]

---

[8] As posited by Hamilton (1976), intrajurisdictional tax and benefit capitalization increases the value of low-priced houses and decreases the value of high-priced houses. The local public sector would thus contribute to the increase in land values with distance to the CBD in the city of Chicago if less expensive houses were located at greater distances to the CBD. Such is not the case, as was shown in Chapter 3.

A Model of the Chicago
Housing Market

To this point this study has, in a sense, consisted of preliminary work. We have attempted to discover which basic assumptions, or building blocks, have received strong empirical support. Then we examined time series and cross section data for Chicago in order to establish as best we can the basic patterns of population density and land values that a model should explain. Now all of these elements must be brought together to produce a "state of the science" model for the Chicago housing market. In the first section of this chapter a summary of the empirical findings for Chicago is presented. This is a list of the key results from Chapters 6 and 7. In the next section is presented a class of analytical models that will serve the purpose at hand. This class of models draws upon the material presented in Chapters 1–5, and begins with the standard model augmented by the "putty–clay" model of housing capital. A selection is made from the class of analytical models that is consistent with the empirical findings. The chapter concludes with suggestions for further research.

1 Population Density and Land Values in Chicago:
A Summary

The purpose of this section is to present, based upon the work contained in Chapters 6 and 7, a list of key empirical facts that a model of the housing market should be able to explain. Statements concerning population density are listed first, the key results for land values are listed next, and the relationship of population density to land values is considered last.

1. Population density can be described by a negative exponential function of distance to the CBD at all points in time.
2. Since 1940, the central density has declined steadily over time.
3. Since 1900, the density gradient has steadily become flatter over time.
4. Density is negatively related to income.
5. As of 1970, density is greater in areas with more old houses and lower in areas with a larger fraction of owner occupants.
6. As of 1970, density is greater in black neighborhoods, ceteris paribus. This possibility results from a comparatively low income elasticity of demand for housing on the part of black households.
7. Land values originally could be described by a negative exponential function of distance to the CBD, but at some time prior to 1960 the pattern changed to include a region in which land values *increase* with distance to the CBD. This region is 4 to 10 miles in 1960 and 1970.
8. The complex land value function is, in part, related to the location pattern for old housing. The largest concentrations of old housing are located near the local minimum for land values.
9. Land values are lower in black and low income areas, ceteris paribus.
10. Land values decline with distance to Lake Michigan, but this effect does not extend very far inland.
11. The intensity of land use (population density or capital–land ratio) is strongly positively related to land values for newly constructed housing.
12. Population density and capital–land ratio are only weakly related to land values in areas occupied by older housing structures, ceteris paribus.

While this list glosses over some complications in the results in Chapters 6 and 7, it is a fair representation of the general patterns. Furthermore, this list is the most extensive set of "facts" that anyone has tried to explain though the use of an analytical model of urban housing. Let us now turn to a class of models that can explain most of these facts.

2   A Class of Vintage Housing Models

Since the specification of the supply side of the market is of such crucial importance and has been the subject of so much recent research (Chapter 4), the development of the model shall begin with the supply side. In this model housing is considered to be a homogeneous commodity—no distinction is made between quantity and quality. In the simplest version of the vintage model, housing output at time j of a structure constructed at time i $(i \leq j)$ is

$$h_{ij}(u) = a l_{ij}(u)^\alpha k_{ij}(u)^{1-\alpha}, \tag{1}$$

where l and k are the services of land and capital and u is the distance to the CBD. This is the simplest version of the model because no maintenance is permitted and operating inputs do not substitute for land and capital. We assume that the structure built at time i can house a variable number of families or can be abandoned. Myopic expectations are assumed. Following Hufbauer and Severn (1974) and Evans (1975), the building will be abandoned at time j if

$$R_{ij}(u) > p_{ij}(u)h_{ij}(u), \tag{2}$$

where $R_{ij}(u)$ is the rent on land that a new developer would be willing to pay and $p_{ij}(u)$ is the price of a unit of housing services provided by the old structure. The rent a new developer would be willing to pay is the value of the marginal product of land in its best use minus some fraction b of the charge for demolition and site preparation. Demolition cost may be a function of k_{ij}/l_{ij}, the size of the original building. Land rent at time j on sites occupied by structures built at time i is thus

$$R_{ij}(u) = p_{jj}(u)\frac{\partial h_{jj}(u)}{\partial l_{jj}(u)} - b r_j D(k_{ij}/l_{ij}), \tag{3}$$

where r_j is the cost of capital, b is a constant with $0 \leq b \leq 1$, and $r_j D(k_{ij}/l_{ij})$ is the annual capital charge for demolition and site preparation.[1] Note that in this formulation demolition can be caused either by a fall in $p_{ij}(u)$ or an increase in $R_{ij}(u)$.

We assume that the city is monocentric and closed in the sense that the size of the population is assumed to be unrelated to the operation of the housing market. All CBD workers have the same income level. Population and income change exogenously. The analytic strategy is that of comparative statics. We shall assume that a city has been constructed at time 0, and then we shall examine the effects of once and for all changes in certain exogenous variables assuming that the housing previously constructed is of the "putty–clay" variety.[2] The structure of the model can most simply be presented as an extension of the standard model in Chapter 5.

[1] This formulation for demolition and site preparation costs assumes that the new building will last forever. Also, $D(k_{ij}/l_{ij}) = 0$ if $k_{ij} = 0$.

[2] In a recent article, White (1978b) has developed a model of the monocentric housing market in the short run in order to describe a plausible mechanism for the transition from one

On the demand side we assume a simple Cobb–Douglas utility function

$$U = Z^{\gamma}h^{\beta}, \tag{4}$$

from which we can derive the demand functions for housing h and the composite commodity Z by maximizing U given the constraint $y = Z + p(u)h + tu$, where $p(u)$ is the price of housing at distance u and t is the constant marginal cost of commuting. The demand functions are of unitary elasticity, or

$$Z(u) = \gamma(y - tu) \tag{5}$$

and

$$h(u) = \beta(y - tu)/p(u). \tag{6}$$

These simplifying assumptions will be relaxed below. At time 0, the demand side of the housing market can be described by

$$h_{00}(u) = \beta(y_0 - t_0u)/p_{00}(u) \tag{7}$$

and

$$h_{00}(u)p'_{00}(u) + t_0 = 0. \tag{8}$$

On the supply side, land rent $R_{00}(u)$ and the cost of capital r_0 are equal to the values of their respective marginal products, or

$$R_{00}(u) = \alpha p_{00}(u)h_{00}(u)/l_{00}(u) \tag{9}$$

and

$$r_0 = (1 - \alpha)p_{00}(u)h_{00}(u)/k_{00}(u). \tag{10}$$

Land rent at the urban fringe $\bar{u}_0$ is

$$R_{00}(\bar{u}_0) = \bar{R}_0 = A_0 + S_0, \tag{11}$$

where A_0 is the agricultural rent and S_0 is the annualized cost of converting farm land to land suitable for housing. Included in S_0 are the costs of streets, utility lines, etc. Total population N_0 is simply

$$N_0 = \int_0^{\bar{u}_0} N_0(u)\, du. \tag{12}$$

---

long-run equilibrium to another. In the short run in her model, only the price of housing adjusts to exogenous demand shifts. In response to the price adjustment, the entire city is rebuilt in the long run. The nature of expectations plays an important role in determining the short-run price. The model in this chapter differs from the White (1978b) model in that new construction will occur in my model in response to an increase in demand while the older housing structures remain intact. The price of older housing in this chapter is thus determined by the price of new housing.

Using these conditions, the land rent and population density functions are derived:

$$R_{00}(u) = R_{00}(0)y_0^{-1/(\beta\alpha)}(y_0 - t_0 u)^{1/(\beta\alpha)} \tag{13}$$

and

$$d_{00}(u) = N_0(u)/l_{00}(u) = R_{00}(u)/[\alpha\beta(y_0 - t_0 u)]. \tag{14}$$

In the next "time period" there are changes in exogenous variables N, y, t, and $\bar{R}$ which cause an increase in the demand for housing at $\bar{u}_0$, and the housing market must adapt to these changes. There are two extreme cases possible; there may be no demolition of the housing stock or the entire stock may be demolished and replaced. The intermediate case is also possible. Consider first the case in which no demolition occurs. At no location does $R_{01}(u)$ exceed $p_{01}(u)h_{01}(u)$, where p_{01} is the new price of old housing. The price of the housing services provided by the old structures must adjust so that the utility level achieved is equal to the utility level that might be achieved if the household were to move into a new structure beyond the urban fringe, $\bar{u}_0$. The properties of the model can be examined by setting the utility level in period 1 achieved beyond $\bar{u}_0$ equal to the utility level in period 1 inside distance $\bar{u}_0$. Both utility levels are evaluated at distance $\bar{u}_0$. Solving for the indirect utility functions yields

$$[\gamma(y_1 - t_0\bar{u}_0)]^\gamma [\beta(y_1 - t_1\bar{u}_0)/p_{11}(\bar{u}_0)]^\beta =$$
$$= [\gamma(y_1 - t_1\bar{u}_0)]^\gamma [\beta(y_1 - t_1\bar{u}_0)/p_{01}(\bar{u}_0)]^\beta. \tag{15}$$

Clearly, $p_{11}(\bar{u}_0) = p_{01}(\bar{u}_0)$.

The effect of an increase in the population is shown in Figure 8.1. The household located at distance $\bar{u}_0$ maximizes utility at U_0 in period 0 at

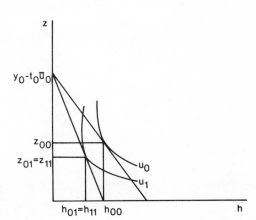

Figure 8.1. An increase in population increases the price of housing and population density.

Z_{00}, h_{00}. In period 1, as a result of an increase in population, the utility level for a household that locates at distance $\bar{u}_0$ in newly constructed housing is U_1. The price of new housing at $\bar{u}_0$ is greater than $p_{00}(\bar{u}_0)$ because the land rent at $\bar{u}_0$ has increased. The price of old housing at $\bar{u}_0$ has increased to equal $p_{01}(\bar{u}_0)$. Thus households in new or old housing at $\bar{u}_0$ consume the same amount of housing. Population density in old housing has increased as a result.

An increase in income (holding the other exogenous variables constant) will tend to make $h_{01}(\bar{u}_0)$ exceed $h_{00}(\bar{u}_0)$, but the increase in land rent will make the price of old housing rise, or $p_{01}(\bar{u}_0)$ exceed $p_{00}(\bar{u}_0)$, thus tending to cause $h_{01}(\bar{u}_0)$ to be less than $h_{00}(\bar{u}_0)$. However, the consumption of old housing per household at $\bar{u}_0$ must rise because some new construction will occur beyond $\bar{u}_0$. There will thus be a general decline in density inside $\bar{u}_0$.

A reduction in marginal transportation cost from t_0 to t_1 will tend to reduce population density (except at distance zero) by inducing some households to move beyond $\bar{u}_0$ into new housing. A reduction in $\bar{R}$, land rent at the urban fringe, will also induce new construction beyond the urban fringe and cause a general decline in population density inside $\bar{u}_0$. These comparative statics results are summarized in Table 8.1. Land rent changes inside $\bar{u}_0$ are also summarized in Table 8.1.

One interesting feature of the model involves the comparison of population density and land rents at $\bar{u}_0$ for sites occupied by older and new housing. The results for land rents follow immediately from Eq. (3), which states that the new land rent at $\bar{u}_0$ for land on which housing was constructed in period 0 must be less than the rent on land previously unused for housing by the annual cost of demolition and site preparation charged to land rent. For the population density comparison, we find that $d_{11}(\bar{u}_0)$ exceeds $d_{01}(\bar{u}_0)$ if population increases, income increases, or marginal transportation cost decreases. These results occur because all three changes cause an increase in the demand for housing at $\bar{u}_0$. A decrease in land rent at the urban fringe makes $d_{11}(\bar{u}_0)$ less than $d_{01}(\bar{u}_0)$. These results are similar to those found by Anas (1976, p. 270). An example of a new land rent profile is shown in Figure 8.2 and the results are also summarized in Table 8.1.

The case in which all of the old housing is demolished reduces to the model with malleable capital. This is so because, with myopic expectations, the fact that demolition cost must be incurred does not influence the subsequent value of the land or the intensity of its use. The comparative statistics of this case have been explored fully by Wheaton (1974). According to Eqs. (2) and (3), demolition will occur if

$$p_{11}(u) \frac{\partial h_{11}(u)}{\partial l_{11}(u)} - br_1 D(u) > p_{01}(u)h_{01}(u), \tag{16}$$

TABLE 8.1
Summary of Comparative Statics Results: Model with No Demolition

Effect on	Population increase	Income increase	Marginal transportation cost decrease	Urban fringe land rent decrease
1. Population density inside $\bar{u}_0$	$d_{01}(u) > d_{00}(u)$	$d_{01}(u) < d_{00}(u)$	$d_{01}(u) < d_{00}(u)$ (except at 0)	$d_{01}(u) < d_{00}(u)$
2. Land rent inside $\bar{u}_0$	?	?	$R_{01}(u) < R_{00}(u)$	$R_{01}(u) < R_{00}(u)$
3. Population density at $\bar{u}_0$	$d_{11} > d_{01}$	$d_{11} > d_{01}$	$d_{11} > d_{01}$	$d_{11} < d_{01}$
4. Land rent at $\bar{u}_0$	$R_{11} > R_{01}$	$R_{11} > R_{01}$	$R_{11} > R_{01}$	$R_{11} > R_{01}$

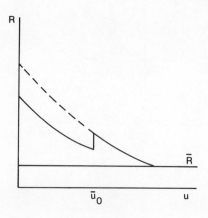

Figure 8.2.   Land rent in period 1.

where $D(u)$ represents demolition costs at distance u. Since $0 \le b \le 1$ and $p_{11}(u) = p_{01}(u)$, a requirement for demolition is that

$$\frac{\partial h_{11}(u)}{\partial l_{11}(u)} > h_{01}(u), \qquad (17)$$

or that the marginal product of land for new housing exceed the output of the older housing stock. Implied by this condition is an increase in the demand for housing at distance u. Assuming the Cobb–Douglas production function with constant returns to scale of Eq. (1), this requirement for demolition simply reduces to $\alpha h_{11}(u) > h_{01}(u)$. Large increases in population or income will tend to generate complete demolition.

In the case of partial demolition, we must first discover where demolition is most likely to begin. The answer depends upon the location of an increase in demand and the demolition cost function. Increases in population and income increase the demand for housing at all locations, but a decline in marginal transportation costs reduces the demand for housing near the CBD and increases housing demand near the urban fringe, ceteris paribus. On these grounds, demolition is more likely near the urban fringe. No empirical evidence is available about the demolition cost function. Perhaps the most likely assumption to make about demolition costs is that the cost increases at a decreasing rate as $k_{01}(u)/l_{01}(u)$ increases. Assuming a general increase in the demand for housing, this means that demolition may occur at the edge of the CBD.[3] Let us suppose that some demolition takes place just inside the urban fringe and near the CBD as a result of increases in population and income and a decline in marginal transportation costs. The new land rent function implied is shown in Figure 8.3. Demolition has occurred from dis-

---

[3] It is also likely that some residential land near the CBD has been converted to business use. This contributed to the decline in population near the CBD.

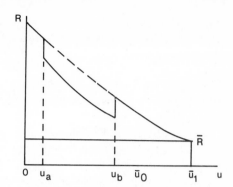

Figure 8.3. Land rent function after partial demolition.

tance 0 to u_a and from distance u_b to $\bar{u}_o$. The new urban fringe is $\bar{u}_1$. Population density at a site may increase or decrease depending upon the relative increase in population and income and decline in marginal transportation costs. However, we can state that, at distances u_a and u_b in Figure 8.3, population density in period 1 is greater in the new housing than in the older housing at that same distance. Remember that the prices of old and new housing must be equal at the same distance and that demolition at any distance cannot occur unless housing demand at that distance has increased. The increase in housing supply after demolition implies that density is greater in new housing than in older housing at the same distance. These results mean that land rent and population density at a given distance will be strongly positively correlated because land rent and population density are both lower in the older housing. However, if we consider housing sites at all distances, the relationship between land rent and population density is more complex. A given population density is not associated with a unique land rent because the land rent in areas occupied by older housing is determined partly by demolition costs, but the population density in such areas is not influenced by demolition costs. This means that, for a density level that exists both in an older housing area and a new housing area (more distant from the CBD), there are two land rent levels. Thus we have demonstrated that, in a simple vintage model, the perfect correlation between land rent and population density of the malleable capital model is broken.

A further complication of the vintage model might be considered at this point. It has been assumed that an older structure can house a variable number of households in period 1. We can consider constraints on malleability in this sense. We might assume that increasing the number of households in an older housing structure is a relatively cheap conversion problem, but that making a satisfactory conversion to lower density is costly. As suggested by the data in the appendix to Chapter 6, it seems to be the case that the subdivision of housing units is more common than the aggregation of units into larger units. The existence of asymmetrical conversion costs means, for example, that new housing near the CBD may be constructed at a lower density than the older housing at the same distance. This outcome could occur if the increase in income is a dominant feature. There will be an incentive to build at a lower density, but density in the older housing may be constrained to a higher level. This result is consistent with the findings in Chapter 6.[4]

As indicated in Chapters 5 and 6, homeownership may be an important factor to add to a vintage model of the housing market. A simple method to expand the model in this direction is to assume that the income tax benefits of homeownership are substantially greater in period 1 than in period 0. According to the theoretical treatment in Chapters 1 and 5, an increase in the benefits of homeownership will cause both the construction of a larger proportion of new housing in period 1 that is designed for homeownership and the generation of lower levels of population density in areas occupied by homeowners. Assume that the housing constructed in period 0 cannot be modified easily to facilitate owner occupancy. This means that the households that occupy the older housing in period 1 will mainly be renters and the occupants of new housing will mainly be owners.

For example, let us consider the case of partial demolition discussed above. Income and population have increased and marginal transportation costs have decreased. The income tax benefits of homeownership have increased from period 0 to period 1. Assume that the new housing is designed for owner occupancy, while the older housing is occupied by renters. At distance u_a in Figure 8.3 the price of rental (old) housing will fall in response to a subsidy to homeowners. This result is obtained because the supply of older housing is fixed (if not demolished) at distance u_a. Depicted in Figure 8.4, which is a modification of Figure 1.1, is the market for housing at distance u_a. The inelastic supply of rental (older) units is S_R and the demand for rental units prior to the introduction of a subsidy to homeowners is D_R. The total supply of housing, including owner occupied housing, is S, D represents the total demand for housing, and D_o is the demand curve for reductions in the price of owner occupied housing. Price p_1 is established for both rental and owner occupied housing in period one. Now we introduce the subsidy to homeowners; the supply curve shifts from S to S'. The net price paid by homeowners falls, causing the demand for rental housing to decline to D_R' as some renters shift to the homeowner market. The net price paid by homeowners will equal p_1^*, and the price received by suppliers of new housing will

---

[4] The constraint on reducing density in older housing means that households that occupy older housing must be compensated for being forced to consume a suboptimal amount of housing by paying a lower price. Thus $p_{01}(u_a) < p_{11}(u_a)$.

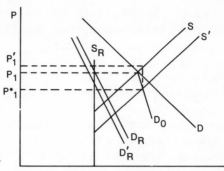

Figure 8.4.   The effects of a subsidy
to homeowners.

equal p_1'. The rent paid by renters will be less than p_1, and could be as low as p_1^*. The exact result depends upon the elasticity of rental demand with respect to the homeowners' price. These results mean that population density will probably be higher in the new housing. New housing is built at a higher capital–land ratio than older housing at the same distance, and the net price of owner occupied housing may be no lower than the rental price.

Thus far the analysis of the effect of a subsidy to homeowners has included the assumption that the population density in older housing can be changed costlessly. As was discussed above, it may be costly to permit a reduction in the number of households that occupy an older housing structure and consume all of the housing services produced by that structure. If this constraint exists, then the subsidy to homeowners examined in Figure 8.4 will reduce the population density in new housing and have little impact on the density in older housing. It is thus possible to have greater density in older housing than in new housing at distance u_a. Land rent is higher in areas occupied by new housing, so higher land rent may be associated with lower population density at distance u_a. This result is roughly consistent with the results in Chapter 6.

The next task is to add race to the model. Recall that, ceteris paribus, population density is greater and land values lower in black areas than in white areas. As pointed out in Chapters 3 and 5, prejudice on the part of whites leads to an expansion of black housing areas and to lower housing prices and land values for blacks, ceteris paribus. However, in the malleable capital model, the effect of white prejudice on land values should lead to lower population density in black areas, ceteris paribus. In addition, there is reason to assume that discrimination against blacks in the housing market confines blacks to certain areas and limits the expansion of black residential areas to locations that are contiguous to the existing black neighborhoods. No further attempt will be made to explain analytically the location pattern of blacks. The areas to which blacks are confined are nearly all within the city of Chicago, which means that blacks are largely confined to older housing.[5] Assuming that there are costs of conversion of older housing to lower density, this could explain why blacks appear to have a low income elasticity of demand for housing because many black households have their consumption of housing services constrained by the nature of the old stock. Kain and Quigley (1975) have made the same point, but the argument is made much more simply in the context of the two-period model used here. However, this argument encounters a difficulty because, in Chapter 6, it was found that population density in 1970 was higher in black areas holding constant the proportion of houses constructed prior to 1940. One possibility is that the housing vintage effect is imperfectly measured by the variable. Such would be the case if blacks tend to occupy the older housing that is located nearer to the CBD. In period 0 the city had the standard negatively sloped land rent function and population density function. Thus it is possible that, in period 1, black densities are higher than white densities, ceteris paribus, because of the difference in the old housing stocks occupied by the two groups.

Based on the evidence reviewed in Chapters 1–3, several other assumptions made in the standard model on the demand side should be relaxed.[6] These changes include

1. Adding commuting time and leisure time to the utility function
2. Considering environmental and other possible external effects
3. Taking the local public sector into account

In Chapter 2 we saw that the marginal cost of commuting increases as commuting time increases. Because the model in this chapter assumes a constant money income for all CBD workers, we have implicitly assumed that work time is fixed and, hence, that the amount of time left to divide between leisure and commuting is fixed. Thus, the marginal cost of commuting time is

$$(U_L/\lambda) - (U_c/\lambda) + g,$$

where U_L is the marginal utility of leisure, U_c is the marginal utility of com-

---

[5] Exceptions to this are the recent movement of blacks to the far South Side of the city of Chicago and the movement of some blacks into new high-rise buildings near the CBD.

[6] An additional assumption that might be relaxed is the unitary price and income elasticities of demand for housing. A recent survey by Mayo (1978) has shown that recent estimates of both elasticities are significantly less than 1.0. However, the model in chapter 5 from Mills (1972b) shows that relaxation of these assumptions has no profound effect on the results of the basic monocentric model.

muting, λ is the marginal utility of income, and g is the money costs of vehicle operation or the transit fare per unit of time. In this formulation, it is reasonable to presume that the empirical results in Chapter 2 imply a rising marginal commuting cost because the change in the marginal cost of commuting time is

$$\frac{\partial(U_L/U_z)}{\partial L} - \frac{\partial(U_c/U_z)}{\partial L} + \frac{\partial(U_c/U_z)}{\partial c} - \frac{\partial(U_L/U_z)}{\partial c},$$

where U_z is the marginal utility of z, the composite commodity. We can suppose that $\partial(U_c/U_z)/\partial c$ and $\partial(U_L/U_z)/\partial L$ are both less than zero. However, if L and c are substitutes, it may be that $\partial(U_c/U_z)/\partial L$ and $\partial(U_L/U_z)/\partial c$ are both less than zero. Thus, the empirical results in Chapter 2 can be consistent with the model used here if we simply assume a rising marginal cost of commuting time. This change has no profound effect on the results of the model, as Amson (1972) showed.

A more important change is the addition of environmental and other possible external effects. As we saw in Chapter 3, there are strong correlations between measures of air pollution (particulates and SO_2) and distance to the CBD. Furthermore, the analysis of the data on a sample of single-family houses by Bednarz (1975) and Berry (1976) indicated that a higher neighborhood income increases house value holding constant the age of the house and the racial composition of the neighborhood. Neighborhood income is strongly positively correlated with distance to the CBD. Other external effects such as crime are negatively correlated with distance to the CBD. Furthermore, crime rates have increased more in the central city than in the suburbs. School quality probably increases with distance to the CBD. While they provided no empirical justification for their models, these facts make the contributions by Polinsky and Shavell (1976) and Richardson (1977b) relevant. It is a simple matter to add to the model an "amenity" that increases more sharply with distance to the CBD in period 1 than in period 0. Finally, the model can be expanded to incorporate the local public sector. As was pointed out in Chapter 3, the local fiscal surplus (value of services minus taxes) is capitalized into the value of land. However, it is not clear that the fiscal surplus is related to distance to the CBD. It is reasonably clear that the quality of some services, such as schools, increases with distance to the CBD. However, in part because the assessment–value ratio on nonresidential property is relatively high in the city of Chicago, the property tax rate on residential property in Chicago is not particularly high. Furthermore, following the argument of Hamilton (1976), within the city it is the less expensive houses that tend to have the greater fiscal surplus. House value is *positively* correlated with distance to the CBD in the sample of single-family houses examined in Chapter 3. Because of this ambiguity, further consideration of the local public sector will not be pursued in the context of the model.

The most important addition to the demand side of the model is, then, the external effects that are related to distance to the CBD. As Polinsky and Shavell (1976) and Richardson (1977b) have pointed out, such external effects may imply that land rent increases with distance to the CBD in the malleable capital model. This result is obtained if the value of the external effects increases with distance to the CBD at a rate greater than the increase in commuting costs. The distance range of increasing land rent is reduced by the rising marginal cost of commuting. However, in the malleable capital model, low land rents that result from negative external effects result in low population densities. Thus, the malleable capital model with externalities added cannot explain both the land value and population density patterns in Chicago. A vintage model is needed.

Let us add an amenity that increases with distance to the CBD in period 1 to the version of the model in which no demolition takes place. Land rent at any distance inside $\bar{u}_0$ can now be expressed as

$$R_{01}(u) = p_{11}(u, a) \frac{\partial h_{11}(u, a)}{\partial l_{11}(u, a)} - br_1 D(k_{01}/l_{01}), \tag{18}$$

where a is the amenity. The land rent profile may now appear as in Figure 8.5a or (perhaps) 8.5b. The exact shape of the land rent function will depend upon the shape of the amenity function. The price of housing function will exhibit a similar shape. Assuming population density can adjust costlessly, the population density function will also have the shape of the land-rent

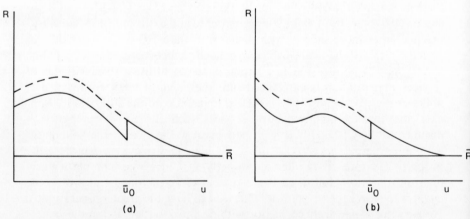

Figure 8.5.   (a) Land rent in period 1. (b) Land rent in period 1.

function. However, if population density cannot be easily adjusted, then the density function will continue to have the shape it had in period 0. Thus, the cost function for converting older units to units of a different size is a critical part of the analysis.

A final extension of the model can be made by allowing for more complex behavior on the supply side of the housing market. Based upon the empirical work examined in Chapter 4, it is reasonable to assume that

1. Housing depreciates, and
2. Maintenance can be used to overcome the effects of depreciation

The possible use of operating inputs will be ignored in this model because, in a two-period model, maintenance and operating inputs for old housing are the same analytically. Thus the structure of the model is the same as that employed by de Leeuw and Struyk (1975) in the Urban Institute simulation model. Their production function is of the form

$$h_{01}(u) = \beta_1 h_{00}(u) + m(M_1, h_{00}), \qquad (19)$$

where M_1 is maintenance in period 1, $1 - \beta_1$ is the depreciation from period 0 to period 1 if no maintenance is used, and $\partial h_{01}/\partial M_1$ is the (declining) marginal product of maintenance. This production function implies a supply function of the form

$$h_{01}(u) = S(h_{00}(u), p_{01}(u), p_m), \qquad (20)$$

where p_m is the price of a unit of maintenance. The results of the model will be modified if the elasticity of $h_{01}(u)$ with respect to $p_{01}(u)$ is significantly different from zero. In particular, the effects of increases in income or population or reductions in commuting costs will be muted by the fact that some increase in $h_{01}(u)$ over $h_{00}(u)$ is possible. However, the basic results of the model will not be altered as long as the distinction between old and new housing is maintained. Older housing is, in this case, defined as housing with a lower supply elasticity than new housing.[7]

It is now useful to suggest the sequence of events that, in the context of the model, will tend to generate the observed patterns of land values and population densities. Period 0 will refer to the time before about 1940–1950, and period 1 will refer to the periods after 1950. From period 0 to period 1, the SMSA experienced a modest increase in population, incomes increased

---

[7] The short-run supply model implies a more reasonable model of housing abandonment, of course. Housing is abandoned if $p_{01}h_{01}$ is less than the maintenance and operating expenditures necessary to produce quantity h_{01}. An exogenous decline in p_{01} at a particular site can result in abandonment and is caused by an increase in disamenities or a decline in access to employment.

substantially, commuting costs declined considerably as the expressway system was put into place, and the homeownership subsidy increased. In addition, it is reasonable to assume that there was an increase in the negative external effects associated with many locations near the CBD such as air pollution, crime, and lower quality of the public schools. Added to these effects are the effects of employment decentralization. The facts of employment decentralization in the Chicago SMSA have been summarized in the appendix to Chapter 1. It is well known that in Chicago employment opportunities in the CBD have remained strong, but that some of the areas in the central city have lost a great number of jobs since the late 1940s. In the context of a vintage model, a further weakening of the demand for residential land in the central city will result. However, it is not known whether the emergence of the fourth-degree land value function occurred after the decline of job opportunities in the central city outside the CBD. This might be a topic for future investigation. There was a little demolition of older housing structures and replacement with new housing. Some demolition occurred to permit the construction of the expressway system, and some sites were abandoned. These changes were concentrated near the CBD. In other areas of the SMSA, population density continued basically to reflect the nature of the older housing stock.

3   Conclusion

The model in this chapter shows that the use of a vintage model of housing capital is the key element in explaining the patterns of population density and land values observed for Chicago in 1970. Models of a perfectly malleable capital stock, even when combined with externalities or the assumption of a multicenter city, cannot generate the result that net population density is unrelated to land values. However, this result can be derived from the "putty–clay" model if changing the density level in older housing is costly. Given this basic building block, it then makes sense to add further complications to the model of the demand for housing. However, as was shown in Chapter 1, the degree of complexity that receives strong empirical support is rather limited. More important perhaps are the effects of neighborhood amenities and disamenities on the demand for land and housing at a particular location. In addition, the racial composition of a neighborhood is a very important influence on the housing demand in Chicago. Difficulties have been encountered in this study in the effort to include race in the model in a way that is consistent with all of the facts listed at the beginning of this chapter. This area of research should be pursued further. While this problem is important, it does not prevent me from concluding that a reasonably simple model has been developed in this study that is based upon assumptions that have received empirical support and is consistent with most of the basic facts of the Chicago housing market.

This study would be incomplete without an enumeration of the new questions that have been raised in the process of developing the model discussed in this chapter. Many of these questions involve the empirical testing of the vintage model of housing supply. The empirical nature of demolition and site preparation costs should be examined. The theory of the firm as related to housing demolition and replacement should be tested empirically. The nature of the costs of changing the population density in older housing should be examined. The conclusions of this study would be strengthened by the finding that these costs are substantial. An extension of the model might seek to explain the long lags observed in some inner city areas between building abandonment, demolition, and replacement. This is a phenomenon that has particularly perplexed policy makers. To what extent does speculation lead to vacant land for long periods? What are the causes of land speculation in the inner city? In addition, it would be interesting to establish the relative importance of the various factors that cause land values to increase with distance to the CBD. In particular, housing vintage effects and external effects both make a contribution to this result, but I am not prepared to assess their relative importance.

References

Aaron, H. (1970). Income taxes and housing. *American Economic Review, 60,* 789–806.

Aaron, H. (1972). *Shelter and Subsidies.* The Brookings Institution, Washington, D.C.

Allen, R. (1967). *Mathematical Analysis for Economists.* St. Martin's Press, New York.

Alonso, W. (1964). *Location and Land Use: Toward a General Theory of Land Rent.* Harvard University Press, Cambridge, Mass.

Amson, J. (1972). The dependence of population distribution on location costs. *Environment and Planning, 4,* 163–181.

Anas, A. (1976). Short-run dynamics in the spatial housing market, in G. Papageorgiou, ed., *Mathematical Land Use Theory.* D. C. Heath, Lexington, Mass.

Anas, A. (1978). Dynamics of urban residential growth. *Journal of Urban Economics, 5,* 66–87.

Anas, A. and D. Dendrinos (1976). The new urban Economics: A brief survey, in G. Papageorgiou, ed., *Mathematical Land Use Theory.* D. C. Heath, Lexington, Mass.

Anderson, R. and T. Crocker (1970). A comment on "Property values and air pollution: A cross section analysis of the St. Louis area," in G. Tolley and J. Gardner, eds., *Proceedings of the Second Research Conference of the Inter-University Committee on Urban Economics.* University of Chicago, Chicago.

Anderson, R. and T. Crocker (1971). Air pollution and residential property values. *Urban Studies, 8,* 171–180.

Anderson, R. and T. Crocker (1972). Air pollution and property values: A reply. *Review of Economics and Statistics, 54,* 470–473.

Avrin, M. (1977). Some economic effects of residential zoning in San Francisco, in G. Ingram, ed., *Residential Location and Urban Housing Markets.* Ballinger, Cambridge, Mass.

Babcock, R. (1957). The new Chicago zoning ordinance. *Northwestern University Law Review, 52,* 174–201.

187

Bailey, M. (1959). A note on the economics of residential zoning and urban renewal. *Land Economics*, *35*, 288–292.

Bailey, M. (1966). Effects of race and other demographic factors on the value of single-family homes. *Land Economics*, *42*, 215–220.

Ball, M. and R. Kirwan (1977). Accessibility and supply constraints in the urban housing market. *Urban Studies*, *14*, 11–32.

Bargen, M. and H. Walberg (1974). School performance, in H. Walberg, ed., *Evaluating Educational Performance*. McCutchan, Berkeley.

Becker, G. (1965). A theory of the allocation of time. *Economic Journal*, *75*, 493–517.

Beckmann, M. (1969). On the distribution of urban rent and residential density. *Journal of Economic Theory*, *1*, 60–67.

Beckmann, M. (1974). Spatial equilibrium in the housing market. *Journal of Urban Economics 1*, 99–107.

Bednarz, R. (1975). The effect of air pollution on property value in Chicago. The University of Chicago, Department of Geography, Research Paper No. 166.

Beesley, M. (1965). The value of time spent travelling: Some new evidence. *Economica*, *32*, 174–185.

Berry, B. (1976). Ghetto expansion and single-family housing prices: Chicago, 1968–1972. *Journal of Urban Economics*, *3*, 397–423.

Berry, B. and R. Bednarz (1975). A hedonic model of prices and assessments for single-family homes: Does the assessor follow the market or the market follow the assessor? *Land Economics*, *51*, 21–40.

Berry, B. and R. Bednarz (forthcoming). The disbenefits of neighborhood and environment to urban property. *Michigan Geographical Publications*.

Blackburn, A. (1971). Equilibrium in the market for land: Obtaining spatial distributions by change of variable. *Econometrica*, *39*, 641–644.

Box, G. and D. Cox (1964). An analysis of transformations. *Journal of the Royal Statistical Society, Series B 26*, 211–243.

Bradbury, K., R. Engle, O. Irwine and J. Rothenberg (1977). Simultaneous estimation of supply and demand for housing location in a multizoned metropolitan area, in G. Ingram, ed., *Residential Location and Urban Housing Markets*. Ballinger, Cambridge, Mass.

Brueckner, J. (1978a). Urban general equilibrium models with non-central production. *Journal of Regional Science*, *18*, 203–215.

Brueckner, J. (1978b). *A Vintage Growth Model for an Open City*. Mimeo, Dept. of Economics, University of Illinois at Urbana-Champaign.

Brunk, H. (1965). *An Introduction to Mathematical Statistics*. Blaisdell, Waltham, Mass.

Burkhead, J. (1969). *Input and Output in Large-City High Schools*. Syracuse University Press, Syracuse.

Casetti, R. (1969). Alternative population density models: An analytical comparison of their validity range, in A. Scott, ed., *Studies in Regional Science*. Pion, London.

Claffey, P. (1961). Characteristics of passenger car travel on toll roads and comparable free roads. *Highway Research Board Bulletin*, *306*, 1–22.

Clark, C. (1951). Urban population densities. *Journal of the Royal Statistical Society*, *114*, 490–494.

Courant, P. (1973). *Economic Aspects of Racial Prejudice in Urban Housing Markets*. Ph.D. Dissertation, Princeton University.

Courant, P. (1976). On the effect of fiscal zoning on land and housing values. *Journal of Urban Economics*, *3*, 88–94.

Courant, P. and J. Yinger (1977). On models of racial prejudice and urban residential structure. *Journal of Urban Economics*, *4*, 272–291.

Crecine, J., O. Davis and R. Jackson (1967). Urban property markets: Some empirical results and their implications for municipal zoning. *Journal of Law and Economics, 10,* 79–99.

Dalvi, M. and N. Lee (1969). Variations in the value of travel time. *The Manchester School of Economics and Social Studies, 37,* 213–236.

Dalvi, M. and N. Lee (1971). Variations in the value of travel time: Further analysis. *The Manchester School of Economics and Social Studies, 39,* 187–201.

David, M. (1962). *Family Composition and Consumption.* North–Holland Publishing Co., Amsterdam.

Davies, G. (1974). An econometric analysis of residential amenity. *Urban Studies, 11,* 217–225.

deDonnea, F. (1972). Consumer behavior, transport mode choice, and value of time: Some microeconomic models. *Regional and Urban Economics, 1,* 355–382.

de Leeuw, F. (1971). The demand for housing: A review of cross-section evidence. *Review of Economics and Statistics, 53,* 1–10.

de Leeuw, F. and N. Ekanem (1971). The supply of rental housing. *American Economic Review, 61,* 806–817.

de Leeuw, F. and N. Ekanem (1973). The supply of rental housing: Reply. *American Economic Review, 63,* 437–438.

de Leeuw, F. and R. Struyk (1975). *The Web of Urban Housing.* The Urban Institute, Washington, D.C.

Delson, J. (1970). Correction on the boundary conditions in Beckmann's model of urban rent and residential density. *Journal of Economic Theory, 2,* 314–318.

Diamond, D. (1978a). *The Analysis of Residential Land Prices.* Unpublished.

Diamond, D. (1978b). *Income and Residential Location: Muth Revisited* Unpublished paper presented at the AREUEA Meetings.

Dildine, L. and F. Massey (1974). Dynamic model of private incentives to housing maintenance. *Southern Economic Journal, 40,* 631–639.

Domencich, T. and D. McFadden (1975). *Urban Travel Demand: A Behavioral Analysis.* North–Holland Publishing Co., Amsterdam.

Edel, M. and E. Sclar (1974). Taxes, spending, and property taxes: Supply adjustment in a Tiebout–Oates model. *Journal of Political Economy, 82,* 941–954.

Epple, D., A. Zelenitz and M. Visscher (1978). A search for testable implications of the Tiebout hypothesis. *Journal of Political Economy, 86,* 405–525.

Evans, A. (1973). *The Economics of Residential Location.* Macmillan, London.

Evans, A. (1975). Rent and housing in the theory of urban growth. *Journal of Regional Science, 15,* 113–125.

Federal Bureau of Investigation (1941, 1951, 1961, 1971.). *Uniform Crime Reports for the United States.* Washington, D.C.

Finney, D. (1941). On the distribution of a variate whose logarithm is normally distributed. *Journal of the Royal Statistical Society, Supplement, 7,* 155–161.

Fisch, O. (1977). Dynamics of the housing market. *Journal of Urban Economics, 4,* 428–447.

Fountain, J., (1977). *Empirical Estimation of the Housing Production Function.* Mimeo.

Frankena, M. (1978). A bias in estimating urban population density functions. *Journal of Urban Economics, 5,* 35–45.

Freeman, A. (1971). Air pollution and property values: A methodological comment. *Review of Economics and Statistics, 53,* 414–415.

Friedman, M. (1953). The methodology of positive economics, in *Essays in Positive Economics.* Chicago University Press, Chicago.

Goldberger, A. (1964). *Econometric Theory.* Wiley, New York.

Goldberger, A. (1968). The interpretation and estimation of Cobb–Douglas Functions. *Econometrica, 36,* 464–472.

Greene, D. and J. Barnbrock (1978). A note on problems in estimating exponential density models. *Journal of Urban Economics, 5*, 285–290.

Grether, D. and P. Mieszkowski (1974). Determinants of real estate values. *Journal of Urban Economics, 1*, 127–145.

Grieson, R. (1973). The supply of rental housing: Comment. *American Economic Review, 63*, 433–436.

Gustely, R. (1976). Local taxes, expenditures and urban housing: A reassessment of the evidence. *Southern Economic Journal, 42*, 659–665.

Guttman, J. (1975). Avoiding specification errors in estimating the value of time. *Transportation, 4*, 19–42.

Hamilton, B. (1976). Capitalization of intrajurisdictional differences in local tax prices. *American Economic Review, 66*, 743–753.

Hamilton, B. (1978). Zoning and the exercise of monopoly power. *Journal of Urban Economics, 5*, 116–130.

Harris, R., G. Tolley and C. Harrell (1968). The residence site choice. *Review of Economics and Statistics, 50*, 241–247.

Harrison, B. (1974). *Urban Economic Development.* Urban Institute, Washington, D.C.

Harrison, D. and J. Kain (1974). Cumulative urban growth and urban density functions. *Journal of Urban Economics, 1*, 61–98.

Heffley, D. (1972). The quadratic assignment problem: A note. *Econometrica, 40*, 1155–1163.

Heffley, D. (1976). Efficient spatial allocation in the quadratic assignment problem. *Journal of Urban Economics, 3*, 309–322.

Heien, D. (1968). A note on log-linear regression. *Journal of the American Statistical Association, 63*, 1034–1038.

Heinberg, J. and W. Oates (1970). The incidence of differential property taxes on urban housing: A comment and some further evidence. *National Tax Journal, 23*, 92–98.

Henderson, J. (1977). *Economic Theory and the Cities.* Academic Press, New York.

Hoyt, H. (1933). *One Hundred Years of Land Values in Chicago.* University of Chicago Press, Chicago.

Hufbauer, G. and B. Severn (1974). The economic demolition of old buildings. *Urban Studies, 11*, 349–351.

Hyman, D. and E. Pasour (1973a). Real property taxes, local public services, and residential property values in North Carolina. *Southern Economic Journal, 39*, 601–611.

Hyman, D. and E. Pasour (1973b). Property tax differentials and residential rents in North Carolina. *National Tax Journal, 26*, 303–307.

Ingram, G., J. Kain and J. Ginn (1972). *The Detroit Prototype of the NBER Urban Simulation Model.* National Bureau of Economic Research, New York.

Ingram, G.and Y. Oron (1977). The production of housing services from existing dwelling units, in G. Ingram, ed., *Residential Location and Urban Housing Markets.* Ballinger, Cambridge, Mass.

Johansen, L. (1959). Substitution versus fixed production coefficients in the theory of economic growth. *Econometrica, 27*, 157–176.

Johnson, M. (1966). Travel time and the price of leisure. *Western Economic Journal, 4*, 135–145.

Johnston, J. (1972). *Econometric Models and Methods*, 2nd ed. McGraw–Hill, New York.

Kain, J. (1968). Housing market segregation, negro employment, and metropolitan decentralization. *Quarterly Journal of Economics, 82*, 175–197.

Kain, J. (1970). The distribution and movement of jobs and industry, in J. Wilson, ed., *The Metropolitan Enigma.*, pp. 1–43. Doubleday, New York.

Kain, J. and J. Quigley (1970a). Evaluating the quality of the residential environment. *Environment and Planning, 2*, 23–32.

Kain, J. and J. Quigley (1970b). Measuring the value of housing quality. *Journal of the American Statistical Association, 45,* 532–548.

Kain, J. and J. Quigley (1972). Housing market discrimination, homeownership, and savings behavior. *American Economic Review, 62,* 263–277.

Kain, J. and J. Quigley (1975). *Housing Markets and Racial Discrimination: A Microeconomic Analysis.* National Bureau of Economic Research, New York.

Katzner, D. (1970). *Static Demand Theory.* Macmillan, New York.

Kau, J. and C. Lee (1976a). Capital-land substitution and urban land use. *Journal of Regional Science, 16,* 83–92.

Kau, J. and C. Lee (1976b). Functional form, density gradient, and price elasticity of demand for housing. *Urban Studies, 13,* 193–200.

Kau, J. and C. Sirmans (1979). Urban land value functions and the price elasticity of demand for housing. *Journal of Urban Economics, 6,* 112–121.

Kelejian, H. and W. Oates (1974). *Introduction to Econometrics.* Harper & Row, New York.

King, A. T. (1973). *Property Taxes, Amenities, and Residential Land Values.* Ballinger, Cambridge, Mass.

King, A. T. (1976). The demand for housing: Integrating the roles of journey-to-work, neighborhood quality, and prices, in N. Terleckyj, ed., *Household Production and Consumption.* National Bureau of Economic Research, New York.

King, A. T. (1977). The demand for housing: A Lancastrian approach. *Southern Economic Journal, 43,* 1077–1087.

King, A. T. and P. Mieszkowski (1973). Racial discrimination, segregation, and the price of housing. *Journal of Political Economy, 81,* 590–606.

Kitagawa, E. and K. Taeuber (1963). *Local Community Fact Book, Chicago Metropolitan Area: 1960.* City of Chicago.

Koenker, R. (1972). An empirical note on the elasticity of substitution between land and capital in a monocentric housing market. *Journal of Regional Science, 12,* 299–305.

Koopmans, T. and M. Beckmann (1957). Assignment problems and the location of economic activities. *Econometrica, 25,* 53–76.

Ladd, G. (1966). Linear probability functions and discriminant functions. *Econometrica, 34,* 873–885.

Laidler, D. (1969). Income tax incentives for owner-occupied housing, in A. Harberger and M. Bailey, eds., *The Taxation of Income from Capital,* pp. 50–76. The Brookings Institution, Washington, D.C.

Lancaster, K. (1966). A new approach to consumer theory. *Journal of Political Economy, 74,* 132–157.

Lancaster, K. (1971). *Consumer Demand: A New Approach.* Columbia University Press, New York.

Lave, C. (1969). A behavioral approach to modal split forecasting. *Transportation Research, 3,* 463–480.

LeRoy, S. (1976). Urban land rent and the incidence of property taxes. *Journal of Urban Economics, 3,* 167–179.

Lisco, T. (1967). *The Value of Commuters' Travel Time.* Ph.D. Dissertation, University of Chicago.

Little, J. (1976). Residential preferences, neighborhood filtering and neighborhood change. *Journal of Urban Economics, 3,* 68–81.

Lowry, I. (1960). Filtering and housing standards: A conceptual analysis. *Land Economics, 36,* 362–370.

MacRae, C. and R. Struyk (1977). The Federal Housing Administration (FHA), tenure choice, and residential land use, *Journal of Urban Economics, 4,* 360–378.

Maddala, G. (1977). *Econometrics*. McGraw–Hill, New York.

Madden, J. (1977). A spatial theory of sex discrimination. *Journal of Regional Science, 17,* 369–380.

Martin, R. (1973). The spatial distribution of the population: Cities and suburbs. *Journal of Regional Science, 13,* 269–278.

Maser, S., W. Riker and R. Rosett (1977). The effects of zoning and externalities on the prices of land in Monroe County, New York. *Journal of Law and Economics, 20,* 111–132.

Mayo, S. (1978). *Theory and Estimation in the Economics of Housing Demand.* Mimeo, Abt Associates, Inc.

McCallum, B. (1971). Relative asymptotic bias from errors of omission and measurement. *Econometrica, 40,* 757–758.

McDonald, J. (1974). Housing market discrimination, homeownership and savings behavior: Comment. *American Economic Review, 64,* 225–229.

McDonald, J. (1975). Variations in the value of reductions in commuting time. *Journal of Urban Economics, 2,* 265–277.

McDonald, J. and H. Bowman (1976). Some tests of alternative urban population density functions. *Journal of Urban Economics, 3,* 422–452.

McDonald, J. and H. Bowman (1979). Land value functions: A reevaluation. *Journal of Urban Economics, 6,* 25–41.

McGillivray, R. (1972). Binary choice of urban transport mode in the San Francisco Bay region. *Econometrica, 40,* 827–848.

Mieszkowski, P. (1969). Tax incidence theory: The effects of taxes on the distribution of income. *Journal of Economic Literature, 7,* 1103–1124.

Mieszkowski, P. (1972). The property tax: An excise tax or a profits tax?" *Journal of Public Economics, 1,* 73–96.

Mills E. (1967). An aggregative model of resource allocation in a metropolitan area. *American Economic Review, Papers and Proceedings, 57,* 197–210.

Mills, E. (1969). The value of urban land, in H. Perloff, ed., *The Quality of the Urban Environment.* Resources for the Future, Inc., Washington, D.C.

Mills, E. (1972a). *Studies in the Structure of the Urban Economy.* Johns Hopkins Press, Baltimore.

Mills, E. (1972b). *Urban Economics.* Scott, Foresman, Glenview, Illinois.

Montesano, A. (1972). A restatement of Beckmann's model of urban rent and residential density. *Journal of Economic Theory, 4,* 329–354.

Moses, L. and H. Williamson (1963). Value of time, choice of mode and the subsidy issue in urban transportation. *Journal of Political Economy, 71,* 247–264.

Moss, W. (1977). Large lot zoning, property taxes, and metropolitan area. *Journal of Urban Economics, 4,* 408–427.

Muellbauer, J. (1974). Household production theory, quality, and the "Hedonic Technique." *American Economic Review, 64,* 977–994.

Murray, M. (1978). Hedonic prices and composite commodities. *Journal of Urban Economics, 5,* 188–197.

Muth, R. (1960). The demand for non-farm housing, in A. Harberger, ed., *The Demand for Durable Goods.* The University of Chicago Press, Chicago.

Muth, R. (1964). The derived demand curve for a productive factor and the industry supply curve. *Oxford Economic Papers (New Series), 16,* 221–234.

Muth, R. (1966). Household production and consumer demand functions. *Econometrica, 34,* 699–708.

Muth, R. (1969). *Cities and Housing.* University of Chicago Press, Chicago.

Muth, R. (1971a). The derived demand for urban residential land. *Urban Studies, 8,* 243–254.

Muth, R. (1971b). *Capital and Current Expenditures in the Production of Housing.* Mimeo, Stanford University.

Muth, R. (1975). Numerical solution of urban residential land-use models. *Journal of Urban Economics*, 2, 307–332.

Muth, R. (1976). A vintage model of housing production, in G. Papageorgiou, ed., *Mathematical Land Use Theory*. D. C. Heath, Lexington, Mass.

Muth, R. (1977). Recent developments in the theory of urban spatial structure, in M. Intriligator, ed., *Frontiers of Quantitative Economics, Vol. IIIB*. North–Holland, Amsterdam.

Nagel, E. (1961). *The Structure of Science*. Harcourt, Brace & World, New York.

Nagel, E. (1963). Assumptions in economic theory. *American Economic Review, Papers and Proceedings*, 53, 211–219.

Nelson, R. (1972). Housing facilities, site advantages and rent. *Journal of Regional Science*, 12, 249–259.

Newling, B. (1969). The spatial variation of urban population densities. *Geographical Review*, 59, 242–252.

Oates, W. (1969). The effects of property taxes and local public spending on property values: An empirical study of tax capitalization and Tiebout hypotheses. *Journal of Political Economy*, 77, 957–971.

Ohls, J. (1975). Public policy toward low income housing and filtering in housing markets. *Journal of Urban Economics*, 2, 144–171.

Ohls, J., R. Weisberg and M. White (1974). The effect of zoning on land value. *Journal of Urban Economics*, 1, 428–444.

Olcott, G. (1911–1971). *Olcott's Land Values Blue Book of Chicago and Suburbs*. G. Olcott, Chicago.

Oort, C. (1969). The evaluation of travelling time. *Journal of Transport Economics and Policy*, 3, 279–286.

Orr, L. (1968). The incidence of differential property taxes on urban housing. *National Tax Journal*, 21, 253–262.

Orr, L. (1970). The incidence of property taxes: A response. *National Tax Journal*, 23, 99–101.

Orr, L. (1975). *Income, Employment, and Urban Residential Location*. Academic Press, New York.

Owen, J. (1969). The value of commuter speed. *Western Economic Journal*, 7, 164–172.

Papageorgiou, G. (1971). A generalization of the population density gradient concept. *Geographical Analysis*, 3, 121–127.

Papageorgiou, G. and E. Casetti (1971). Spatial equilibrium residential land values in a multi-center setting. *Journal of Regional Science*, 11, 385–389.

Parzen, E. (1960). *Modern Probability Theory and Its Applications*. Wiley, New York.

Polinsky, A. and D. Rubinfeld (1978). The long-run effects of a residential property tax and local public services. *Journal of Urban Economics*, 5, 241–262.

Polinsky, A. and S. Shavell (1975). The air pollution and property value debate. *Review of Economics and Statistics*, 57, 100–104.

Polinsky, A. and S. Shavell (1976). Amenities and property values in a model of an urban area. *Journal of Public Economics*, 5, 119–129.

Pollakowski, H. (1973). The effects of property taxes and local public spending on property values: A comment and further results. *Journal of Political Economy*, 81, 994–1003.

Popper, K. (1968). *The Logic of Scientific Inquiry*. Harper and Row, New York.

Quarmby, D. (1967). Choice of travel mode for the journey to work. *Journal of Transport Economics and Policy*, 1, 273–314.

Quigley, J. (1972). *The Influence of Workplaces and Housing Stocks Upon Residential Choice: A Crude Test of the Gross Price Hypothesis*. Mimeo.

Quigley, J. (1976). Comments on the paper by C. Peter Rydell. *Papers of the Regional Science Association*, 37, 87–90.

Reid, M. (1962). *Housing and Income*. University of Chicago Press, Chicago.

Revankar, N. (1971). A class of variable elasticity of substitution production functions. *Econometrica, 39*, 61–71.

Richardson, H. (1977a). *The New Urban Economics: and Alternatives.* Pion, London.

Richardson, H. (1977b). On the possibility of positive rent gradients. *Journal of Urban Economics, 4*, 60–68.

Ridker, R. and J. Henning (1967). The determinants of residential property values with special reference to air pollution. *Review of Economics and Statistics, 49*, 246–257.

Rose-Ackerman, S. (1975). Racism and urban structure. *Journal of Urban Economics, 2*, 85–103.

Rose-Ackerman, S. (1977). The political economy of a racist housing market. *Journal of Urban Economics, 4*, 150–169.

Rosen, S. (1974). Hedonic prices and implicit markets: Product differentiation in pure competition. *Journal of Political Economy, 82*, 34–55.

Rothenberg, J. (1967). *Economic Evaluation of Urban Renewal.* The Brookings Institution, Washington, D.C.

Rotwein, E. (1959). On the methodology of positive economics. *Quarterly Journal of Economics, 73*, 554–575.

Rueter, R. (1973). Externalities in urban property markets: An empirical test of the zoning ordinance in Pittsburgh. *Journal of Law and Economics, 16*, 313–349.

Rydell, C. (1971). Maintenance and operating costs in public housing. *Papers of the Regional Science Association, 27*, 229–245.

Rydell, C. (1976). Measuring the supply response to housing allowances. *Papers of the Regional Science Association, 37*, 31–57.

Sabella, E. (1974). The effects of property taxes and local public expenditures on the sales price of residential buildings. *Appraisal Journal, 42*, 114–125.

Samuelson, P. (1963). Problems of methodology—Discussion. *American Economic Review, Papers and Proceedings, 53*, 231–236.

Schafer, R. (1976). *Racial Discrimination in the Boston Housing Market.* Mimeo.

Schnare, A. (1976). Racial and ethnic price differentials in an urban housing market. *Urban Studies, 13*, 107–120.

Schnare, A. and R. Struyk (1976). Segmentation in urban housing markets. *Journal of Urban Economics, 3*, 146–166.

Shelton, J. (1968). The cost of renting versus owning a home. *Land Economics, 44*, 59–72.

Simon, H. (1963). Problems of methodology—Discussion. *American Economic Review, Papers and Proceedings, 53*, 229–231.

Sirmans, C., J. Kau and C. Lee (forthcoming). The elasticity of substitution in urban housing production: A VES approach. *Journal of Urban Economics.*

Small, K. (1975). Air pollution and property values: Further comment. *Review of Economics and Statistics, 57*, 105–107.

Smith, B. (1976). The supply of urban housing. *Quarterly Journal of Economics, 90*, 389–405.

Smith, B. (1978). Measuring the value of urban amenities. *Journal of Urban Economics, 5*, 370–387.

Solow, R. (1972). Congestion, density and the use of land in transportation. *The Swedish Journal of Economics, 74*, 161–173.

Solow, R. (1973). On equilibrium models of urban locations, in J. Parkin, ed., *Essays in Modern Economics.* Longmans, London.

Starrett, D. (1978). Market allocations of location choice in a model of free mobility. *Journal of Economic Theory, 17*, 21–37.

Steinnes, D. (1977). Alternative models of neighborhood change. *Social Forces, 55*, 1043–1057.

Stopher, P. (1969). A probability model for the journey to work. *Highway Research Record, 283*, 57–65.

Straszheim, M. (1974). Hedonic estimation of housing market prices: A further comment. *Review of Economics and Statistics, 56,* 404–406.

Straszheim, M. (1975). *An Econometric Analysis of the Urban Housing Market.* National Bureau of Economic Research, New York.

Stull, W. (1974). Land use and zoning in an urban economy. *American Economic Review, 64,* 337–347.

Stull, W. (1975). Community environment, zoning and the market value of single-family homes. *Journal of Law and Economics, 18,* 535–557.

Sweeney, J. (1974). A commodity hierarchy model of the rental housing market. *Journal of Urban Economics, 1,* 288–323.

Tiebout, C. (1956). A pure theory of local expenditures. *Journal of Political Economy, 64,* 416–424.

Thaler, R. (1978). A note on the value of crime control: Evidence from the property market. *Journal of Urban Economics, 5,* 137–145.

Thomas, T. and G. Thompson (1970). The value of time for commuting motorists as a function of their income level and amount of time saved. *Highway Research Record, 314,* 1–15.

Tobin, J. (1958). Estimation of relationships for limited dependent variables. *Econometrica, 26,* 24–36.

Tolley, G. and A. Cohen (1976). Air pollution and urban land use policy. *Journal of Environmental Economics and Management, 2,* 247–254.

Walberg, H. and M. Bargen (1974a). School equality, in H. Walberg, ed., *Evaluating Educational Performance* McCutchan, Berkeley.

Walberg, H. and M. Bargen (1974b). Urban spatial models, in H. Walberg, ed., *Evaluating Educational Performance.* McCutchan, Berkeley.

Warner, S. (1962). *Stochastic Choice of Mode in Urban Travel: A Study in Binary Choice.* Northwestern University Press, Evanston.

Watson, P. (1974). *The Value of Time: Behavioral Models of Modal Choice.* D. C. Heath, Lexington, Mass.

Wendt, P. and W. Goldner (1966). Land values and the dynamics of residential location, in *Essays in Urban Land Economics,* pp. 188–213. University of California, Los Angeles.

Wheaton, W. (1974). A comparative static analysis of urban spatial structure. *Journal of Economic Theory, 9,* 223–237.

Wheaton, W. (1977a). Income and urban residence: An analysis of consumer demand for location. *American Economic Review, 67,* 620–631.

Wheaton, W. (1977b). A bid rent approach to housing demand. *Journal of Urban Economics, 4,* 200–217.

White, L. (1977). How good are two-point estimates of urban density gradients and central densities? *Journal of Urban Economics, 4,* 292–309.

White, M. (1975). The effect of zoning on the size of metropolitan areas. *Journal of Urban Economics, 2,* 279–290.

White, M. (1976). Firm suburbanization and urban subcenters. *Journal of Urban Economics, 3,* 323–342.

White, M. (1977a). A model of residential location choice and commuting by men and women workers. *Journal of Regional Science, 17,* 41–52.

White, M. (1977b). On cumulative urban growth and urban density functions. *Journal of Urban Economics, 4,* 104–112.

White, M. (1978a). Job suburbanization, zoning and the welfare of urban minority groups. *Journal of Urban Economics, 5,* 219–240.

White, M. (1978b). On the short-term effects of a long-term change in cities. *Journal of Urban Economics, 5,* 485–504.

White, M. and L. White (1977). The tax subsidy to owner-occupied housing: Who benefits? *Journal of Public Economics, 7,* 111–126.

Wickens, M. (1971). A note on the use of proxy variables. *Econometrica, 40,* 759–761.

Wieand, K. (1973). Air pollution and property values: A study of the St. Louis area. *Journal of Regional Science, 13,* 91–95.

Wilkie, L. (1962). Congress Street Expressway traffic characteristics. *Highway Research Board Bulletin, 351,* 24–32.

Wilkinson, R. (1973). House prices and the measurement of externalities. *Economic Journal, 83,* 72–86.

Yamada, H. (1972). On the theory of residential location: Accessibility, space, leisure and environmental quality. *Papers of the Regional Science Association, 29,* 125–135.

Yeates, M. (1965). Some factors affecting the spatial distribution of Chicago land values. *Economic Geography, 41,* 57–70.

Yinger, J. (1976). Racial prejudice and racial residential segregation in an urban model. *Journal of Urban Economics, 3,* 383–396.

Yinger, J. (1978). The black–white differential in housing: Some further evidence. *Land Economics, 54,* 187–206.

Zerbe, R. (1969). *The Economics of Air Pollution: A Cost–Benefit Approach.* Ontario Dept. of Public Health, Toronto.

Index

A

Aaron, H., 24, 27
Abandonment, 99, 108, 183, 185
Air pollution, 62–68
   and vintage model, 181–183
Alexis, M., 61n
Allen, R., 13
Alonso, W., 14
Amenity demand, income elasticity, 22
Amson, J., 104, 181
Anas, A., 75, 90, 91, 107, 108, 109, 115n, 174
Anderson, R., 62, 63, 64, 67, 68
Assignment model, 88, 89
Avrin, M., 159

B

Babcock, R., 160
Bailey, M., 53, 111
Ball, M., 90n
Bargen, M., 73
Barnbrock, J., 119n
Becker, G., 8
Beckmann, M., 75, 89, 109, 111, 112

Bednarz, R., 57, 63, 64, 65, 66, 67, 70, 129, 141, 145, 166, 181
Beesley, M., 36, 38, 42, 46
Berry, B., 54, 55, 57, 59, 60, 61, 62, 65, 129, 141, 145, 146, 166, 181
Blackburn, A., 109n
Black–white border, movement, 61, 62
Bowman, H., 104, 105, 129, 135, 146n
Box, G., 79, 106
Bradbury, K., 76, 84, 85, 94, 98
Brueckner, J., 103n, 109
Brunk, H., 120
Burkhead, J., 73

C

Casetti, R., 105, 115
Claffey, P., 36, 42
Clark, C., 121, 122n
Cohen, A., 65, 68n
Commuting time, 35–49, 180, 181
   driving speed, 47–49
   value, 38–47
Conversion of land use, 115, 116
Crime, 68, 69

Crime (*Continued*)
  city–suburb comparison, 68, 69
  and property value, 68
  and vintage model, 181–183
Courant, P., 111, 112, 114, 160, 161
Cox, D., 79, 106
Crecine, J., 159
Crocker, T., 62, 63, 64, 67, 68

D

Dalvi, M., 36, 38, 46
David, M., 16, 20
Davies, G., 18, 70
deDonnea, F., 8n
deLeeuw, F., 76, 85, 86, 87, 88, 94, 95, 99
Delson, J., 109n
Demand for housing, *see* Housing demand
Demolition
  complete, 175, 176
  cost function, 171
  location, 176
  partial, 176, 177
Dendrinos, D., 1, 115n
Diamond, D., 21, 22, 63, 67, 68, 69
Dildine, L., 93, 96
Domencich, T., 45

E

Edel, M., 71
Ekanem, N., 85, 86, 87, 88
Elasticity of substitution
  estimation, 77–84
  measurement error bias, 82, 83
Empirical facts, summary, 170
Employment
  access, 29–33
  manufacturing, 29–32
  retail, 32
  services, 32
  wholesale, 32
Evans, A., 15, 16, 23, 107, 108, 171
Expectations in vintage model, 107, 172n
  myopic, 107, 108, 171
  perfect foresight, 107, 108
Experimental law, 3, 4

F

Filtering, 92, 93
Finney, D., 120

Floor-area ratio, 161, 163, 164
Fountain, J., 77, 79, 81, 83, 128, 131
Frankena, M., 121n
Freeman, A., 63
Friedman, M., 3, 4

G

Goldberger, A., 44, 120, 121
Goldner, W., 78
Greene, D., 119n
Grieson, R., 85, 86, 87, 88
Gustley, R., 72
Guttman, J., 37n

H

Hamilton, B., 71, 159, 167n, 181
Harris, R., 14, 15
Harrison, B., 32, 33
Harrison, D., 115, 117, 123, 124, 125
Heffley, D., 89
Heien, D., 120
Heinberg, J., 72
Henderson, J., 9n, 70, 71, 101, 110, 111
Henning, J., 62
Homeownership
  compared to renting, 24–27
  favorable tax treatment, 26–29
  and population density, 113, 114, 135–137
  vintage model, 178, 179
Housing demand
  income elasticity, 13, 18, 20, 103, 180n
  price elasticity, 13, 18, 20, 103, 105, 180n
  and race, 52–62
  simplified example, 12, 13
  survey of studies, 14–24
  synthesis, 7–11
Housing stock age structure, 137–140
Hoyt, H., 141, 142
Hufbauer, G., 91, 109, 135, 171
Hyman, D., 72

I

Ingram, G., 94, 97, 98
Instrumentalism, 3, 4

J

Johansen, L., 90

Johnson, M., 8n
Johnston, J., 82n

K

Kain, J., 2, 4, 9n, 16, 17, 18n, 19, 23, 26, 32, 33n, 52, 53, 61, 68, 70, 75, 89, 90, 115, 117, 123, 124, 125, 136, 180
Katzner, D., 100
Kau, J., 105, 106, 131, 141, 142n
King, A., 18, 19, 21, 52, 61, 75, 90
Kirwan, R., 90n
Kitagawa, E., 118
Koenker, R., 77, 79, 81, 82, 83, 91, 128, 131
Koopmans, T., 75, 89

L

Ladd, G., 45
Laidler, D., 26n
Lancaster, K., 8
Land demand, 14, 22
  income elasticity, 22
  price elasticity, 22
Land value
  and age of housing stock, 157, 158
  complex functional form, 146–158
  determinants, 147
  fourth-degree polynomial, 148–150
  historical record, 142–146
  and neighborhood income, 158
  and noncentral employment, 151–154
  and race, 155–157
  summary of empirical results, 170
  and zoning, 150, 151, 159–166
Lave, C., 36, 38, 46
Lee, C., 105, 106, 131
Lee, N., 36, 38, 46
LeRoy, S., 111
Lisco, T., 36, 38, 46, 48
Little, J., 18n
Lowry, I., 92, 93

M

McCallum, B., 57
McDonald, J., 9n, 36, 37n, 104, 105, 129, 135, 136
McFadden, D., 45
McGillivray, R., 45
MacRae, C., 24, 27, 112, 113

Maddala, G., 57
Madden, J., 8
Maintenance, 93–98
  and vintage model, 183
Martin, R., 128, 129, 133
Maser, S., 70, 159, 162
Massey, F., 93, 96
Mayo, S., 180n
Methodology, economics, 2–5
Mieszkowski, P., 52, 61, 70
Mills, E., 2, 11, 101n, 105, 107, 115, 121, 127, 128, 129, 141, 142, 144, 145, 154, 180n
Monocentric model, 101–106
  and amenity, 110, 111
  and homeownership, 112, 113
  and income variations, 109
  land rent, 104, 105
  population density, 104–106
  and property tax, 111
  and public services, 111
  and race, 111, 112
  and taste variations, 109, 110n
  and vintage model, 107–109
  and zoning, 114, 115
Montesano, A., 109n
Moses, L., 37
Moss, W., 114n
Muellbauer, J., 99
Multicenter model, 115
Murray, M., 90, 99, 100
Muth, R., 1, 2, 3, 4, 5, 8, 9n, 12, 13, 15, 16, 18, 23, 24, 28, 35n, 53, 75, 76, 77, 79, 81, 82, 90, 95, 101, 105, 106, 107, 108, 112, 115, 117, 121, 123, 125, 126, 127, 128, 129, 131

N

Nagel, E., 3, 4
Neighborhood income and property value, 70
Nelson, R., 10, 11, 12
Newling, B., 122n

O

Oates, W., 71, 72
Ohls, J., 94, 114, 161
Olcott, G., 83, 91, 129, 133, 141, 144, 145, 147, 163
Omitted variables bias, 56–61
Oort, C., 8n
Operating inputs, 94–98

Oron, Y., 94, 97, 98
Orr, L., 71, 72, 160, 161
Owen, J., 8n

P

Papageorgiou, G., 115
Parzen, E., 119
Pasour, E., 72
Polinsky, A., 63, 110, 111, 181, 182
Pollakowski, H., 71
Popper, K., 1
Population density
  and age of housing, 135
  components, 125–127
  and cumulative urban growth, 123–125
  historical record, 117–122
  and homeownership, 113, 114, 135–137
  and land value, 128–134
  negative exponential form, 119–122
  summary of empirical results, 170
Production function
  Cobb-Douglas, 90, 98, 103, 130, 171
  constant elasticity of substitution, 76–79,
    96, 97, 131, 132
  returns to scale, 77
  variable elasticity of substitution, 78, 79
Property tax, 70–72
Proxy variable, 56–61
Public expenditures, 70–73

Q

Quarmby, D., 36, 38, 45, 46
Quigley, J., 2, 4, 9n, 16, 17, 18n, 19, 23, 26,
    52, 53, 61, 68, 70, 75, 82, 89, 90, 136, 180

R

Racial price differential, 52–61
  aversion, 52, 61
  discrimination, 52
  omitted variables bias, 56–61
Reid, M., 9n
Residential location demand
  simplified example, 12, 13
  survey of studies, 14–24
  synthesis, 7–11
Revankar, N., 78
Richardson, H., 1, 115n, 181, 182

Ridker, R., 62
Rose-Ackerman, S., 111, 112, 155, 157
Rosen, S., 8
Rothenberg, J., 129
Rotwein, E., 4
Rubinfeld, D., 111
Rueter, R., 159
Rydell, C., 77, 79, 81, 82, 83, 94, 96, 97, 99,
    128, 131

S

Sabella, E., 72
Samuelson, P., 4
Schafer, R., 53, 61
Schnare, A., 53, 90
School quality, 73, 74
  and vintage model, 181–183
Sclar, E., 71
Severn, B., 91, 109, 135, 171
Shavell, S., 63, 110, 111, 181, 182
Shelton, J., 25, 26
Simon, H., 4
Sirmans, C., 78, 79, 81, 105n, 128, 141, 142n
Small, K., 63
Smith, B., 63, 65, 66, 67, 68, 69, 72, 79, 81, 83,
    84, 141, 166
Starrett, D., 89n
Steinnes, D., 61
Stopher, P., 36, 38, 46
Straszheim, M., 2, 4, 9n, 16, 17, 18, 20, 23,
    63, 75, 90
Struyk, R., 24, 27, 76, 90, 94, 95, 99, 112, 113
Stull, W., 114, 159, 161
Supply of housing
  long run, 76–88
  market period, 88–92
  short run, 92–98
Sweeney, J., 94

T

Taeuber, K., 118
Thaler, R., 68
Theory in economics, 3, 4
Thomas, T., 36, 37n, 38, 42, 45n, 46
Thompson, G., 36, 37n, 38, 42, 45n, 46
Tiebout, C., 38, 70
Tobin, J., 163
Tolley, G., 65, 68n

V

Vintage model, 90–92, 107–109, 170–177
  and air pollution, 181–183
  comparative statics, 173, 174
  and conversion to lower density, 177–179
  and crime, 181–183
  and demolition, 173, 174–177
  and homeownership, 178, 179
  and land value, 171–173
  and maintenance, 183
  and population density, 173
  and race, 179, 180
  and school quality, 183

W

Walberg, H., 73
Warner, S., 45
Watson, P., 45

Wendt, P., 78
Wheaton, W., 9, 14, 22, 23, 107, 110, 174
White, L., 27, 121
White, M., 8, 27, 114, 115, 124, 161, 171n, 172n
Wickens, M., 57
Wieand, K., 62n
Wilkie, L., 47, 48
Wilkinson, R., 18n
Williamson, H., 37

Y

Yamada, H., 8n, 11
Yeates, M., 129, 141, 142, 143, 166
Yinger, J., 53, 111, 112

Z

Zerbe, R., 62
Zoning ordinance, 151, 160, 161